HENRY STEDMAN has been writing guidebooks for more than a decade and is the author or co-author of half a dozen titles including Trailblazer's guides to *Kilimanjaro*, the *Coast to Coast Path*, *Dolomites Trekking – Alta Via 1 & Alta Via 2*, *Hadrian's Wall Path*, *The Bradt Guide to Palestine* and the *Rough Guide to Indonesia and Southeast Asia*.

When not trekking or travelling, Henry lives in Hastings, editing other people's guidebooks and putting on weight.

JIM MANTHORPE has trekked in many of the world's mountainous regions from Patagonia to the Himalaya and Scandinavia to the Canadian Rockies. He has been a travel writer, photographer, editor and lecturer for the best part of ten years, penning four Trailblazer guidebooks, including *Scottish Highlands – The Hillwalking Guide*, and contributing to a further five.

Following stints at Stanfords Travel Books and Maps in London and on *The Scotsman* newspaper in Edinburgh he is now living on the west coast of Scotland in Knoydart, accessible only by boat. When not writing, he works as a ranger. He can be contacted at ⌨ www.jim manthorpe.com.

Pembrokeshire Coast Path
First edition: 2004; this second edition: 2007

Publisher
Trailblazer Publications
The Old Manse, Tower Rd, Hindhead, Surrey, GU26 6SU, UK
Fax (+44) 01428-607571, info@trailblazer-guides.com
www.trailblazer-guides.com

British Library Cataloguing in Publication Data
A catalogue record for this book is available from the British Library

ISBN 978-1-905864-03-4

© **Trailblazer 2004, 2007**
Text and maps

Editor: Anna Jacomb-Hood
Additional research: Jenny Hill
Layout: Anna Jacomb-Hood
Illustrations: © Nick Hill (pp59-60); Rev CA Johns (p63)
Photographs (flora): C2 Row 1, middle, © Jane Thomas;
C3 Row 2, right, © Henry Stedman; all others © Bryn Thomas
Other photographs: © as credited
Cartography: Nick Hill
Index: Anna Jacomb-Hood and Jane Thomas

The maps in this guide were prepared from out-of-Crown-
copyright Ordnance Survey maps amended and updated by Trailblazer.

Warning: coastal walking can be dangerous
Please read the notes on when to go (p21) and outdoor safety (pp48-51).
Every effort has been made by the author and publisher to ensure that the information
contained herein is as accurate and up to date as possible. However, they are unable
to accept responsibility for any inconvenience, loss or injury sustained by anyone
as a result of the advice and information given in this guide.

Printed on chlorine-free paper by
D2Print (☎ +65-6295 5598), Singapore

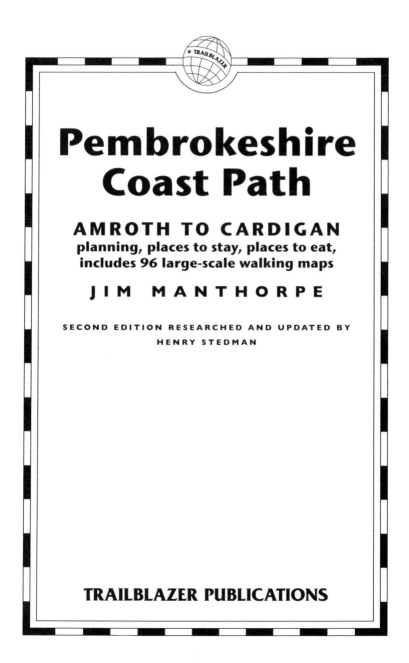

Pembrokeshire Coast Path

AMROTH TO CARDIGAN
planning, places to stay, places to eat, includes 96 large-scale walking maps

JIM MANTHORPE

SECOND EDITION RESEARCHED AND UPDATED BY
HENRY STEDMAN

TRAILBLAZER PUBLICATIONS

Para Nuria
Gracias por todo

Acknowledgements

From Jim Manthorpe I'd like to thank Henry Stedman for such dedicated work on this edition of the Pembrokeshire Coast Path. Many thanks, as always, to Bryn Thomas for giving me such wonderful opportunities to write and travel. Also at Trailblazer, many thanks to Anna Jacomb-Hood, Nick Hill and Jane Thomas for editing, mapping and indexing. Finally, thank you to Mum, Dad, Sam, Amy and Jack for their unstinting encouragement and just for being there.

From Henry Stedman Thanks to Sam Turner for his fortitude and company on the first part of the walk, and for being such a good photographic model! And to Tam Lush for performing a similar role on the latter half of the walk.

I'd particularly like to thank the Pembrokeshire Coast Path National Trail Officer, Dave Maclachlan, for his helpful advice. Thanks also to the readers who wrote to us with suggestions, including Andrea Reinacher, Mrs A Richards, Emma Stewardson, Brian Shelley, Andrew Heath, Chris Tobitt, Robert Harris, Nigel Smith, Anson Paul, Tony Phelps

A request

The author and publisher have tried to ensure that this guide is as accurate and up to date as possible. However, things change even on these well-worn routes. If you notice any changes or omissions that should be included in the next edition of this guide, please write to Trailblazer (address on p2) or email us at 🖥 info@trailblazer-guides.com). A free copy of the next edition and an acknowledgement in the front of that edition will be sent to those persons making a significant contribution.

Updated information will shortly be available on
🖥 **www.trailblazer-guides.com**

Front cover: Looking out from Stackpole Head (see p89).
These precipitous limestone cliffs are popular with climbers. © Henry Stedman

CONTENTS

MAP KEYS 6

INTRODUCTION 7

PART 1: PLANNING YOUR WALK
   About the Pembrokeshire Coast Path 9
   Practical information for the walker 10
   Budgeting 20
   When to go 21
   Itineraries 23
   What to take 30
   Getting to and from the Pembrokeshire Coast Path 36

PART 2: MINIMUM IMPACT WALKING AND OUTDOOR SAFETY
   Minimum impact walking 42
   Outdoor safety 48

PART 3: THE ENVIRONMENT AND NATURE
   Conserving Pembrokeshire 52
   Flora and fauna 56

PART 4: ROUTE GUIDE AND MAPS
   Using this guide 65
   Pembrokeshire Coast Path
   Kilgetty 66 – Kilgetty to Amroth 67 – Amroth to Tenby 71 – Tenby to
   Manorbier Bay 79 – Manorbier Bay to Freshwater East 86 – Freshwater
   East to Broad Haven 86 – Broad Haven to Castlemartin via Stack Rocks 90
   Detour route: Broad Haven to Castlemartin via Bosherston 94
   Castlemartin to Angle 96 – Angle to Hundleton 100 – Hundleton to
   Hazelbeach 106 – Hazelbeach to Sandy Haven 118 – Sandy Haven to
   Dale 126 – Dale to Musselwick Sands 133 – Musselwick Sands to Broad
   Haven 138 – Broad Haven to Newgale 144 – Newgale to Caerfai Bay 152
   Caerfai Bay to Whitesands Bay 160 – Whitesands Bay to Trefin 162
   Trefin to Pwll Deri 172 – Pwll Deri to Fishguard 176 – Fishguard to
   Newport 184 – Newport to St Dogmaels 194 – Cardigan 203

INDEX 205

Trail map key

		𝄙𝄙𝄙	Stone wall	🌲	Trees/woodland
⫽	Coast Path	∼ ∼ ∼	Water	〰 〰	Rough grassland
⫽	Other path	⋰⋱⋰	Sand or mudflats	■	B&B/guesthouse/youth hostel
⫽	4 x 4 track	∘∘∘	Pebbly beach	⋇	Campsite
⫽⫽	Tarmac road	▼▼▼▲	Cleft/small valley	▢	Building
⫼⫼⫼	Steps	⟋⟋	Cliffs	⎋	Lighthouse/beacon
↗	Slope/Steep slope	⚑	Blue Flag beach	†	Church/religious site
⤬	Stile and fence	⚐	Safe for swimming	⊘	Public toilet
⫽	Gate and fence	⌣	Stream	⊤	Public telephone
⫽▯	Cattle grid	⌇	River	⊕	Bus stop
⤳	Bridge	↓ ↓ ↓	Bog or marsh	CP	Car park
〰〰	Hedge	⌇⌇	Sand dunes	🔵80	Map continuation

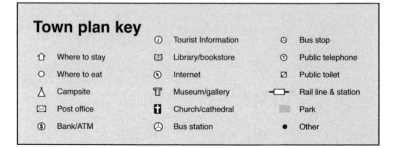

Town plan key

⌂	Where to stay	ⓘ	Tourist Information	☉	Bus stop
○	Where to eat	📖	Library/bookstore	⊤	Public telephone
△	Campsite	ⓢ	Internet	⊘	Public toilet
✉	Post office	⛪	Museum/gallery	▭	Rail line & station
Ⓢ	Bank/ATM	✝	Church/cathedral		Park
		⊘	Bus station	●	Other

INTRODUCTION

I must go down to the sea again, for the call of the running tide,
Is a wild call and a clear call that may not be denied;
... And all I ask is a windy day with the white clouds flying,
And the flung spray and the blown spume, and the seagulls crying.

I must go down to the sea again, to the vagrant gypsy life,
To the gull's way and the whale's way where the wind's like a whetted knife;
... And all I ask is a merry yarn from a laughing fellow-rover,
And quiet sleep and a sweet dream when the long trick's over.
Sea Fever (selected lines, post-1902 version) – **John Masefield** (1878-1967)

The Pembrokeshire coast is not generally well known yet in its obscurity it is outstanding. More and more people, however, are discovering this magnificent coastline on the extreme western point of Wales. What better way to explore it than to pull on your boots and walk the cliff tops and beaches of this superb 186-mile (299km) route.

The Pembrokeshire Coast Path begins in the seaside village of Amroth and takes you across the contorted sandstone cliffs of south Pembrokeshire past the colourful houses set above Tenby Harbour and on to the dramatic limestone cliffs at Stackpole. Around every corner the cliffs surprise you with blowholes, sea caves and spectacular natural arches such as the famous Green Bridge of Wales (see p90).

Then it's on across the immaculate sands of Freshwater West and through the patchwork fields around the lazy waters of the Daugleddau estuary to the town of Pembroke with its Norman castle and ancient town walls. North of the estuary everything changes. The scenery is wilder and the walking tougher. The path leaves the Norman south and enters true Welsh country crossing spectacular beaches at Broad Haven and Newgale to reach the beautiful village of Solva, its busy little harbour tucked in a fold in the cliffs.

Next is St David's, the smallest city in Britain, where you can hear the bells of the cathedral echoing across the wooded valley while paying homage to the patron saint of Wales. Leading towards the most westerly point at St David's Head the path takes you past Ramsey Island, a haven for dolphins and seals, and up the rugged heathery coastline to the curious little fishing village of Porthgain. At Fishguard you can learn about the Last Invasion of Britain, or catch a ferry over to Ireland.

The final stretch takes you beneath the shadow of the Preseli Hills, bluestone country, the source of some of the raw material for Stonehenge. Continuing over the highest, most spectacular cliffs in West Wales brings you to the end of the path at St Dogmaels, near Cardigan. The Pembrokeshire coast has everything – from endless, sandy beaches and rugged cliffs festooned with wild flowers to lonely hills and sleepy waterways; a beautiful blend of sand, sea and scents.

About this book

This guidebook contains all the information you need. The hard work has been done for you so you can plan your trip from home without the usual pile of books, maps, guides and tourist brochures. It includes:

● All standards of accommodation from campsites to luxurious guesthouses
● Walking companies if you want an organized tour
● Suggested itineraries for all types of walkers
● Answers to all your questions: when to go, degree of difficulty, what to pack and how much will the whole walking holiday cost me?

When you're all packed and ready to go, there's comprehensive information to get you to and from the coast path and 96 detailed maps (1:20,000) and town plans to help you find your way along it. The route guide section includes:

● Walking times in both directions
● Reviews of campsites, bunkhouses, hostels, B&Bs and guesthouses
● Cafés, pubs, tea shops, takeaways, restaurants and shops for buying supplies
● Rail, bus and taxi information for all the villages and towns along the coast path
● Street maps of the main towns: Saundersfoot, Tenby, Pembroke, Pembroke Dock, Milford Haven, St David's, Fishguard, Newport and Cardigan
● Historical, cultural and geographical background information

Minimum impact for maximum insight

Everybody needs a break; climb a mountain or jump in a lake.
Christy Moore, *Lisdoonvarna*

Why is walking in wild and solitary places so satisfying? Partly it is the sheer physical pleasure: sometimes pitting one's strength against the elements, sometimes relaxing on the springy turf or sand. The beauty and wonder of the natural world restore our sense of proportion, freeing us from the stresses and strains of everyday life.

All this the countryside gives us and the least we can do is to safeguard it by supporting rural economies, local businesses and environmentally sensitive forms of transport, and low-impact methods of farming and land use. In this book there is a detailed and illustrated chapter on the wildlife and conservation of Pembrokeshire and a chapter on minimum impact walking with ideas on how to tread lightly in this fragile environment. By following these principles we can help to preserve our natural heritage for future generations.

PART 1: PLANNING YOUR WALK

About the Pembrokeshire Coast Path

HISTORY

It was in 1952 that the Pembrokeshire coast received National Park status. At the same time naturalist Ronald Lockley proposed a long-distance footpath that would provide an uninterrupted walking route through the length of the park. But it was not until 1970 that the coast path was finally opened.

A number of problems arose when choosing the best route for the path, particularly around the, quite frankly, ugly industrial stretches among the power stations and oil refineries on either side of the Milford Haven estuary. It is hard to avoid these eyesores, but the path designers have done a good job in choosing a route that keeps the chimneys and towers out of sight for as long as possible. In many places trees and shrubs have been planted alongside the perimeter fences to act as a screen. At times it is only by looking at the map or sensing the acrid smell that you realize you are walking right next to a major refinery.

Nevertheless many walkers quite justifiably choose to leave out this uninspiring section between Angle and Milford Haven. For the rest of its length the path hugs the coastline where possible but inland diversions are inevitable to avoid private land, geographical obstacles and the artillery range at Castlemartin.

The official length of the path has changed over the years. It presently stands at 186 miles (299km) but the distance that any one person walks really depends on how many detours or shortcuts they choose to take.

HOW DIFFICULT IS THE PEMBROKESHIRE COAST PATH?

This is not a technically difficult walk and most reasonably fit people should be able to tackle it without any problems. However, the distance should not be underestimated; although it is not a mountainous path there are many steep up-and-down sections. On completion you will have ascended more than the height of Everest.

The southern section is tamer than the northern stretch with its mighty cliffs where the sense of exposure is more marked and the distances between villages are greater. Always be aware of the ever-present danger of the cliff edge. Accidents often happen late in the day when fatigue sets in and people lose their footing. Be aware of your capabilities and limitations and plan each day accordingly. Don't try to do too much in one day: taking it slowly allows you to relax, see a lot more and you'll enjoy the walk without becoming exhausted or fed up.

Waymarker

Route finding

This should not be a problem since the path is well trodden and obvious. The entire length is waymarked with 'finger-posts' marked with an acorn symbol. For the most part the path hugs the coastline, although detours are sometimes necessary due to erosion of the cliff. Every year at least one large cliff section gives way but the park authorities are usually very quick to realign the path.

Check the tide times (see p50) to avoid lengthy detours around bays and estuaries. You will need to carefully plan crossing the river mouths at Sandy Haven and The Gann, just to the north of Dale, as they are flooded at high tide. If you time it right you will be able to cross them both on the same day (see box p126 for further details). One other area for confusion is the Castlemartin MoD range. When firing is taking place a detour must be taken along the road (see p94).

HOW LONG DO YOU NEED?

This depends on your fitness and experience. Do not try to do too much in one day if you are new to long-distance walking. Most people find that two weeks is enough to complete the walk and still have time to look around the villages and enjoy the views along the way. Alternatively the entire path can be done in eleven days or less if you are fit enough.

If you're camping don't underestimate how much a heavy pack laden with camping gear will slow you down. It is also worth bearing in mind that those who take it easy on the path tend to see a lot more than those who sweat out long days and only ever see the path in front of them. When deciding how long you need remember to allow a few extra days for side trips or simply to rest. On pp26-8 there are some suggested itineraries covering different walking speeds.

If you have only a few days available concentrate on the best parts of the coast path; there is a list of recommended day and weekend walks on p29.

Practical information for the walker

ACCOMMODATION

Most of the coast path is well served with accommodation for all budgets, from campsites to luxurious hotels. The route guide (Part 4) lists a selection of places to stay along the full length of the trail. It's advisable to book all accommodation in advance, particularly during the high season (Easter to August). The most barren area for accommodation is from Manorbier to Pembroke where pre-planning is even more crucial. Remember that the advantages of walking at less busy times are countered by the fact that many places are closed during the winter months.

Camping

Wild camping is not strictly allowed in the national park but a kind landowner may let you camp in a field (see p45). There are a number of official campsites with basic facilities such as toilets and the all-important showers with prices from £2.50 to £10 per person making this the cheapest accommodation option.

In the summer there are usually plenty of places to camp along the length of the coast path, but if you are planning short days you may have to find alternative accommodation on two or three nights. This is particularly true around Bosherston and the Dale peninsula where you can stay in bed and breakfasts instead (see box p26). Those hardy souls who plan to walk in winter (November to Easter) will find many of the campsites closed, although there are a few that remain open all year.

Camping is like being a snail; carrying your home on your back and travelling at a similar speed. However, there is great satisfaction to be had from spending not just the day but the night in the great outdoors, watching the stars and witnessing the sunset and sunrise. Those who shy away from tented travel because of its perceived disadvantages really miss out on an enlightening experience.

Hostels and bunkhouses

The hostels on the coast path are cheap (£10-14, £7-10 for under 18s) and allow you to travel on a budget without having to carry cumbersome camping equipment. YHA hostels vary greatly in style; St David's hostel, above Whitesands Bay, is an old farmhouse while the one at Manorbier is a converted NATO storage building. The hostel at Newgale is now run in partnership with YMCA Wales.

Youth hostels are good places to meet fellow walkers and in many cases are just as comfortable as B&Bs. However, there is a problem. With the exception of Manorbier Youth Hostel (Lydstep) there aren't any other hostels or bunkhouses for the first 70 miles or so between Amroth and Marloes Sands. Depending on your speed, you will need to use B&Bs for the first 3-7 nights and again in St David's itself if you plan to stop there (see box p27).

On the positive side there are six youth hostels conveniently spaced a day apart from Marloes Sands to the end of the coast path at St Dogmaels. All the youth hostels on the coast path provide bedding so there is no need to carry a sleeping bag. Increasingly youth hostels have (en suite) rooms with locks as well as the traditional dorms. Additionally they all have self-catering kitchens; most on the route are self-catering only but a couple provide meals. All hostels provide toilets and washing facilities, most have a sitting area and a drying room, some also have a games room/tv lounge. A few have a small shop for emergency groceries. Most youth hostels will only save your booked bed until 6pm which puts you in an uncomfortable rush if you have a lot of walking to do. It's worth phoning ahead to let them know if you're going to arrive later.

Youth hostels (YHAs) are, despite their name, for anyone of any age as long as you are a member. You can join the **Youth Hostels Association of England and Wales** (☎ 0870-770 8868, 🖳 www.yha.org.uk) at any of the hostels, or over the phone or online, for £15.95 per year for an individual (£22.95 for two people living at the same address or a family, £9.95 for people under 26).

In addition to the youth hostels there is an **independent hostel** at Fishguard. This is privately owned so you do not need to be a member of any association and it also has the welcome advantage of having few rules and no curfew, unlike YHA youth hostels. Otherwise it is similar to YHA hostels with accommodation in small dormitories with bed linen provided and a fully equipped self-catering kitchen.

Finally you could try one of the **bunkhouses** on the coast path (at Dale, Cyffredin, near Abereiddy, Trefin, and Newport; also possibly by the time you read this at Castlemartin) which provide more basic accommodation. They are full of character and eccentricity and are well worth visiting, if only for one night. The drawback is that you need your own sleeping bag.

By using hostels on the northern half of the walk and bed and breakfasts on the southern half you can cut out the need to pack a sleeping bag altogether, thus significantly lightening your load.

If you are planning to walk in **winter** you should bear in mind that some or all of the YHA hostels may be closed, especially during the week. However, if there is enough demand they may open so it is always worth checking.

Bed and breakfast

Anyone who has not stayed in a bed and breakfast (B&B) has missed out on something very British. They vary greatly in quality, style and price but usually consist of a bed in someone's house and a big cooked breakfast in the morning. For visitors from outside Britain it can provide an interesting insight into the Welsh way of life as you often feel like a guest of the family.

What to expect All the coastal walker wants is a warm bed and a hot bath. For this reason most B&Bs listed in this guide are recommended because of their usefulness to the walker and their proximity to the path.

Many bed and breakfasts offer en suite rooms or at least have the choice. However, for a few pounds less you can usually get a standard room and it's never far to the bathroom. Anyone walking alone may find it hard to find establishments with **single** rooms. **Twin** rooms and **double** rooms are often confused but a twin room usually comprises two single beds while a double room has one double bed. **Family** rooms are for three or more people.

Virtually all B&Bs provide a hefty cooked breakfast as part of the room rate, some also provide a packed lunch and/or evening meal if requested in advance (see also p12).

Tariffs B&Bs in this guide vary in price from £17 per person for the most basic accommodation to over £40 for the most luxurious en suite places. Most charge around £25 per person. Remember that many places do not have single rooms and will usually charge a supplement of between £5 and £10 for single occupancy in a double or twin room.

Rates can be substantially lower during the winter months and if you are on a budget you could always ask to go without breakfast which will usually result in a lower price.

❑ **Booking accommodation**

You should always book your accommodation. In summer there can be stiff competition for beds and in winter there's the distinct possibility that the place could be closed. Bookings for any YHA hostel can be made through the centralized reservation service (☎ 0870-770 8868) but some hostels can be booked online (🖥 www.yha .org.uk, or through 🖥 www.hihostels.com for instant confirmation) through the booking request facility. Many B&Bs and hotels can also now be booked online – some only through an agency but others have their own website; however, phoning is probably best because you can check details more easily.

In most cases you will have to pay a deposit or the full charge at the time of booking. Always let the establishment know if you have to cancel your booking so they can offer the bed to someone else.

Since April 2007 there has been a ban on smoking in all public places in Wales. While places to stay are able to designate rooms for smokers, do check this if it's important to you. See also box p17.

Many B&Bs ban dogs and young children so it is worth checking in advance if any of these are likely to be a problem.

Guesthouses, hotels, pubs and inns

Guesthouses and hotels are usually more sophisticated than bed and breakfasts offering evening meals and a lounge for guests. Pubs and inns offer bed and breakfast of a medium to high standard and have the added advantage of having a bar downstairs, so it's not far to stagger back to bed. However, the noise from tipsy punters might prove a nuisance if you want an early night. Rates usually range from £20 to £30 per person per night.

Hotels are usually aimed more for the motoring tourist rather than the muddy walker and the tariff (£35 to £60 per person) is likely to put off the budget traveller. A few hotels have been included in the trail guide for those feeling they deserve at least one night of luxury during their trip.

Holiday cottages

Self-catering cottages are ideal for small groups who want to base themselves in the same place for a week or more. This can be a good way to walk parts of the coast path using public transport (see pp38-41) to travel to and from each day's stage.

A good base for a week's walking in south Pembrokeshire would be the seaside town of Tenby which has good public transport links. If you prefer something quieter you could try Freshwater East which has lots of holiday cottages.

St David's, or somewhere close to Fishguard, would be a convenient place to base yourself for walks in north Pembrokeshire. Try the tiny holiday village of Cwm-yr-eglwys which has a good bathing beach.

Prices for holiday cottages usually start at £120 per person for the week based on four to six people sharing. Cottages haven't been listed in this book; contact the tourist information centre (see box p35) in the area you want to go to for details.

FOOD AND DRINK

Breakfast and lunch

If staying in a B&B or hotel you can be sure to enjoy a full Welsh cooked break-fast which may be more than you are used to. Ask for a lighter continental or veg-etarian breakfast if you'd prefer.

Many B&Bs and youth hostels can also provide you with a packed lunch at an additional cost; if you want an early start or have had enough of cooked break-fasts it may be worth asking for a packed lunch instead of a cooked breakfast. Alternatively, breakfast and packed lunches can be bought and made yourself. There are some great cafés and bakeries along the way which can supply both eat-in or takeaway; many pubs also offer lunches. Remember that stretches of the walk are devoid of anywhere to eat so check the information in Part 4 to make sure you don't go hungry.

Evening meals

Hotels and guesthouses almost always offer evening meals; some B&Bs and YHA youth hostels may also but you will almost always need to book in advance and eat at a set time. Youth hostels always have self-catering kitchens so you can make your own meal. Most B&Bs are close enough to a pub or restaurant and if they are not, the owner may sometimes give you a lift to and from the nearest eating place.

The Pembrokeshire coast is blessed with some outstanding **pubs** and inns. There is nothing quite like the lure of a pint to get you through those last few miles of the day. Most pubs offer lunch and evening meals and usually have some vegetarian options. The standard varies from basic pub grub from the bar menu to à la carte restaurant food. Most walkers will be happy with whatever is put in front of them after working up an appetite.

There are some quality **restaurants** in most of the towns, with menus vary-ing from French and Italian to the ubiquitous seafood. In addition most towns and some of the larger villages are riddled with cheap **takeaway** joints offering kebabs, pizzas, Chinese and fish and chips. They can come in handy if you fin-ish your walk late in the day since they usually stay open until at least 11pm.

Buying camping supplies

If you are camping, fuel for your stove, outdoor equipment and food supplies are important considerations. The best places for outdoor gear are the TYF out-door adventure shops in Tenby and St David's. In the summer many of the campsites have shops that sell fuel as do most of the general stores along the route but remember that in the winter months many of the smaller ones open for a shorter time or not at all. Check the services details in Part 4 for more infor-mation. Particularly barren areas for supplies of any kind are from Tenby to Pembroke and St David's to Fishguard.

Drinking water

Depending on the weather you will need to drink as much as two to four litres of water a day. If you're feeling lethargic it may well be that you haven't drunk

❏ Local food and drink

Many of the pubs promote **real ales**. There are plenty of the well-known brands from across the border but for a Welsh ale try Brains SA, Buckley's, Cousin Jack or Reverend James.

As for food, it would be easy to walk the entire coast path surviving on a diet of fish and chips and junk food and, like the rest of Britain, West Wales seems to have claimed Indian food as its own. All the towns have at least one curry house, many of them of very high quality. Even the old traditional pubs have got in on the act with chicken tikka masala ever present on the menu.

But Welsh cuisine should not be overlooked, as it so often is. The coast path gives you the perfect opportunity to try it for yourself. Unsurprisingly seafood is a speciality in these parts with many restaurants and pubs serving local **cockles** and **mussels**, **sea trout** and **pints of prawns**. If this is not your thing there is always the famous **Welsh lamb**. Here are some other Welsh delicacies:

● **Laver bread** Has been described as Welsh caviar but equally as a seaweed pancake; take your pick. It is certainly seaweed based and is mixed with oatmeal and fried in fat. Even supermarkets stock it now.
● **Bara brith** A rich fruity bread made by soaking fruit in tea and then adding marmalade, spices and other ingredients
● **Welsh cakes** Tasty cakes full of currants and sultanas; you can find them in supermarkets and in most tea shops and cafés
● **Welsh rarebit** Melted cheese with a hint of mustard poured over buttered toast, though recipes vary
● **Cawl cennin a phersli** (Leek and parsley broth) A soup made from root vegetables such as parsnips, carrots, swede, potatoes) with leeks and parsley in a lamb stock
● **Cawl mamgu Tregaron** (Tregaron granny's broth) Another soup full of vegetables with shin beef and bacon
● **Stuffed leeks with cheese and mustard sauce** Leeks stuffed with sausagemeat and served with a cheese and mustard sauce
● **Gorfoledd y glowyr** (Miner's delight) A rabbit casserole
● **Oggy** The Welsh equivalent of the Cornish pasty containing Welsh beef, leeks, potato, onions and gravy in a thick pastry crust. It was originally the standard lunch for miners.
● **Preseli cheese** Goat's cheese, two soft cow cheeses and smoked cheese are all made at Pant Mawr Farm (☎ 01437-532627, 🖳 www.pantmawrcheeses.co.uk), Rosebush, Clynderwen, in the Preseli Hills. All the cheeses carry the Pembrokeshire Produce seal of approval and are made from pasteurized milk with vegetarian rennets.

enough, even if you're not feeling particularly thirsty. Drinking directly from streams and rivers is tempting, but is not a good idea. Streams that cross the path tend to have flowed across farmland where you can be pretty sure any number of farm animals have relieved themselves. Combined with the probable presence of farm pesticides and other delights it is best to avoid drinking from these streams.

Drinking-water taps and fountains are marked in the trail guide. Where these are thin on the ground you can usually ask a friendly shopkeeper or pub barman to fill your bottle or pouch for you, from the tap of course.

MONEY

On some sections of the coast path there is a distinct lack of banks. There are no banks along the 53-mile (85km) stretch between Tenby and Pembroke (though there is an ATM in the shop at Manorbier), for example, and there are only a couple of ATMs – one at Marloes, just off the path, and one in the post office/shop at Broad Haven – between Milford Haven and St David's, a distance of 47 miles (76km). Be aware that some Link ATMs are 'pay to use' though the charges are clearly displayed outside the machine and on the screen.

It is a good idea therefore to carry plenty of cash with you, maybe keeping it in a money belt for security. Small independent shops rarely accept payment by card and will require you to pay in cash or by cheque, as will most B&Bs,

---

❑ **Information for foreign visitors**

● **Currency** The British pound (£) comes in notes of £100, £50, £20, £10, £5 and coins of £2 and £1. The pound is divided into 100 pence (usually referred to as 'p', pronounced 'pee') which comes in silver coins of 50p, 20p, 10p, and 5p and copper coins of 2p and 1p. The design of the pound coin is different in Wales, the Welsh coin carrying a leek.

● **Rates of exchange** Up-to-date rates of exchange can be found on 🖳 www.xe.com/ucc, at some post offices, or at any bank or travel agent.

● **Business hours** Most **shops** and main **post offices** are open at least from Monday to Friday 9am-5pm and Saturday 9am-12.30pm but many choose longer hours and some open on Sunday as well. Occasionally, especially in rural areas, you'll come across a local shop that closes at midday during the week, usually a Wednesday or Thursday, a throwback to the days when all towns and villages had an 'early closing day'. Many **supermarkets** remain open 12 hours a day; the Spar chain usually displays '8 till late' on the door. **Banks** typically open Monday to Friday at 9.30am until 3.30pm or 4pm, but of course ATM machines are open all the time. **Pub** hours are less predictable, but common opening hours are 11am-2.30pm and 6-11pm Mon-Sat, opening an hour later on Sunday evenings.

● **National holidays** Most businesses in Wales are shut on 1 January, Good Friday (March/April), Easter Monday (March/April), first and last Monday in May, last Monday in August, 25 December and 26 December.

● **School holidays** State-school holidays in England and Wales are generally as follows: a one-week break late October, two weeks over Christmas and the New Year, a week mid-February, two weeks around Easter, one week at the end of May/early June (to coincide with the bank holiday at the end of May) and five to six weeks from late July to early September. Private-school holidays fall at the same time, but tend to be slightly longer.

● **EHICs and travel insurance** Although Britain's National Health Service (NHS) is free at the point of use, that is only the case for residents. All visitors to Britain should be properly insured, including comprehensive health coverage. The European Health Insurance Card (EHIC) entitles EU nationals (on production of the EHIC card so ensure you bring it with you) to necessary medical treatment under the NHS while on a temporary visit here. For details, contact your national social security institution.

(cont'd opposite)

bunkhouses and campsites. Shops that do take cards, such as supermarkets, will sometimes advance cash against a card as long as you buy something at the same time. **Travellers' cheques** can only be cashed at banks, foreign exchange offices and some large hotels.

See also p33 and the town and village facilities table, pp24-5.

Using the post office for banking Several banks in Britain have agreements with the Post Office allowing customers to make cash withdrawals using a chip and pin debit card, or a chequebook and debit card at post offices throughout the country. As there are plenty of post offices along the coast path this is a useful facility for the walker. For a full list of banks offering these facilities call ☎ 08457-223344.

(cont'd from opposite) However, this is not a substitute for proper medical cover on your travel insurance and for unforeseen bills and for getting you home should that be necessary. Also consider cover for loss and theft of personal belongings, especially if you are camping or staying in hostels, as there will be times when you'll have to leave your luggage unattended.

● **Weights and measures** Britain is moving slowly into the metric system but there is resistance. Most food is now displayed and sold in metric (g and kg) but most people still think and talk in the imperial weights of pounds (lb) and ounces (oz). Milk is sold in pints, as is beer in the pub, yet most other liquid including petrol (gasoline) is sold in litres.

The population remains split between those who still use inches and feet and those who are happy with centimetres and millimetres. Road distances are shown in miles rather than kilometres, and you'll often be told that 'it's only a hundred yards or so'. The weather – a frequent topic of conversation – is also an issue: while most forecasts predict temperatures in °C, many people continue to think in terms of °F.

● **Smoking** A ban on smoking in public places came into force in Wales in April 2007. The ban relates not only to pubs and restaurants, but also to B&Bs, hostels and hotels. These latter have the right to designate one or more bedrooms where the occupants can smoke, but the ban will be in force in all enclosed areas open to the public – even if they are in a private home such as a B&B. Should you be foolhardy enough to light up in a no-smoking area, which includes pretty well any indoor public place, you could be fined £50, but it's the owners of the premises who carry the can if they fail to stop you, with a potential fine of £2500.

● **Time** During the winter, the whole of Britain is on Greenwich Meantime (GMT). The clocks move one hour forward on the last Sunday in March, remaining on British Summer Time (BST) until the last Sunday in October.

● **Telephone** From outside Britain the international country access code for Britain is ☎ 44 followed by the area code minus the first 0, and then the number you require. Within Britain, to call a number with the same code as the phone you are calling from, the code can be omitted: dial the number only. It is cheaper to ring at weekends, and after 6pm and before 8am on weekdays. If you're using a mobile phone that is registered overseas, consider buying a local SIM card to keep costs down.

● **Emergency services** For police, ambulance, fire brigade and coastguard dial ☎ 999.

PLANNING YOUR WALK

OTHER SERVICES

Most villages and all the towns have at least one public **telephone**, a small **shop** and a **post office**. Other than for withdrawing money (see p17) post offices can be used for sending unnecessary clothes and equipment home which may be weighing you down.

In Part 4 special mention is given to services that may be of use to the walker such as the above as well as **banks**, **cash machines** (cashpoints), **outdoor equipment shops**, **laundrettes**, **internet access**, **pharmacies**, and **tourist information centres** which can be used for finding and booking accommodation among other things.

WALKING COMPANIES

For walkers wanting to make their holiday as easy and trouble-free as possible there are several specialist companies offering a range of services from accommodation booking to fully guided group tours.

Expect to pay between £335 for a 5-day/6-night self-guided holiday and £920 for a 16-day/17-night fully guided tour. These prices are for two sharing a room; walkers on their own are likely to be charged an additional single supplement of £15-20 per night.

Baggage carriers
Some of the **taxi** firms listed in this guide (see Part 4) can provide a baggage-carrying service within a local area. See also Self-guided holidays below.

Group/guided walking tours
Fully guided tours are ideal for individuals wanting to travel in the company of others and for groups of friends wanting to be guided. The packages usually include meals, accommodation, transport arrangements, minibus back-up, baggage transfer, as well as a qualified guide. Companies' specialities differ widely with varying size of groups, standards of accommodation, age range of clients, distances walked and professionalism of guides. In the list of companies below we have indicated which offer a complete guided walking package.

Self-guided holidays
Self-guided holidays are all-in customized packages for walkers which usually include detailed advice and notes on itineraries and routes, maps, accommodation booking, daily baggage transfer and transport arrangements at the start and end of your walk. If you don't want the whole all-in package some companies will gladly arrange the **accommodation booking** or **baggage-carrying** services on their own. The following companies provide self-guided holidays and where specified fully guided tours:

● **Celtic Trails** (☎ 0800-970 7585 or from overseas ☎ 01600-860846, 🖥 www .celtrail.com; PO Box 11, Chepstow, NP16 6DZ) Itineraries from 3 to 13 days.
● **Contours Walking Holidays** (☎ 017684 80451, 🖥 www.contours.co.uk; Gramyre, 3 Berrier Rd, Greystoke, CA11 OUB) Offers both the complete path,

taking between 12 and 16 days (with optional rest days) and shorter trails covering either the northern (St Dogmaels to St David's; 66 miles), central (St David's to Milford Haven; 48 miles) or southern (Milford Haven to Amroth; 66 miles) sections of the path.

● **Footpath Holidays** (☎ 01985-840049; ▨ www.footpath-holidays.com; 16 Norton Bavant, nr Warminster, Wilts BA12 7BB) Walkers are based at St David's Warpool Court Hotel (see p158) for the duration of their holiday. Fully guided tours also available.

● **Greenways Holidays** (☎ 01834-862109, ▨ www.greenwaysholidays.com; The Old School, Station Rd, Narberth, SA67 7DU) This company is managed by PLANED (Pembrokeshire Local Action Network for Enterprise and Development so it supports locally owned facilities and uses the coastal buses and trains, ie sustainable means of transport, on its Explorer breaks. They also offer cycling holidays around the region.

● **HF Holidays** (☎ 020-8905 9556, ▨ www.hfholidays.co.uk; Imperial House, The Hyde, Edgware Rd, London, NW9 5AL) Provides guided-trail holidays, such as six days/seven nights from St Dogmaels to St David's.

● **InStep Linear Walking Holidays** (☎ 01903-766475, ▨ www.instephols .co.uk; 35 Cokeham Rd, Lancing, West Sussex BN15 0AE) Offers a 13-day trek covering the entire path.

● **Xplore Britain** (☎ 01740-650900, ▨ www.xplorebritain.com; 6 George St, Ferryhill, Co Durham DL17 0DT) Self-guided treks along the coast path include a six-night Dale to St David's trail.

● **The Discerning Traveller** (☎ 01865-0516518, ▨ www.chycor.co.uk; 24 Cardigan St, Oxford OX2 6BP) This company specializes in week-long tours; their tour on the Pembrokeshire Coast Path is from Dale to St David's.

TAKING DOGS ALONG THE COAST PATH

The National Park trail officers have worked hard to make the path more dog friendly. Dog stiles, or doggy stiles as they are affectionately known, have been installed all along the path to prevent damage to the fences caused by dogs squeezing their way through. This acceptance shown towards the dog-walking fraternity is thanks in part to the responsible attitude that they have shown.

Dogs should always be kept on leads while on the footpath to avoid disturbing wildlife, livestock and other walkers. Dog excrement should be cleaned up and not left to decorate the boots of other walkers. Bear in mind that between 1 May and 30 September dogs are not allowed on certain parts of the following beaches: Amroth, Saundersfoot, Tenby Castle, Tenby South, Lydstep, Newgale and Poppit Sands. Between the same dates complete bans exist on Tenby's North Beach and at Whitesands Bay. However, these restrictions do not pose any great obstacle to coast-path walkers with dogs since the path only occasionally crosses a beach and where it does there is always an alternative route a short way inland.

Remember when planning and booking your accommodation you will need to phone ahead to check if your dog will be welcome. Not all places to stay accept dogs and of those that do, some charge extra (up to £10).

DISABLED ACCESS

Taking the coast path's undulating and rough terrain into account, it may come as a surprise to learn that short sections of it are accessible by wheelchair. The National Park Authority was awarded the BT Access for All Award in 2000 and their guide *Easy Access Routes in the Pembrokeshire Coast National Park* (£2.95) details 19 routes for wheelchair users ranging from 600m to 3km, all but one of which lies within the national park. Some of these routes include: Tenby South beach to Penally (pp79-80), St Govan's car park to St Govan's Head (pp89-91), Abereiddy to The Blue Lagoon (pp167-8) and Pwllgwaelod to Cwm-yr-eglwys (pp184-6).

Budgeting

The amount of money you are likely to spend depends on your accommodation plans and how you're going to eat. If you camp and cook your own meals your expenses can stay very low but most people prefer to have at least some of their meals cooked for them and even the hardy camper may be tempted into the occasional B&B when the rain is falling.

CAMPING

You can survive on as little as £9 per person if you use the cheapest sites and cook all your own food from staple ingredients. Nevertheless, most people find that the best-laid plans to survive on the bare minimum soon fall flat after a couple of hard days' walking. Always budget for unforeseen expenses as well as for the end-of-day drink (a pint of beer costs around £2). Assuming such liquid treats and the occasional pub meal or takeaway a budget of £10-15 per day is more realistic.

BUNKHOUSES AND HOSTELS

YHA hostels on the route charge between £9.50/7 and £14/10 per adult/child per night; most places have a self-catering kitchen allowing you to create your own meals from food bought at local shops or supermarkets. Some YHA hostels provide meals (breakfast costs £4.20/2.45 adult/child, a picnic lunch costs £4.80/3.80 and an evening meal costs £8.40/6.15). Bunkhouses cost £10-20 per person; sometimes this includes breakfast. There may also be an additional charge if you want to rent bed linen.

Now and then you will need, or want, to eat out which adds to your daily costs. Around £25-30 per day should be enough to cover the cost of accommodation while still allowing for the occasional bar meal and end of day tipple. If you are planning on eating out most nights you should clearly increase your budget to around £35 per day.

B&Bs, INNS, GUESTHOUSES AND HOTELS

B&B prices can be as little as £17 per night but are usually nearer half as much again but this will almost always include breakfast. Add on the price of a packed lunch, pub evening meal, drink and other expenses and you can expect to need around £30-50 per day, and probably more if you are walking on your own. If staying in a guesthouse or hotel expect to pay £40-60 per day.

EXTRAS

Don't forget all those little things that secretly push up your daily costs: post-cards, stamps, souvenirs, beer, camera film, buses here, buses there, more beer and getting to and from the trail in the first place; it all adds up!

When to go

SEASONS

Pembrokeshire is subjected to the full force of the weather sweeping in from the Atlantic so you can expect rain and strong winds at any time of year. Equally you can be blessed with blazing sunshine; the climate is unpredictable. The **main walking season** in Pembrokeshire is from Easter to the end of September.

Spring

Walking in Pembrokeshire from March to June has many rewards, the greatest of which is the chance to appreciate the spectacular wild flowers which come into bloom at this time. Spring is also the time of year when you are most like-ly to have dry weather. Easter can be a busy time since it is the first major hol-iday of the year but at other times the path is relatively quiet.

Summer

Unsurprisingly, summer is when every man and his dog descend on the coun-tryside with July and August, when the heather colours the hillsides purple, being the busiest months. At this time many of the beaches are packed and the coast path too. This isn't always a bad thing. Part of the enjoyment of walking is meeting like-minded people and there are plenty of them about. However, accommodation can be hard to come by, so do book well in advance.

Summer weather in west Wales is notoriously unpredictable. One day you can be sweating in the midday sun, the next day battling against the wind and rain. Remember to take clothes for any eventuality.

Autumn

Come September the tourists return home. Autumn can be wild with the first storms of winter arriving towards the end of September. Don't let this put you off. Although the likelihood of rain and wind increases as winter approaches, sunny days are still possible and the changing colours of the hillsides make the coastline spectacular.

Winter

There are a number of disadvantages of walking the coast path in winter; winter storms are common, the daylight hours are short and many of the places to stay are closed until spring. Experienced walkers who are not afraid of getting wet may appreciate the peace and quiet and may be rewarded with one of those beautifully crisp, clear winter days.

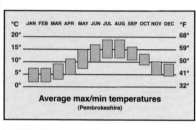

Average max/min temperatures
(Pembrokeshire)

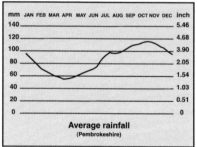

Average rainfall
(Pembrokeshire)

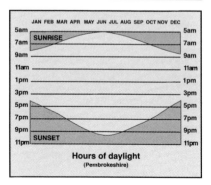

Hours of daylight
(Pembrokeshire)

TEMPERATURE

The Welsh climate is temperate and even in winter the air temperature is relatively mild thanks to the warm Gulf Stream sea current. Consequently the temperature is usually quite comfortable at any time of year although on rare occasions in summer it can get a little too hot for walking.

RAINFALL

Pembrokeshire bears the brunt of the violent weather systems that sweep in from the North Atlantic. As a result, the rainfall is usually higher here than in the more sheltered areas further east. The total annual rainfall for west Wales is 1000mm with most of it falling from late summer through into the winter with spring being the driest period.

DAYLIGHT HOURS

If walking in autumn, winter or early spring, you must take account of how far you can walk in the available light. The sunrise and sunset times in the table opposite are based on information for Milford Haven on the first of each month. This gives a rough picture for the rest of Pembrokeshire. Also bear in mind that you will get a further 30-45 minutes of usable light before and after sunrise and sunset depending on the weather.

ANNUAL EVENTS

The free national park newspaper *Coast to Coast* has a comprehensive 'What's On' page updated annually. Check with tourist information centres for details and times.

    The National Park Authority also organizes events, see their website (🖳 www.pcnpa.org.uk) for details. Below is a taster of what can be found to distract you along the way:

● **Fishguard Folk Festival** (☎ 01348-872514, 🖳 www.pembrokeshire-folk-music.co.uk/festival.htm) The sound of fiddles and *bodhrans* fill the town in the last weekend of May. Concerts and workshops are also organized. The main venue is The Royal Oak Inn in Market Sq.

● **Fishguard International Music Festival** (☎ 01348-873612, 🖳 www.fishguardfestival.org.uk) Lots of strings and brass in the last week of July. A number of orchestras perform during the week.

● **St David's Cathedral Festival** (☎ 01437-720271, 🖳 www.stdavidscathedral.org.uk/festivals) Nine days of music in the wonderful St David's Cathedral, beginning the last weekend of May; widely considered to be one of the best music festivals in Wales.

● **Tenby Arts Festival** (☎ 01834-842404, 🖳 www.tenbyartsfest.co.uk) Exhibitions in various venues around town in the last week of September. Dance workshops, kite-flying competitions, sand sculptures, music and drama.

Itineraries

This guidebook has not been divided up into rigid daily stages. Instead, it's structured to make it easy for you to plan your own itinerary. The Pembrokeshire Coast Path can be tackled in any number of ways, the most challenging of which is to do it all in one go. This does require around two weeks, time which some people just don't have.

    Most people do the walk over a series of short breaks coming back year after year to do a bit more. Others just walk the best bits, avoiding the ugly industrial stretches around the Milford Haven estuary and others use the path for linear day-walks using public transport there and back.

    To help you plan your walk see the **planning map** (opposite the inside back cover) and the **table of village/town facilities** on pp24-5; the latter gives a run down on the essential information you will need regarding accommodation possibilities and services.

PLANNING YOUR WALK

Place name Places in (brackets) are a short walk off the path	Distance from previous place approx miles/km	ATM/ Bank	Post Office	VILLAGE AND Tourist Information Centre/ National Park Centre
(Kilgetty)		ATM only	✔	TIC
Amroth	3/5			
Wiseman's Bridge	2/3			
Saundersfoot	1/1.5	✔	✔	TIC
Tenby	4/6.5	✔	✔	TIC
Penally	2.5/4		✔	
Lydstep	4/6.5			
Manorbier	4/6.5	ATM only		
Freshwater East	4/6.5			
Bosherston	6.5/10.5			
Merrion, Warren & Castlemartin	10/16		✔	
Angle	10.5/17		✔	
Hundleton	9/14.5			
Pembroke	2.5/4	✔	✔	TIC
Pembroke Dock	3/5	✔	✔	TIC
Neyland & Hazelbeach	4/6.5		✔	
Milford Haven	5.5/9	✔	✔	TIC
Sandy Haven (& Herbrandston)	4/6.5		✔	
(St Ishmael's)	2.5/4		✔	
Dale	3/5		✔	
Marloes Sands (& Marloes)	8/13		✔	
Little Haven	12/19.5		✔	
Broad Haven	0.5/1	ATM only	✔	
Nolton Haven	3.5/5.5			
Newgale	3.5/5.5			
Solva	5/8		✔	
Caerfai Bay	4/6.5			
(St David's)	(1)/(1/5)	✔	✔	TIC/NPC
Porthclais	1.5/2.3			NT kiosk
St Justinian's/Porthselau	5/8			
Whitesands Bay	2/3.2			
Abereiddy	7.5/12			
Porthgain	2/3			
Trefin	2/3		✔	
Pwll Deri & Strumble Head	9.5/15.5			
Goodwick & Fishguard	10.5/17	✔	✔	TIC
Pwllgwaelod (& Dinas Cross)	4.5/7		✔	
Newport	7/11	✔	✔	TIC/NPC
Ceibwr Bay (for Moylgrove)	9/14.5			
Poppit Sands	5/8			
St Dogmaels	2/3		✔	
(Cardigan)	(1)/(1.5)	✔	✔	TIC
TOTAL DISTANCE	186 miles (299km)			

PLANNING YOUR WALK

TOWN FACILITIES

Eating Place ✔=one; ✔✔=a few; ✔✔✔=4+	Food Store	Campsite or area where can camp	Hostels* YHA =Youth Hostel; H = Ind hostel B = Bunkhouse	B&B-style accommodation ✔=one ✔✔=a few; ✔✔✔=4+	Place name (places in brackets are a short walk off the path)
✔✔	✔	✔		✔	(Kilgetty)
✔✔✔	(✔)			✔✔	**Amroth**
✔		✔		✔	**Wiseman's Bridge**
✔✔✔	✔	✔		✔✔✔	**Saundersfoot**
✔✔✔	✔	✔		✔✔✔	**Tenby**
✔✔	✔	✔		✔✔	**Penally**
✔			YHA		**Lydstep**
✔✔✔	✔	✔		✔✔	**Manorbier**
✔				✔✔	**Freshwater East**
	(✔)			✔✔	**Bosherston**
✔		✔		✔✔	**Merrion, Warren &Castlemartin**
✔	✔	✔		✔✔	**Angle**
✔				✔✔	**Hundleton**
✔✔✔	✔	✔		✔✔✔	**Pembroke**
✔✔✔	✔			✔✔✔	**Pembroke Dock**
✔	✔			✔	**Neyland & Hazelbeach**
✔✔✔	✔			✔✔✔	**Milford Haven**
✔	✔	✔		✔✔	**Sandy Haven** (& Herbrandston)
✔					(St Ishmael's)
✔✔	✔		B	✔✔	**Dale**
✔✔	✔	✔	YHA	✔✔✔	**Marloes Sands** (& Marloes)
✔✔✔	✔	✔		✔✔✔	**Little Haven**
✔✔	✔		YHA	✔✔	**Broad Haven**
✔				✔	**Nolton Haven**
✔✔		✔	YMCA*	✔✔✔	**Newgale**
✔✔✔	✔	✔		✔✔✔	**Solva**
	✔	✔		✔	**Caerfai Bay**
✔✔✔	✔			✔✔✔	(St David's)
		✔			**Porthclais**
		✔			**St Justinian's & Porthselau**
(✔)	(✔)	✔	YHA	✔	**Whitesands Bay**
(✔)		✔	B	✔✔	**Abereiddy**
✔✔				✔	**Porthgain**
✔✔		✔	B	✔✔	**Trefin**
		✔	YHA		**Pwll Deri & Strumble Head**
✔✔✔	✔	✔	H	✔✔✔	**Goodwick & Fishguard**
✔✔	✔			✔	**Pwllgwaelod** (& Dinas Cross)
✔✔✔	✔	✔	YHA & B	✔✔✔	**Newport**
(✔)				✔	**Ceibwr Bay** (for Moylgrove)
		✔	YHA	✔	**Poppit Sands**
✔✔✔	✔				**St Dogmaels**
✔✔✔	✔			✔✔✔	(Cardigan)

* Newgale YMCA (Wales) is run in partnership with the YHA

PLANNING YOUR WALK

	CAMPING					
	Relaxed pace		**Medium pace**		**Fast pace**	
Night	Place	Approx Distance miles/km	Place	Approx Distance miles/km	Place	Approx Distance miles/km
0	Amroth		Amroth		Amroth	
1	Penally	9.5/15	Penally (nr Manorbier)	9.5/15	Swanlake Bay	20/32
2	Swanlake Bay (nr Manorbier)	10.5/17	Swanlake Bay (nr Manorbier)	10.5/17	Castlemartin	18/29
3	Bosherston*	8/13	Castlemartin	18/29	Hundleton*	19.5/31
4	Castlemartin	10/16	Angle	10.5/17	Sandy Haven	19/31
5	Angle	10.5/17	Pembroke (nr Marloes Sands)	11.5/19	Martin's Haven (nr Marloes)	16/26
6	Pembroke	11.5/19	Sandy Haven	16.5/27	Newgale	17/27
7	Sandy Haven	16.5/27	Martin's Haven (nr Marloes)	16/26	Whitesands Bay (nr Marloes Sands)	17.5/28
8	Dale*	5.5/9	Newgale	17/27	Strumble Head	23.5/38
9	Martin's Haven (nr Marloes)	10.5/17	Whitesands Bay	17.5/28	Newport	19.5/3
10	Little Haven	9.5/15	Trefin	11.5/18	Poppit Sands	14/23
11	Newgale	7.5/12	Strumble Head	12/19	St Dogmaels*	2/3
12	Caerfai Bay	9/14	Fishguard Bay (nr Fishguard)	10/16		
13	Whitesands Bay	8.5/14	Newport	9.5/15		
14	Trefin	11.5/18	Poppit Sands	14/23		
15	Strumble Head	12/19	St Dogmaels*	2/3		
16	Fishguard Bay (nr Fishguard)	10/16				
17	Newport	9.5/15				
18	Poppit Sands	14/23				
19	St Dogmaels*	2/3				

* There are no campsites at places marked with an asterisk but there is alternative accommodation available

The **suggested itineraries** in the boxes above, opposite and on p28 may also be useful; they are based on different accommodation types – camping, hostels and B&Bs – with each one divided into three alternatives depending on your walking speed. They are only suggestions, feel free to adapt them to your needs. **Don't forget** to add your travelling time before and after the walk.

There is also a list of recommended linear day and weekend walks on p29; these cover the best stretches of the coast and those which are well served by public transport. The **public transport map and table** are on pp39-41.

Once you have an idea of your approach turn to **Part 4** for detailed information on accommodation, places to eat and other services in each village and

STAYING IN BUNKHOUSES/HOSTELS

Night	Relaxed pace Place	Approx Distance miles/km	Medium pace Place	Approx Distance miles/km	Fast pace Place	Approx Distance miles/km
0	Amroth		Amroth		Amroth	
1	Lydstep	13.5/22	Lydstep	13.5/22	Lydstep	13/22
2	Freshwater East*	8/13	Bosherston*	14.5/23	Castlemartin*	24.5/39
3	Bosherston*	6.5/10	Castlemartin*	10/16	Pembroke*	22/35
4	Castlemartin*	10/16	Angle*	10.5/17	Sandy Haven*	16.5/27
5	Angle*	10.5/17	Pembroke*	11.5/19	Marloes Sands	13.5/22
6	Pembroke*	11.5/19	Milford Haven*	12.5/20	Newgale**	19.5/31
7	Milford Haven*	12.5/20	Marloes Sands	17.5/28	Whitesands	17.5/28
8	Dale	9.5/15	Broad Haven	12.5/20	Pwll Deri	21/34
9	Marloes Sands	8/13	Newgale**	7/11	Newport	22/35
10	Broad Haven	12.5/20	Whitesands Bay	17.5/28	Poppit Sands	14/23
11	Newgale**	7/11	Trefin	11.5/18	St Dogmaels*	2/3
12	St David's*	9/14	Fishguard	20/32		
13	Whitesands Bay	8.5/14	Newport	11.5/18		
14	Trefin	11.5/18	Poppit Sands	14/23		
15	Pwll Deri	9.5/15	St Dogmaels*	2/3		
16	Fishguard	10.5/17				
17	Newport	11.5/18				
18	Poppit Sands	14/23				
19	St Dogmaels*	2/3				

*No bunkhouses or hostels but alternative accommodation is available
**Newgale YMCA hostel is 45 minutes from Newgale

town on the route. Also in Part 4 you will find summaries of the route to accompany the detailed trail maps.

WHICH DIRECTION?

There are a number of advantages in tackling the path in a south to north direction. An important consideration is the prevailing south-westerly wind which will, more often than not, be behind you, helping rather than hindering you.

On a more aesthetic note the scenery is tamer in the south, while more dramatic and wild to the north, so there is a real sense of leaving the best until last. In addition a south to north direction allows you to get used to the walking on easier ground before confronting the more strenuous terrain further north.

Some may choose to walk in the opposite direction, perhaps preferring to get the hard stuff out of the way at the beginning. The maps in Part 4 give timings for both directions so the guide can easily be used back to front, or for day trips.

PLANNING YOUR WALK

			STAYING IN B&Bs		
	Relaxed pace		**Medium pace**		**Fast pace**
Place	**Approx Distance**	**Place**	**Approx Distance**	**Place**	**Approx Distance**
Night	miles/km		miles/km		miles/km
0 Amroth		Amroth		Amroth	
1 Tenby	7/11	Penally	9.5/15	Manorbier	17.5/28
2 Manorbier	10.5/17	Freshwater East	12/19	Castlemartin	20.5/33
3 Bosherston	10.5/17	Castlemartin	16.5/27	Pembroke	22/35
4 Castlemartin	10/16	Angle	10.5/17	Herbrandston	16.5/27
5 Angle	10.5/17	Pembroke	11.5/19	Marloes	13.5/22
6 Pembroke	11.5/19	Milford Haven	12.5/20	Solva	24.5/39
7 Milford Haven	12.5/20	Marloes	17.5/28	Trefin	24/39
8 Dale	9.5/15	Broad Haven	12.5/20	Fishguard	20/32
9 Marloes	8/13	Solva	12/19	Newport	11.5/18
10 Broad Haven	12.5/20	Whitesands Bay	12.5/20	St Dogmaels*	16/26
11 Solva	12/19	Trefin	11.5/18		
12 St David's	4/6	Fishguard	20/32		
13 Whitesands Bay	8.5/14	Newport	11.5/18		
14 Trefin	11.5/18	St Dogmaels*	16/26		
15 Pwll Deri	9.5/15				
16 Fishguard	10.5/17				
17 Newport	11.5/18				
18 Poppit Sands	14/23				
19 St Dogmaels*	2/3				

* There is no B&B-style accommodation at St Dogmaels but there is plenty a mile
away in Cardigan

SIDE TRIPS

The coast path gives a fairly thorough impression of what the national park has
to offer. However, there are some other hidden gems to be discovered both
inland and off-shore for those with some time to spare.

One of the wildest and most beautiful places is the Preseli Hills (see pp192-
4) rising above Newport offering extensive views over the whole peninsula with
gentle walks in the Cwm Gwaun valley. Closer to Tenby are the Bosherston Lily
Ponds (see p90) for short woodland walks; a great place to spot otters. Over on
the islands of Skomer, Skokholm and Grassholm (see box p134) and Ramsey
(see box p157) gannets, gulls and puffins festoon the cliffs while the lazy creeks
of the Daugleddau estuary (see pp111-12) make a relaxing change from the
seething Atlantic surf. It is worth planning a few extra days on your trip to take
in one or two, if not all of these side trips. A boat trip to one of the islands makes
for a good day off since it is not too strenuous.

The Pembrokeshire Coast National Park website (🖳 www.pcnpa.org.uk)
lists 200 circular walks in the National Park many of which are based around
the coast path.

❏ HIGHLIGHTS – THE BEST DAY AND WEEKEND WALKS

If you don't have the time to walk the whole trail the following day and weekend walks highlight the best of the coast path and most are well served by public transport (see pp38-41); details of some services are given below. For the more experienced walker many of the weekend walks suggested here can be completed in a day.

Day walks

● **Amroth to Tenby** 7 miles/11km (see pp71-9) An easy day passing through beautiful coastal woodland culminating in one of the prettiest seaside towns in Wales. Bus services to Amroth are limited but bus/rail connections from Tenby are good.

● **Freshwater East to Bosherston** 6.5 miles/10km (see pp86-91) A short day, passing from a twisting sandstone coastline to spectacular limestone cliffs ending at the banks of the wooded lily ponds at Bosherston. Coastal Cruiser services call at Freshwater West and Bosherston.

● **Freshwater West to Angle** 8 miles/13km (see pp96-102) Starting at a wonderful beach this is one of the quietest stretches of the coast path. Both ends are stops on the Coastal Cruiser routes.

● **Dale to Marloes Sands (Marloes)** 8 miles/13km (see pp133-8) Varied scenery around the Dale peninsula, beginning with gentle wooded slopes leading to wild scenery around the vast sands of Marloes. On the Puffin Shuttle route.

● **Musselwick Sands (Marloes) to Little Haven** 8 miles/13km (see pp138-42) An easy start to this walk but a strenuous finale over high wooded cliffs with spectacular views over St Bride's Bay. Little Haven is a stop on the Puffin Shuttle route.

● **Nolton Haven to Solva** 8.5 miles/14km (see pp144-53) A short day, taking in the fantastic Newgale Sands, passing through spectacular coastal scenery and finishing at the prettiest village on the coast. On the Puffin Shuttle route.

● **Circular walk from St David's via Caerfai Bay and St Justinian's** 6.5 miles/ 10km (see pp155-62) Wild scenery and wildlife on this short stretch with views of Ramsey Island, starting and finishing in the tiny cathedral city of St David's. On the Celtic Coaster bus route.

● **St Justinian's to Abereiddy** 9.5 miles/15km (see pp162-8) A beautiful stretch around the wild St David's peninsula passing Whitesands Bay and St David's Head. Both ends are stops on the Strumble Shuttle.

● **Newport to Poppit Sands** 14 miles/23km (see pp194-200) The toughest and most spectacular stretch of the coast path with the highest cliffs. On the Poppit Rocket route.

Weekend walks

● **Amroth to Freshwater East** 21.5 miles/35km (see pp71-86) Easy walking passing through woodland with tiny hidden beaches and pretty villages in the coves. Bus services to both Amroth and Freshwater East are limited.

● **Freshwater East to Angle** 27 miles/43km (see pp86-102) A long stretch which takes in the spectacular limestone scenery around St Govan's and Castlemartin and the wonderful beach at Freshwater West. Angle is on the Coastal Cruiser route.

● **Dale to Broad Haven** 20.5 miles/33km (see pp138-44) Fantastic beaches and cliffs with the potential to include a trip over to Skomer Island to see the puffins. Both stops are on the Puffin Shuttle route.

● **Newgale to Trefin** 29 miles/47km (see pp152-72) Wild and rugged scenery around the St David's peninsula with a useful halfway point at the tiny cathedral city of St David's. Newgale is on the Puffin Shuttle and Trefin on the Strumble Shuttle route.

● **Trefin to Fishguard** 20 miles/32km (see pp172-84). Pwll Deri and its jaw-dropping cliff scenery make a good halfway point on this beautiful stretch that takes in the rugged coast around Strumble Head. Both are stops on the Strumble Shuttle.

What to take

Deciding how much to take with you can be difficult. Experienced walkers know that you should take only the bare essentials but at the same time you must ensure you have all the equipment necessary to make the trip safe and comfortable.

KEEP IT LIGHT

Carrying a heavy rucksack really can ruin your enjoyment of a good walk and can also slow you down, turning an easy seven-mile day into an interminable slog. Be ruthless when you pack and leave behind all those little home comforts that you tell yourself don't weigh that much really. This advice is even more pertinent to campers who have added weight to carry.

HOW TO CARRY IT

The size of your **rucksack** depends on where you plan to stay and how you plan to eat. If you are camping and cooking you will probably need a 65- to 75-litre rucksack which can hold the tent, sleeping bag, cooking equipment and food.

Make sure your rucksack has a stiffened back and can be adjusted to fit your own back comfortably. This will make carrying the weight much easier. When packing the rucksack make sure you have all the things you are likely to need during the day near the top or in the side pockets, especially if you don't have a bum bag or daypack (see below). This includes water bottle, packed lunch, waterproofs and this guidebook (of course). Make sure the hip belt and chest strap (if there is one) are fastened tightly as this helps distribute the weight with most of it being carried on the hips.

Rucksacks are decorated with seemingly pointless straps but if you adjust them correctly it can make a big difference to your personal comfort while walking.

Consider taking a small **bum bag** or **daypack** for your camera, guidebook and other essentials for when you go sightseeing or for a day walk.

Hostellers should find a 40- to 60-litre rucksack sufficient. If you have gone for the B&B option you will find a 30- to 40-litre day pack is more than enough to carry your lunch, warm and wet weather clothes, camera and guidebook.

A good habit to get into is to always put things in the same place in your rucksack and memorize where they are. There is nothing more annoying than having to pull everything out of your pack to find that lost banana when you're starving, or your camera when there is a seal basking on a rock ten feet away from you.

It's also a good idea to keep everything in **canoe bags**, **waterproof rucksack liners** or strong plastic bags. If you don't it's bound to rain.

FOOTWEAR

Boots

Your boots are the single most important item of gear that can affect the enjoyment of your trek.

In summer you could get by with a light pair of trail shoes if you're only carrying a small pack, although this is an invitation for wet, cold feet if there is any rain and they don't offer much support for your ankles. Some of the terrain can be quite rough so a good pair of walking boots is a safer bet. They must fit well and be properly broken in. It is no good discovering that your boots are slowly murdering your feet three days into a two-week trek. See p50 for more blister-avoidance advice.

Socks

The traditional wearing of a thin liner sock under a thicker wool sock is no longer necessary if you choose a high-quality sock specially designed for walking. A high proportion of natural fibres makes them much more comfortable. Three pairs are ample.

Extra footwear

Some walkers have a second pair of shoes to wear when they are not on the trail. Trainers, sport sandals or flip flops are all suitable as long as they are light.

CLOTHES

Experienced walkers will know the importance of wearing the right clothes. Don't underestimate the weather: Pembrokeshire pokes its nose into a wet and windy Atlantic so it's important to protect yourself from the elements. The weather can be quite hot in the summer but spectacularly bad at any time of the year. Modern hi-tec outdoor clothes can seem baffling but it basically comes down to a base layer to transport sweat from your skin; a mid-layer or two to keep you warm; and an outer layer or 'shell' to protect you from the wind and rain.

Base layer

Cotton absorbs sweat, trapping it next to the skin and chilling you rapidly when you stop exercising. A thin lightweight **thermal top** of a synthetic material is better as it draws moisture away keeping you dry. It will be cool if worn on its own in hot weather and warm when worn under other clothes in the cold. A spare would be sensible. You may also like to bring a **shirt** for wearing in the evening.

Mid-layers

In the summer a woollen jumper or mid-weight polyester **fleece** will suffice. For the rest of the year you will need an extra layer to keep you warm. Both wool and fleece, unlike cotton, have the ability to stay reasonably warm when wet.

Outer layer

A **waterproof jacket** is essential year-round and will be much more comfortable (but also more expensive) if it's also 'breathable' to prevent the build up of condensation on the inside. This layer can also be worn to keep the wind off.

P L A N N I N G   Y O U R   W A L K

Leg wear

Whatever you wear on your legs it should be light, quick-drying and not restricting. Many British walkers find polyester tracksuit bottoms comfortable. Poly-cotton or microfibre trousers are excellent. Denim jeans should never be worn; if they get wet they become heavy and cold, and bind to your legs. A pair of **shorts** is nice to have on sunny days. Thermal **longjohns** or thick tights are cosy if you're camping but are probably unnecessary even in winter. **Waterproof trousers** are necessary most of the year. In summer a pair of wind-proof and quick-drying trousers is useful in showery weather. **Gaiters** are not really necessary but may come in useful in wet weather when the vegetation around your legs is dripping wet.

Underwear

Three changes of what you normally wear is fine. Women may find a **sports bra** more comfortable because pack straps can cause bra straps to dig painfully into your shoulders.

Other clothes

A **warm hat** and **gloves** should always be kept in your rucksack; you never know when you might need them. In summer you should also carry a **sun hat** with you, preferably one which also covers the back of your neck. Another use-ful piece of summer equipment is a **swimsuit**; some of the beaches are irre-sistible on a hot day. Also consider a small **towel**, especially if you are camping or staying in hostels.

TOILETRIES

Only take the minimum: a small bar of **soap** in a plastic container (unless stay-ing in B&Bs) which can also be used instead of shaving cream and for washing clothes; a tiny tube of **toothpaste** and a **toothbrush**; and one roll of **loo paper** in a plastic bag. If you are planning to defecate outdoors you will also need a lightweight **trowel** for burying the evidence (see pp44-5 for further tips). In addition a **razor**; **deodorant**; **tampons/sanitary towels** and a high-factor **sun screen** should cover all your needs.

FIRST-AID KIT

Medical facilities in Britain are excellent so you only need a small kit to cover common problems and emergencies; pack it in a waterproof container. A basic kit should contain: **aspirin** or **paracetamol** for treating mild to moderate pain and fever; **plasters/Band Aids** for minor cuts; **Moleskin**, **Compeed**, or **Second Skin** for blisters; a **bandage** for holding dressings, splints or limbs in place and for supporting a sprained ankle; elastic knee support (tubigrip) for a weak knee; a small selection of different-sized **sterile dressings** for wounds; **porous adhesive tape**; **antiseptic wipes**; **antiseptic cream**; **safety pins**; **tweezers** and **scissors**.

GENERAL ITEMS

Essential

The following should be in everyone's rucksack: a one-litre **water bottle or pouch**; a **torch** (flashlight) with spare bulb and batteries in case you end up walking after dark; **emergency food** which your body can quickly convert into energy; a **penknife**; a **watch** with an alarm; and a **plastic bag** for packing out any rubbish you accumulate. A **whistle** is also worth taking; although you are very unlikely to need it you may be grateful of it in the unlikely event of an emergency.

Useful

Many would list a **camera** as essential but it can be liberating to travel without one once in a while; a **notebook** can be a more accurate way of recording your impressions. Other things you may find useful include a **book** to pass the time on train and bus journeys; a pair of **sunglasses**, particularly in summer; **binoculars** for observing wildlife; a **walking stick** or pole to take the shock off your knees and a **vacuum flask** for carrying hot drinks. Although the path is easy to follow a 'Silva' type **compass** and the knowledge of how to use it is a good idea in case the sea mist comes in or for any side trips in the Preseli Hills.

SLEEPING BAG

A sleeping bag is only necessary if you are camping or staying in one of the bunkhouses on the route. Campers should find that a two- to three-season bag will cope but obviously in winter a warmer bag is a good idea.

CAMPING GEAR

Campers will need a decent **tent** (or bivvy bag if you enjoy travelling light) able to withstand wet and windy weather; a **sleeping mat**; a **stove** and **fuel** (there is special mention in Part 4 of which shops stock fuel); a **pan** with frying pan that can double as a lid/plate is fine for two people; a **pan handle**; a **mug**; a **spoon**; and a wire/plastic **scrubber** for washing up.

MONEY

There are not many banks or cash machines along the coast path so you will have to carry most of your money as **cash**. A **debit card** is the easiest way to withdraw money from banks or cash machines and a **credit card** can be used to pay in larger shops, restaurants and hotels. A **cheque book** is very useful for walkers with accounts in British banks as a cheque will often be accepted where a card is not.

MAPS

The hand-drawn maps in this book cover the trail at a scale of 1:20,000; plenty of detail and information to keep you on the right track. For side trips to the

PLANNING YOUR WALK

❑ SOME WELSH WORDS ON MAPS AND SIGNS

Welcome to
PEMBROKESHIRE

Croeso i
SIR BENFRO

		gors	marsh, bog
		gorsaf tren	railway station
		gorsaf bws	bus station
		heol	road
		llan	church, enclosure
		llyn	lake
		mawr	big
		moel	rocky hill
aber	river mouth	mynydd	mountains, moorland
afon	river		
coed	wood	nant	stream
caer	fort	pen	head, headland, top of hill
castell	castle		
carreg/careg/craig	stone, rock	pont	bridge
cartref	home	pwll	pool/pit
coch	red	rhos	moorland
croes	cross	sgwâr	square
cwm	valley	Sir Benfro	Pembrokeshire
cwm-bach	small valley	swyddfa post	post office
dinas	fort, city	traeth	beach
du	black	tre/tref	homestead, homeland
eglwys	church		
fford	road	ty	house
ffynnon	well, spring	ynys	island
glyn	glen		

Preseli Hills, the Daugleddau estuary, or anywhere else in the national park you will need an Ordnance Survey map (☎ 08456-050 505, 🖥 www.ordsvy.gov.uk). There are two excellent maps of the National Park: OS Outdoor Leisure (OL) Maps (with a yellow or, latterly, orange cover) Nos 35 and 36 for North and South Pembrokeshire at a scale of 1:25,000.

Enthusiastic map buyers can reduce the often considerable expense of purchasing them: members of the **Backpackers' Club** (see box opposite) can purchase maps at a significant discount through their map service. Alternatively, members of the **Ramblers' Association** (see box opposite) can borrow up to 10 maps for a period of four weeks at 50p per map (£1 for weatherproof maps) plus post and packing from their library.

RECOMMENDED READING

Most of the following books can be found in the tourist information centres in Pembrokeshire as well as good bookshops in the rest of Britain.

General guidebooks
The Rough Guide series includes the comprehensive *Wales: The Rough Guide* by Mike Parker. Lonely Planet also produce a guide to the country.

Walking guidebooks

A couple of books cover day walks away from the coast path that explore the hidden corners of Pembrokeshire. The National Park Authority used to publish a guide to *Walking in the Preseli Hills* which you may still find lurking in one of

---

❑ SOURCES OF FURTHER INFORMATION

Trail information
● **Pembrokeshire Coast National Park Authority** (☎ 0845-345 7275, 🖳 www.pcn pa.org.uk; Llanion Park, Pembroke Dock, Pembrokeshire SA72 6DY) The park authority provides a wealth of useful information about the area from specific information about the coast path and outdoor activities to wildlife and beaches. The website is very informative and has a detailed section on the coast path.

Tourist information
● **Tourist information centres (TICs)** TICs are based in towns throughout Britain and provide all manner of locally specific information and an accommodation-booking service. The centres relevant to the coast path, with the ones at St David's and Newport doubling up as national park information centres, are in: **Kilgetty** (see p66), **Saundersfoot** (p72), **Tenby** (p76), **Pembroke** (p108), **Pembroke Dock** (p114), **Milford Haven** (p120), **St David's** (p157), **Goodwick** (p180), **Fishguard** (p181), **Newport** (p190) and **Cardigan** (p203). For further information see 🖳 www.visitpem brokeshire.co.uk/TIC.
● **Wales Tourist Board** (☎ 0870-830 0306, 🖳 www.visitwales.co.uk) The tourist board oversees all the local tourist information centres. It's a good place to find general information about the country and information on outdoor activities and local events. They can also help with arranging holidays and accommodation.

Organizations for walkers
● **The Backpackers' Club** (🖳 www.backpackersclub.co.uk). A club aimed at people who are involved or interested in lightweight camping through walking, cycling, skiing, canoeing, etc. They produce a quarterly magazine, provide members with a comprehensive advisory and information service on all aspects of backpacking, organize weekend trips and also publish a farm-pitch directory. Membership is £12/15/7 per year for an individual/family/anyone under 18 or over 65.
● **Friends of Pembrokeshire National Park** (🖳 http://home.freeuk.com/fpnp; FPNP, PO Box 218, Haverfordwest SA61 1WR) Besides arranging walks on which the members are the guides this organization also gives you the opportunity to give something back to the park. They arrange projects which involve repairing footbridges and dry stone walls and clearing overgrown paths. You do not have to be from the local area to join. There's a minimum 'donation' of £10 to join.
● **Long Distance Walkers' Association** (🖳 www.ldwa.org.uk) An association of people with the common interest of long-distance walking. Membership includes a thrice-yearly magazine, *Strider*, giving details of challenge events and local group walks as well as articles on the subject. Information on over 500 long-distance paths is presented in the their *Long Distance Walkers' Handbook*. Membership is currently £13 per year.
● **Ramblers' Association** (☎ 020-7339 8500, 🖳 www.ramblers.org.uk; 2nd Floor, Camelford House, 87-89 Albert Embankment, London SE1 7BR) Looks after the interests of walkers throughout Britain. They publish a large amount of useful information including their *Walk Britain* yearbook (£5.99 to non-members), a full directory of services for walkers. Membership costs £24/32 individual/joint.

the local bookshops, and Abercastle Publications have a *Short Guide to the Best Walks in Pembrokeshire* by A Roberts for just £2.10. Those who like to round off the day with a pint may appreciate *Pub Walks in Pembrokeshire* published by Sigma with a cover price of £6.95.

Of course, if you are a seasoned long-distance walker or even if you are new to the game and like what you see, check out the other titles in the Trailblazer series; see pp207-8.

Flora and fauna field guides

The National Park Authority publish a small booklet highlighting the more common species along the coastline called *The Birds of the Pembrokeshire Coast* by Peter Knights; it's out of print now but you may be able to find a copy on the trail. Dyfed Wildlife Trust's *Birds of Pembrokeshire* by Donovan and Rees at £17.95 is an expensive yet useful guide but some might prefer a book which is also of use when travelling elsewhere. The AA's *Birds of Britain and Europe* at £9.99 is one of many excellent bird guides that can fit inside a rucksack pocket.

Pembrokeshire is famous for its wild flowers so a guidebook on these may come in handy. At just £3.99 Andrew Branson's *Wild Flowers of Britain and Europe*, published by Bounty Books, is an excellent pocket-sized guide that categorizes flowers according to habitat.

Getting to and from the Coast Path

A glance at any map of Britain gives the impression that Pembrokeshire is a long way from anywhere and hard to get to. In reality road and rail links with the coast path are excellent with Kilgetty, close to the start of the coast path, lying on both the national rail network and the National Express coach network.

Travelling to the start of the coast path by public transport makes sense. There's no need to worry about the safety of your abandoned vehicle while walking, there are no logistical headaches about how to return to your car when you've finished the walk and it's obviously one of the biggest steps you can take towards minimizing your ecological footprint. Quite apart from that, you'll simply feel your holiday has begun the moment you step out of your front door, rather than having to wait until you've slammed the car door behind you.

NATIONAL TRANSPORT

By rail

For those walking the whole path the nearest train stations are Kilgetty (3 miles/5km from the start of the path at Amroth) and Fishguard Harbour (a 50-minute bus ride from the end of the coast path near Cardigan). There are frequent services to Kilgetty from both Cardiff and Swansea which in turn are

❏ GETTING TO BRITAIN

● **By air** Most international airlines serve London Heathrow and London Gatwick. In addition a number of budget airlines fly from many of Europe's major cities to the other London terminals at Stansted and Luton and increasingly to Cardiff (www.cwlfly.com), the nearest airport with international services to the coast path, and to Bristol airport as well.

From London it is 5-6 hours by train to Pembrokeshire; from Bristol or Cardiff it is about $2^{1}/_{2}$-3 hours.

● **From Europe by train** (with or without a car) Eurostar (🖳 www.eurostar .com) operate a high-speed passenger service via the Channel Tunnel between Paris and London, and Brussels and London. Until November 2007 trains arrive and depart from the international terminal at London Waterloo Station (Waterloo has connections to the London Underground and to all other main railway stations in London). From November 2007 services will move to the newly built St Pancras International terminal, which also has good underground links to other railway stations.

For more information about rail services between Europe and Britain contact **Rail Europe** (🖳 www.raileurope.co.uk) or Railteam (🖳 www.railteam.eu). **Eurotunnel** (🖳 www.eurotunnel.com) operates a shuttle train service for vehicles via the Channel Tunnel between Calais and Folkestone taking 35 minutes to cross between the two.

● **From Europe by coach** Eurolines (🖳 www.eurolines.com) have a huge network of services connecting over 500 cities in 25 European countries to London.

● **From Europe by ferry** (with or without a car) Numerous ferry companies operate routes between the major North Sea and Channel ports of mainland Europe and the ports on Britain's eastern and southern coasts. A useful website for further information is 🖳 www.directferries.com.

Visitors from the Republic of Ireland have the choice of two ferry services direct to Pembrokeshire; both operate daily. Irish Ferries (🖳 www.irishferries.com) operates from Rosslare to Pembroke Dock, and Stena Line (🖳 www.stenaline.co.uk) from Rosslare to Fishguard.

served by trains from all over the country. However, services to Fishguard Harbour are fairly limited.

Other points of the path can also be reached by train; there are stations at Tenby, Penally, Pembroke, Pembroke Dock and Milford Haven. Arriva Trains Wales (🖳 www.arrivatrainswales.co.uk) operates most services within Wales, First Great Western (🖳 www.firstgreatwestern.co.uk) has services to Cardiff and Swansea from London Paddington, and Central Trains (🖳 www.centraltrains.co.uk) from Birmingham and central England.

All timetable and fare information can be found at **National Rail Enquiries** (☎ 08457-484950, 24hrs; 🖳 www.nationalrail.co.uk). Tickets can be booked online direct through the companies mentioned above or through 🖳 www.the trainline.com and and 🖳 www.qjump.co.uk.

If you think you may want to book a taxi when you arrive visit 🖳 www .traintaxi.co.uk or phone ☎ 01733-237037 for details of taxi companies operating at rail stations throughout England.

PLANNING YOUR WALK

By coach

National Express (☎ 08705-808080, lines open 8am-10pm daily; 💻 www
.nationalexpress.com) is the principal coach (long-distance bus) operator in
Britain. Coach travel is generally cheaper but takes longer than travel by train.
Kilgetty, which is just three miles (5km) from Amroth and the start of the coast
path, is a stop on the twice-daily (one overnight) NX508 service from London to
Haverfordwest via Tenby, Pembroke and Milford Haven. The NX582 services
operates daily from Birmingham to Haverfordwest via Swansea, Tenby and
Pembroke.

By car

Pembrokeshire has good links to the national road network with the M4 motor-
way stretching as far as Swansea. From here Kilgetty can be reached by following the A48 to Carmarthen, A40 to St Clears and finally the A477. From Kilgetty
it is a short drive down the lane to Amroth and the start of the path. The National
Park Authority have a car park, indicated by a blue 'P' sign, just off the seafront
road near the Amroth Arms pub.

The end of the coast path and the northern half of the coast are reached by
following the A484 from Carmarthen to Cardigan. The best place to park your
car is at the National Park supervised car park at Poppit Sands which is opposite the lifeboat station.

LOCAL TRANSPORT

Pembrokeshire has an excellent public transport system reaching some of the
smallest, most out-of-the-way villages. This is great news for anyone hoping to
do any linear day or weekend walks. Of particular interest are the coastal shuttle bus services (see opposite) that are designed especially for coast-path walkers, serving all the villages along the coast between Milford Haven and St
David's.

The public transport map opposite shows the most useful bus and train
routes and the box on pp40-1 gives details of the frequency of services and
whom you should contact for detailed timetable information.

The whole county is covered in the *Pembrokeshire Bus Timetable*, published each year. It can be picked up for free at any of the tourist information
centres. Alternatively, copies of that and the Coastal Buses timetable, as well as
train information, are available from Pembrokeshire County Council Transport
Unit (☎ 01437-775227, 💻 www.pembrokeshire.gov.uk).

There's also a useful travel information line and website for Wales: ☎ 0870-
608 2608, 💻 www.traveline-cymru .org.uk. Up-to-date information can also be
found at both St David's National Park Information Centre (☎ 01437-720392)
and Newport National Park Information Centre (☎ 01239-820912).

Summer services operate from early May until late September; winter services operate from late September to early May. Sunday services also often operate on Bank Holiday Mondays as well.

PLANNING YOUR WALK

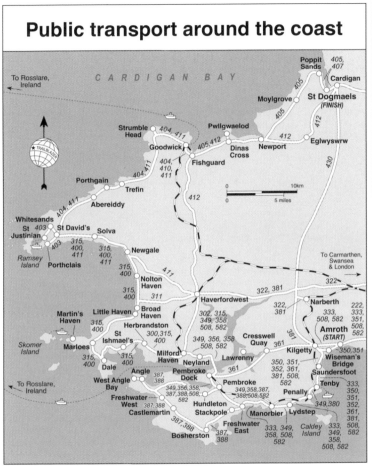

Public transport around the coast

Coastal bus services

The five excellent services (Coastal Cruiser 1 & 2, Puffin Shuttle, Strumble Shuttle, Poppit Rocket and Celtic Coaster 1 & 2; the latter two are powered by eco-friendly liquid petroleum gas; aimed directly at weary coast-path walkers, cover most of the path; see the public transport map (above) and table, pp40-1, for full details. Most operate year-round but services in the winter months are limited. All operate on a Hail and Ride basis in rural areas, as long as you are standing in a safe place for the bus to stop. Buses on the Celtic Coaster and Coastal Cruiser services are accessible for wheelchair users.

❏ PUBLIC TRANSPORT SERVICES

The following list is not completely comprehensive but does cover the most important services. Unless specified otherwise services operate year-round.

Buses

Silcox Coaches (☎ 01646-683143; 🖳 www.silcoxcoaches.co.uk)

222 Amroth to Carmarthen via Pendine, Sun 3/day (services connect with the 350)
300 Milford Haven town service including Herbrandston, Mon-Sat 2/day
322 Haverfordwest bus station to Carmarthen via Narberth, Mon-Sat 3/day
333 Pembroke Dock to Carmarthen via Tenby, Mon-Sat 1/day
350 Tenby to Amroth via Saundersfoot, Wiseman's Bridge & Kilgetty, summer Sun 4/day (connects with the 222, see above)
351 Pendine to Tenby via Amroth, Saundersfoot, Wiseman's Bridge & Kilgetty, Mon-Sat 6-7/day plus 1/day Amroth to Tenby
352 Tenby to Kilgetty via Saundersfoot, Mon-Sat 1/hr
356 Milford Haven to Monkton via Hazelbeach, Neyland, Pembroke Dock & Pembroke, Mon-Sat approx 1/hr
358 Haverfordwest to Tenby via Pembroke Dock, Pembroke, Manorbier, Lydstep & Penally, Fri & Sat 1/night
361 Pembroke Dock to Tenby via Cresswell Quay, Kilgetty & Saundersfoot, Mon-Sat 3/day
380 Tenby town service including Penally, Mon-Sat 8/day
381 Tenby to Haverfordwest via Saundersfoot, Kilgetty & Narberth, Mon-Sat 8-9/day
387 **Coastal Cruiser 1**: circular route to/from Pembroke Dock via Pembroke, Hundleton, West Angle Bay, Angle, Freshwater West, Castlemartin, Bosherston, Stackpole, Stackpole Quay, Freshwater East & Pembroke, summer daily 3/day, winter Mon-Sat 2/day
388 **Coastal Cruiser 2**: circular route to/from Pembroke Dock – route as above but in reverse, summer daily 3/day, winter Mon-Sat 1/day

First (☎ 0870-608 2608; 🖳 www.firstgroup.com/ukbus/swwales/home/index.php)

302 Haverfordwest to Hubberston via Milford Haven, Mon-Sat 2/hr, Sun 7/day
349 Haverfordwest to Tenby via Neyland, Pembroke Dock, Pembroke, Manorbier, Lydstep & Penally, Mon-Sat 1/hr, summer Sun 4/day plus 1/day Haverfordwest to Pembroke, winter Sun 2/day plus 1/day Haverfordwest to Pembroke

Acorn Travel (☎ 01348-874728; 🖳 www.acorntravel.com)

311 Haverfordwest to Broad Haven, Mon-Sat 4-5/day
400/315 **Puffin Shuttle** Milford Haven to St David's via St Ishmaels, Dale, Marloes, Martin's Haven, Little Haven, Broad Haven, Nolton Haven, Newgale & Solva, summer daily 3/day (operated in conjunction with Richards and Edwards, see below, and connects with First's No 302 service to Haverfordwest)
411 Haverfordwest (bus and rail stations) to St David's via Newgale and Solva, Sun 4/day plus 1/day to/from Fishguard (also operates on summer Bank Holiday Mondays) (see Richards Brothers for Mon-Sat services)
412 Cardigan to Haverfordwest via Eglwyswrw, Newport, Dinas Cross & Fishguard, Sun 3/day plus 1/day Fishguard to Haverfordwest (see Richards for Mon-Sat service)

Edwards Brothers (☎ 01437-890230)

315 **Puffin Shuttle** (see Acorn opposite) Haverfordwest to Marloes via Milford
　　　Haven, Herbrandston, St Ishmaels & Dale, winter Tue, Thur, Sat 3-4/day

Richards Brothers (☎ 01239-613756; 💻 www.gobybus.net)

400/315 Puffin Shuttle (see Acorn opposite)

400 **Puffin Shuttle** Marloes to St David's via Broad Haven & Newgale, winter
　　　Tue, Thur and Sat 2/day plus one service to Milford Haven via Dale &
　　　Herbrandston (but only for the St David's to Marloes service)

404 **Strumble Shuttle** Fishguard to St David's via Goodwick, Strumble Head,
　　　Trefin, Porthgain & Abereiddy, summer daily 2/day plus 1/day to/from
　　　Newport via Dinas Cross; winter Mon, Thur, Sat 2/day

405 **Poppit Rocket** Cardigan to Fishguard via St Dogmaels, Poppit Sands,
　　　Moylgrove, Newport, Dinas Cross & Pwllgwaelod summer daily 3/day;
　　　winter Cardigan to Newport only Mon, Thur, Sat 3/day

407 Poppit Sands to Cardigan via St Dogmaels, Mon-Sat 6/day plus 8/day from
　　　Glanteifion/The Moorings (after Poppit Sands)

410 Fishguard town service including Goodwick and Fishguard Harbour,
　　　Mon-Sat 2/hr

411 Fishguard to St David's via Goodwick and Trefin, Mon-Sat 5-7/day **and**

411 Haverfordwest (bus and rail stations) to St David's via Solva and Newgale,
　　　Mon-Sat 11/day (for Sun service see Edwards Brothers No 411)

412 Cardigan to Haverfordwest via Eglwyswrw, Newport, Dinas Cross &
　　　Fishguard, Mon-Sat 1/hr (see Acorn re Sunday service)

Collins (☎ 01437-710337)

403 **Celtic Coaster 1** St David's (Peninsula Shuttle Service, circular route) via
　　　Porthclais, St Justinian & Whitesands, early May to late July and September
　　　daily 1/hr

403 **Celtic Coaster 2** St David's (Peninsula Shuttle Service, circular route) via
　　　Porthclais, St Justinian & Whitesands, late July to early September daily 2/hr

Midway Motors (☎ 01239-831267)

430 Narberth to Cardigan, Mon-Sat 2-3/day

Trains

Arriva Trains Wales (💻 www.arrivatrainswales.co.uk)

● Swansea to Pembroke Dock via Narberth, Kilgetty, Saundersfoot, Tenby, Penally,
Manorbier & Pembroke, Mon-Sat 8-9/day, Sun 2-3/day (late afternoon/evening
only)

● Cardiff Central to Milford Haven via Haverfordwest Mon-Sat 8/day, Swansea to
Milford Haven Sun 4/day

● Cardiff to Fishguard Harbour (Goodwick), Mon-Sat 1/day

Ferry (day trips)

Day trips to Rosslare are perfectly feasible for anyone who fancies a break from the
coast path. Contact **Irish Ferries** (☎ 08705-329543, 💻 www.irishferries.com) for
services from Pembroke Dock or **Stena Line** (☎ 08705-707070, 💻 www.stenaline
.co.uk) for services from Fishguard.

PART 2: MINIMUM IMPACT AND OUTDOOR SAFETY

Minimum impact walking

In this chaotic world in which people live their lives at an increasingly frenetic pace, many of us living in overcrowded cities and working in jobs that offer little free-time, the great outdoors is becoming an essential means of escape. Walking in the countryside is a wonderful means of relaxation and gives people the time to think and re-discover themselves.

Of course as the popularity of the countryside increases so do the problems that this pressure brings. It is important for visitors to remember that the countryside is the home and workplace of many others. Walkers in particular should be aware of their responsibilities. Indeed a walker who respects and understands the countryside will get far more enjoyment from their trip.

By following a few simple guidelines while walking the coast path you can have a positive impact, not just on your own well-being but also on local communities and the environment, thereby becoming part of the solution.

ECONOMIC IMPACT

Rural businesses and communities in Britain have been hit hard in recent years by a seemingly endless series of crises. Most people are aware of the country code; not dropping litter and closing the gate behind you are still as pertinent as ever, but in light of the economic pressures that local countryside businesses are under there is something else you can do: buy local.

Buy local

Look and ask for local produce (see box p15) to buy and eat. Not only does this cut down on the amount of pollution and congestion that the transportation of food creates, (the so-called 'food miles'), but also ensures that you are supporting local farmers and producers; the very people who have moulded the countryside you have come to see and who are in the best position to protect it. If you can find local food which is also organic so much the better.

Support local businesses

It's a fact of life that money spent at local level – perhaps in a market, or at the greengrocer, or in an independent pub – has a far greater impact for good on that community than the equivalent spent in a branch of a national chain store or restaurant. While no-one would advocate that walkers should boycott the larger supermarkets, which after all do provide local employment, it's worth remembering that businesses in rural communities rely heavily on visitors for their very existence. If we want to keep these shops and post offices, we need to use them. The more money that circulates locally and is spent on local labour and materials, the greater the impact on the local economy and the more power the community has to effect the change it wants to see.

Encourage local cultural traditions and skills
No part of the countryside looks the same. Buildings, food, skills, and language evolve out of the landscape and are moulded over hundreds of years to suit the locality. Discovering these cultural differences is part of the pleasure of walking in new places. Visitors' enthusiasm for local traditions and skills brings awareness and pride, nurturing a sense of place; an increasingly important role in a world where economic globalization continues to undermine the very things that provide security and a feeling of belonging.

ENVIRONMENTAL IMPACT

A walking holiday in itself is an environmentally friendly approach to tourism. The following are some ideas on how you can go a few steps further in helping to minimize your impact on the natural environment while walking the Pembrokeshire Coast Path.

Use public transport whenever possible
Public transport in Pembrokeshire is excellent and in many cases specifically geared towards the coast-path walker. By using the local bus you will help to keep the standard high. Public transport is always preferable to using private cars as it benefits everyone: visitors, locals and the environment.

Never leave litter
Leaving litter shows a total disrespect for the natural world and others coming after you. As well as being unsightly litter kills wildlife, pollutes the environment and can be dangerous to farm animals. **Please** carry a plastic bag so you can dispose of your rubbish in a bin in the next village. It would be very helpful if you could pick up litter left by other people too.
● **Is it OK if it's biodegradable?** Not really. Apple cores, banana skins, orange peel and the like are unsightly, encourage flies, ants and wasps and ruin a picnic spot for others. Using the excuse that they are natural and biodegradable just doesn't cut any ice. When was the last time you saw a banana tree in Wales?
● **The lasting impact of litter** A piece of orange peel left on the ground takes six months to decompose; silver foil 18 months; a plastic bag 10 years; clothes 15 years; and an aluminium can 85 years.

Erosion
● **Stay on the main trail** The effect of your footsteps may seem minuscule but when they are multiplied by several thousand walkers each year they become rather more significant. Avoid taking shortcuts, widening the trail or taking more than one path; your boots will be followed by many others.
● **Consider walking out of season** The maximum disturbance by walkers coincides with the time of year when nature wants to do most of its growth and repair. In high-use areas, like that along much of the coast path, the trail never

❏ **Maintaining the Pembrokeshire Coast Path**

Maintenance of the path is carried out by the National Trail officer and is funded largely by the Countryside Council for Wales (who contribute 75%) and 25% by the National Park Authority. Teams of rangers, wardens and volunteers undertake various tasks throughout the year. In summer, for example, there is the constant battle to cut back vigorous growth which would engulf the path if left alone and repairs need to be carried out on some of the footbridges, stiles and kissing gates. Many of the stiles are now being replaced by kissing gates to make access easier for the less able.

Where erosion of the path becomes a problem wooden causeways or steps are constructed and particularly boggy areas are drained by digging ditches. Occasionally the authorities will re-route the path where erosion has become so severe as to be a danger to the walker. In the winter some sections of the path slip into the sea necessitating the realignment of the path, often involving the instalment of new stiles or kissing gates in order to run the path through a field.

Take these potential route changes into account when using the maps in Part 4. They usually cover a very short distance but have the potential to cause a little confusion.

recovers. Walking at less busy times eases this pressure while also generating year-round income for the local economy. Not only that, but it may make the walk a more relaxing experience with fewer people on the path and less competition for accommodation.

Respect all wildlife

Care for all wildlife you come across along the coast path; it has as much right to be there as you. Tempting as it may be to pick wild flowers leave them so the next people who pass can enjoy them too. Don't break branches off or damage trees in any way.

If you come across wildlife keep your distance and don't watch for too long. Your presence can cause considerable stress, particularly if the adults are with young, or in winter when the weather is harsh and food is scarce. Young animals are rarely abandoned. If you come across young birds keep away so that their mother can return. Anyone considering a spot of climbing on the sea cliffs should bear in mind that there are restrictions in certain areas due to the presence of nesting birds. Check with the local tourist information office.

The code of the outdoor loo

'Going' in the outdoors is a lost art worth re-learning, for your sake and everyone else's. As more and more people discover the joys of the outdoors this is becoming an important issue.

In some parts of the world where visitor pressure is higher than in Britain walkers and climbers are required to pack out their excrement. This could soon be necessary here. Human excrement is not only offensive to our senses but, more importantly, can infect water sources.

● **Where to go** Wherever possible **use a toilet**. Public toilets are marked on the trail maps in this guide and you will also find facilities in pubs, cafés and campsites along the coast path.

If you do have to go outdoors choose a site at least **30 metres away from running water**. Carry a small trowel and **dig a small hole** about 15cm (6") deep to bury your excrement in. It decomposes quicker when in contact with the top layer of soil or leaf mould. Use a stick to stir loose soil into your deposit as well as this speeds up decomposition even more. Do not squash it under rocks as this slows down the composting process. If you have to use rocks to cover it make sure they are not in contact with your faeces.

Make sure you do not dig any holes on ground that is, or could be, of historic or archaeological interest.

● **Toilet paper and tampons** Toilet paper takes a long time to decompose whether buried or not. It is easily dug up by animals and may then blow into water sources or onto the path. The best method for dealing with it is to **pack it out**. Put the used paper inside a paper bag which you then place inside a plastic bag (or two). Then simply empty the contents of the paper bag at the next toilet you come across and throw the bag away.

You should also pack out **tampons** and **sanitary towels** in a similar way; they take years to decompose and may also be dug up and scattered about by animals.

Wild camping

Unfortunately, wild camping is not encouraged within the national park. In any case there are few places where it is a viable option. This is a shame since wild camping is an altogether more fulfilling experience than camping on a designated site. Living in the outdoors without any facilities provides a valuable lesson in simple, sustainable living where the results of all your actions, from going to the loo to washing your plates, can be seen.

If you do insist on wild camping **always** ask the landowner for permission. Anyone contemplating camping on a beach should be very aware of the times and heights of the tide. Follow these suggestions for minimizing your impact and encourage others to do likewise.

● **Be discreet** Camp alone or in small groups, spend only one night in each place and pitch your tent late and move off early.

● **Never light a fire** The deep burn caused by camp fires, no matter how small, damages the turf which can take years to recover. Cook on a camp stove instead.

● **Don't use soap or detergent** There is no need to use soap; even biodegradable soaps and detergents pollute streams. You won't be away from a shower for more than a day or so. Wash up without detergent; use a plastic or metal scourer, or failing that, a handful of fine pebbles from the beach or some bracken or grass.

● **Leave no trace** Learn the skill of moving on without leaving any sign of having been there: no moved boulders, ripped up vegetation or dug drainage ditches. Make a final check of your campsite before departing; pick up any litter that you or anyone else has left, so leaving the place in a better state than you found it.

ACCESS

Britain is a crowded cluster of islands with few places where you can wander as you please. Most of the land is a patchwork of fields and agricultural land

MINIMUM IMPACT & OUTDOOR SAFETY

❏ **National Trails**
The Pembrokeshire Coast Path is one of 15 National Trails (🖥 www.national trail.co.uk) in England and Wales. These are Britain's flagship long-distance paths which grew out of the post-war desire to protect the country's special places, a movement which also gave birth to national parks and AONBs (see box p53).

National Trails in Wales are designated and largely funded by the Countryside Council for Wales and are managed on the ground by a National Trail Officer. They co-ordinate the maintenance work undertaken by the local highway authority and landowners to ensure that the trail is kept to nationally agreed standards.

and the Pembrokeshire Coast National Park is no different. However, there are countless public rights of way, in addition to the coast path, that criss-cross the land. This is fine, but what happens if you feel a little more adventurous and want to explore the beaches, dunes, moorland, woodland and hills that can also be found within the national park boundaries?

Right to roam
The Countryside & Rights of Way Act 2000, or 'Right to Roam' as dubbed by walkers, was passed by parliament after a long campaign to allow greater public access to areas of countryside in England and Wales deemed to be uncultivated open country. This essentially means moorland, heathland, downland and upland areas.

In the case of the Pembrokeshire Coast National Park this implies the Preseli Hills and the wild country around the St David's peninsula. It does not mean free access to wander over farmland, woodland or private gardens. The legislation came into effect in October 2005.

Some land is covered by restrictions (ie high-impact activities such as driving a vehicle, cycling, horse-riding are not permitted) and some land is excluded (such as gardens, parks and cultivated land.

If the urge takes you and you feel like tramping the Preseli Hills or getting lost among the sand dunes check with the Countryside Council for Wales (🖥 www.ccw.gov.uk) first.

With more freedom in the countryside comes a need for more responsibility from the walker. Remember that wild open country is still the workplace of farmers and home to all sorts of wildlife. Have respect for both and avoid disturbing domestic and wild animals.

Lambing
Around 80% of the coast path passes through private farmland much of which is pasture for sheep. Lambing takes place from mid-March to mid-May when dogs should not be taken along the path. Even a dog secured on a lead is liable to disturb a pregnant ewe. If you should see a lamb or ewe that appears to be in distress contact the nearest farmer.

The Country Code

The countryside is a fragile place which every visitor should respect. The country code seems like common sense but sadly some people still seem to have no understanding of how to treat the countryside they walk in. Everyone visiting the countryside has a responsibility to minimize the impact of their visit so that other people can enjoy the same

❑ **The Countryside Code**
● Be safe – plan ahead and follow any signs (see pp48-51)
● Leave gates and property as you find them
● Protect plants and animals and take your litter home
● Keep dogs under close control
● Consider other people

peaceful landscapes. It does not take much effort; it really is common sense. The Countryside Code (see box above) has been revised (partly because of the CroW Act 2000) and was launched on 12 July 2004 by the Countryside Agency and Countryside Council for Wales under the themes: Respect, Protect, Enjoy.

● **Enjoy the countryside and respect its life and work** Access to the countryside depends on being sensitive to the needs and wishes of those who live and work there. Being courteous and friendly to those you meet will ensure a healthy future for all based on partnership and co-operation.

● **Guard against all risk of fire** Accidental fire is a great fear of farmers and foresters. Never make a camp fire and take matches and cigarette butts out with you to dispose of safely.

● **Keep your dog under close control** The only place you can safely allow your dog off the lead is along the beaches but there are restrictions in the summer (see p19). Across farmland dogs should be kept on a short lead at all times but must be between 1 March and 31 July on most areas of open country and common land.

If a farm animal starts to chase you/your dog let your dog off the lead. Also take care that your dog does not disturb birds that nest on the ground, or other wildlife. During lambing time they should not be taken with you at all (see opposite).

Don't disturb farm animals

Farmers are permitted to destroy any dog that injures or worries their animals. For further information call the CCW enquiry line (☎ 0845-130 6229.

● **Keep to paths across farmland** Stick to the official coast path across arable or pasture land. Minimize erosion by not cutting corners or widening the path.

● **Use gates and stiles to cross fences, hedges and walls** The coast path is well supplied with gates where it crosses field boundaries. On some of the side trips you may find the paths less accommodating. If you do have to climb over a gate which you can't open always do so at the hinged end.

MINIMUM IMPACT & OUTDOOR SAFETY

● **Leave livestock, crops and machinery alone** Help farmers by not interfering with their means of livelihood.

● **Take your litter home** 'Pack it in, pack it out'. Litter is not only ugly but can be harmful to wildlife. Small mammals often become trapped in discarded cans and bottles. Many walkers think that orange peel and banana skins do not count as litter. Even biodegradable foodstuffs attract common scavenging species such as crows and gulls to the detriment of less dominant species. Carry a plastic bag to put yours and other people's litter and food scraps in and take it home or find a bin.

● **Help keep all water clean** Leaving litter and going to the toilet near a water source can pollute people's water supplies. For information on going to the toilet in the outdoors see p44.

● **Protect wildlife, plants and trees** Care for and respect all wildlife you come across along the coast path. Don't pick plants, break trees or scare wild animals. If you come across young birds that appear to have been abandoned leave them alone. If you visit any of the islands always stick to the designated paths to avoid disturbing nesting seabirds.

● **Take special care on country roads** Cars travel dangerously fast on narrow winding lanes. To be safe walk facing the oncoming traffic and carry a torch or wear highly visible clothing when it's getting dark.

● **Make no unnecessary noise** Enjoy the peace and solitude of the outdoors by staying in small groups and acting unobtrusively.

Outdoor safety

AVOIDANCE OF HAZARDS

With good planning and preparation most hazards can be avoided. This information is just as important for those out on a day walk as for those walking the entire coast path.

Ensure you have suitable **clothes** to keep you warm and dry, whatever the conditions (see p50) and a spare change of inner clothes. A compass, whistle, torch and first-aid kit should be carried and are discussed on pp32-3. The **emergency signal** is six blasts on the whistle or six flashes with a torch. A mobile phone may also be useful.

Take plenty of **food** with you for the day and at least one litre of **water** although more would be better, especially on the long northern stretches. It is a good idea to fill up your bottle whenever you pass through a village since stream water cannot be relied upon. You will eat far more walking than you do normally so make sure you have enough for the day, as well as some high-energy snacks

---

(Opposite) Popular with surfers, Freshwater West (see p96) is one of the best beaches in Pembrokeshire. (Photo © Jim Manthorpe).

(chocolate, dried fruit, biscuits) in the bottom of your pack for an emergency.

Stay alert and know exactly where you are throughout the day. The easiest way to do this is to **regularly check your position** on the map. If visibility suddenly decreases with mist and cloud, or there is an accident, you will be able to make a sensible decision about what action to take based on your location.

If you choose to walk alone you must appreciate and be prepared for the increased risk. It's a good idea to leave word with someone about where you are going and remember to contact them when you have arrived safely.

Safety on the cliff top

Sadly every year people are either injured or killed walking the coast path. Along the full length of the path you will see warning signs urging you to keep well away from the cliff edge. They are there for a reason. Cliffs are very dangerous. In many places it is difficult to see just where the edge is since it is often well hidden by vegetation. Added to this is the fact that, in places, the path is extremely close to the edge. Always err on the side of over-caution and think twice about walking if you are tired or feeling ill. This is when most accidents happen. To ensure you have a safe trip it is well worth following this advice:

● Keep to the path – avoid cliff edges and overhangs
● Avoid walking in windy weather – cliff tops are particularly dangerous in such conditions
● Be aware of the increased possibility of slipping over in wet or icy weather.
● Wear strong sturdy boots with good ankle support and a good grip rather than trainers or sandals
● Be extra vigilant with children
● Keep dogs under close control
● Wear or carry warm and waterproof clothing
● In an emergency dial ☎ 999 and ask for the coastguard

Take note of signs warning of dangerous cliffs

Safety on the beach

Pembrokeshire's beaches are spectacular in any weather but it's when the sun is shining that the sweaty walker gets the urge to take a dip. The sea can be a dangerous environment and care should be taken if you do go for a swim and even if you're just walking along the beach. Follow this common-sense advice:

● If tempted to take a shortcut across a beach be aware of the tides to avoid being cut off or stranded
● Do not sit directly below cliffs and do not climb them unless you are an experienced climber with the right equipment, or with someone who has experience
● Don't swim immediately after eating, or after drinking alcohol; swimming in itself can be dangerous

MINIMUM IMPACT & OUTDOOR SAFETY

(Opposite) Top: On the coast path near St Brides Haven. (Photo © Jim Manthorpe).
Bottom: St Brides Haven (see p138), with the eponymous estate in the background. Note the colourful bands of rock; much of the coastline is of great geological interest and some of the oldest exposed rocks in the world can be seen in Pembrokeshire. (Photo © Henry Stedman).

● Be aware of local tides and currents – don't assume it is safe just because other people are swimming there; if in doubt consult the tide tables (see below) or check with the nearest tourist information centre

● Be extra vigilant with children

● In an emergency dial ☎ 999 and ask for the coastguard

TIDE TABLES

Tide tables are available from newsagents in the area. Between Easter and the end of October they are also published in the free newspaper, *Coast to Coast*, which you can get from tourist information centres.

WEATHER FORECASTS

The Pembrokeshire coast is exposed to whatever the churning Atlantic can throw at it. Even when it's sunny sea breezes usually develop during the course of the day so it's worth taking weather forecasts with a pinch of salt. A warm day can feel bitterly cold when you stop for lunch on a cliff top being battered by the wind. Try to get the local weather forecast from the newspaper, TV or radio, or one of the telephone forecasts before you set off. Alter your plans for the day accordingly.

Telephone forecasts
Weather call ☎ 09068-500414 (extension 1405; 💻 www.weathercall.co.uk) provides frequently updated and generally reliable weather forecasts. However, calls are charged at the expensive premium rate.

BLISTERS

It is important to break in new boots before embarking on a long walk. Make sure the boots are comfortable and try to avoid getting them wet on the inside. Air your feet at lunchtime, keep them clean and change your socks regularly. If you feel any hot spots stop immediately and apply a few strips of zinc oxide tape and leave them on until it is pain-free or the tape starts to come off.

If you have left it too late and a blister has developed you should surround it with 'moleskin' or any other blister kit to protect it from abrasion. Popping it can lead to infection. If the skin is broken keep the area clean with antiseptic and cover with a non-adhesive dressing material held in place with tape.

HYPOTHERMIA

Also known as exposure, this occurs when the body can't generate enough heat to maintain its normal temperature, usually as a result of being wet, cold, unprotected from the wind, tired and hungry. It is usually more of a problem in upland areas. However, even on the Pembrokeshire coast in bad weather the body can be exposed to strong winds and driving rain making the risk a real one. The northern stretches of the path are particularly exposed and there are fewer villages making it difficult to get help should it be needed. Hypothermia is easily avoided by wearing suitable clothing, carrying and eating enough food and drink, being aware of the weather conditions and checking the morale of your companions. Early signs to watch for are feeling cold and tired with involuntary shivering. Find some shelter as soon as possible and warm the victim up with a hot drink and some chocolate or other high-energy food. If possible give them another warm layer of clothing and allow them to rest until feeling better.

If allowed to worsen, strange behaviour, slurring of speech and poor co-ordination will become apparent and the victim can quickly progress into unconsciousness, followed by coma and death. Quickly get the victim out of wind and rain, improvising a shelter if necessary. Rapid restoration of bodily warmth is essential and best achieved by bare-skin contact: someone should get into the same sleeping bag as the patient, both having stripped to their underwear, any spare clothing under or over them to build up heat. Send urgently for help.

HYPERTHERMIA

Heat exhaustion is often caused by water depletion and is a serious condition that could eventually lead to death. Symptoms include thirst, fatigue, giddiness, a rapid pulse, raised body temperature, low urine output and later on, delirium and coma. The only remedy is to re-establish water balance. If the victim is suffering severe muscle cramps it may be due to salt depletion.

Heat stroke is caused by failure of the body's temperature-regulating system and is extremely serious. It is associated with a very high body temperature and an absence of sweating. Early symptoms can be similar to those of hypothermia, such as aggressive behaviour, lack of co-ordination and so on. Later the victim goes into a coma or convulsions and death will follow if effective treatment is not given. To treat heat stroke sponge the victim down or cover with wet towels and vigorously fan them. Get help immediately.

SUNBURN

Even on overcast days the sun still has the power to burn. Sunburn can be avoided by regularly applying sunscreen. Don't forget your lips and those areas affected by reflected light off the ground; under the nose, ears and chin. You may find that you quickly sweat sunscreen off, so consider wearing a sun hat. If you have particularly fair skin wear a light, long-sleeved top and trousers.

DEALING WITH AN ACCIDENT

● Use basic first aid to treat the injury to the best of your ability.
● Work out exactly where you are. If possible leave someone with the casualty while others go to get help. If there are only two people, you have a dilemma. If you decide to get help leave all spare clothing and food with the casualty.
● Telephone ☎ 999 and ask for the coastguard. They will assist in both offshore and onshore incidents.

MINIMUM IMPACT & OUTDOOR SAFETY

PART 3: THE ENVIRONMENT & NATURE

The Pembrokeshire coast is not just about beaches and the sea. The coast path takes you through all manner of habitats from woodland and grassland to heathland and dunes providing habitats for a distinct array of species. This book is not designed to be a comprehensive guide to all the wildlife that you may encounter, but serves as an introduction to the animals and plants that the walker is likely to find within the boundaries of the national park.

Making that special effort to look out for wildlife and appreciating what you are seeing enhances your enjoyment of the walk. To take it a step further is to understand a little more about the species you may encounter, appreciating how they interact with each other and learning a little about the conservation issues that are so essential today. At a time when man seems ever more detached from the natural world it is important to remember that we continue to be a part of this complex web and this brings a responsibility to limit our negative influences.

Conserving Pembrokeshire

Like much of the British Isles, the Welsh countryside has had to cope with a great deal of pressure from the activities of an increasingly industrialized world. It must have been a fascinating place when the broadleaved forests, home to wolves and wild boar, stretched as far as the eye could see. Today the surviving pockets of forest and heathland are still under threat but, thankfully, there is a greater understanding of the value of the natural environment and with it a number of organizations who are actively helping to safeguard what remains of Wales's natural heritage.

As beautiful as the modern-day countryside may be it is sad to note that almost every acre of land has been altered in some way by man. What we have today are fragments of semi-natural woodland and hedgerows stretched across farmland. Aside from the tops of the highest Welsh mountains the only truly untouched land is found on the coast; the cliffs, islands and beaches.

This plundering of the countryside has had a major effect on its biodiversity. Add to the loss of the wolf and wild boar a number of other species lost and others severely depleted in number and one begins to appreciate the influence that man has had over the years.

There is good news, however. In these enlightened times when environmental issues are quite rightly given more precedence, many endangered species, such as the otter, have increased in number thanks to the active work of voluntary conservation bodies. One such success story is the red kite, a beautiful bird of prey which was all but extinct in Britain some ten years ago when just 50 pairs remained in the hills of Mid-Wales. Since then their range has increased to cover greater parts of Wales as well as Scotland and England thanks to an on-going release programme that covers the country.

There is reason to be optimistic. The environment is no longer the least important issue in party politics and this reflects the opinions of everyday people who are concerned about conservation on both a global and local scale. In Wales there are organizations, both voluntary and government based, dedicated to conserving their local heritage; everything from Norman castles to puffins.

GOVERNMENT AGENCIES AND SCHEMES

The Countryside Council for Wales (CCW) and other agencies (see box, below) aim to give protection from modern development and to maintain the countryside in its present state. An effective plan until the government decides a new road or housing estate needs to be built, ignoring their own legislation.

The CCW oversees the Pembrokeshire Coast National Park Authority whose wardens and conservation officers work with landowners, encouraging traditional farming and land-use techniques. The aim is to safeguard the environment and features that make the landscape of Pembrokeshire what it is. The stone walls and cliff-top heathland can only survive through careful grazing methods.

❑ **Government agencies and schemes**
● **Countryside Council for Wales** (CCW ☎ 08451-306229, ⌨ www.ccw.gov.uk; Maes-y-Ffynnon, Penrhosgarnedd, Bangor, Gwynedd, LL57 2DW) Government body responsible for conservation and landscape protection in Wales, including the maintenance of the **Pembrokeshire Coast National Park** and Wales's two other national parks. They also manage a number of **National Nature Reserves** (NNR) within the national park including the limestone cliffs of Stackpole estate on the south coast and the **Marine Nature Reserve** (MNR) around Skomer Island. They are also responsible for the conservation of protected plant, bird and animal species and the designation and maintenance of **Sites of Special Scientific Interest** (SSSI). These range in size from tiny patches set aside for an endangered plant or nesting site, to larger expanses of dunes, saltmarsh, woodland and heathland.
● **Pembrokeshire Coast National Park Authority** (☎ 0845-345 7275, ⌨ www.pcn pa.org.uk; Llanion Park, Pembroke Dock, Pembrokeshire SA72 6DY) Concerned with conserving and managing the national park. Amongst many other roles **The Welsh Association for National Park Authorities** (☎ 029-2049 9966, ⌨ www.an pa.gov.uk or ⌨ www.nationalparks.gov.uk; 126 Bute St, Cardiff Bay, Cardiff CF10 5LE) works with other national park authorities to promote their profile in Wales.
● **Pembrokeshire County Council** (☎ 01437-764551, ⌨ www.pembrokeshire .gov.uk; County Hall, Haverford West, Pembrokeshire SA61 1TP.

Pembrokeshire is not just about the national park. Outside its boundaries the Countryside Council has an array of designations for land of special interest. Being an **Area of Outstanding Natural Beauty** (AONB; ⌨ www.aonb.org.uk) gives some protection to land, though less than that enjoyed by the status national parks. In addition, 500km of the Welsh coast, much of it in Pembrokeshire, has been defined as **Heritage Coast**.

THE ENVIRONMENT & NATURE

They are also responsible for the active protection of endemic species and habitats, as well as geological features, within the national park. If necessary this may involve access restrictions and designating specific areas as Sites of Special Scientific Interest. However, promoting public access and appreciation of Pembrokeshire's natural heritage is also of importance, as is educating locals and visitors about the significance of the local environment.

There is no doubt that the Countryside Council plays a vital role in safeguarding Pembrokeshire for future generations. However, the very fact that we rely on national parks and other such designations for protecting limited areas begs the question: what are we doing to the vast majority of land that remains relatively unprotected? Surely we should be aiming to protect the natural environment outside national parks just as much as within them.

CAMPAIGNING AND CONSERVATION ORGANIZATIONS

The Royal Society for the Protection of Birds (RSPB) was the pioneer of voluntary conservation bodies. It began over a hundred years ago when concern was raised about the use of feathers in ladies' hats. Since then voluntary conservation and environmental organizations have flourished both on a local and global scale. They play a vital role in education, conservation and campaigning and many of the local organizations in Wales are also some of the most significant landowners in the national park.

The **RSPB** manage a number of nature reserves including the islands of Ramsey and Grassholm, as does the **Wildlife Trust West Wales** who manage Skokholm Island and Skomer Island on behalf of the Countryside Council for Wales. The **National Trust** owns many stretches of the mainland coast.

BEYOND CONSERVATION

Pressures on the countryside grow year on year. Western society, whether directly or indirectly, makes constant demands for more oil, more roads, more houses, more cars. At the same time awareness of environmental issues increases and the knowledge that our unsustainable approach to life cannot continue. Some governments appear more willing to adopt sustainable ideals, others less so.

Yet even the most environmentally positive of governments are some way off perfect. It's all very positive to classify parts of the countryside as national parks and Areas of Outstanding Natural Beauty but it will be of little use if we continue to pollute the wider environment; the seas and skies. For a brighter future we need to adopt that sustainable approach to life. It would not be difficult and the rewards would be great.

The individual can play his or her part. Walkers in particular appreciate the value of wild areas and should take this attitude back home with them. This is not just about recycling the odd green bottle or two and walking to the corner shop rather than driving, but about lobbying for more environmentally sensitive policies in local and national government. The first step to a sustainable way of living is in appreciating and respecting this beautiful complex world we live in

❏ Campaigning and conservation organizations

● **Campaign for the Protection of Rural Wales** (☎ 01938-552525, 🖳 www.cprw .org.uk; Ty Gwyn, 31 High St, Welshpool, Powys SY21 7YD) Organization campaigning over a number of local issues from sustainable development to conservation of landscape, historic sites and local traditions.

● **Friends of the Pembrokeshire National Park** (🖳 http://home.freeuk.com/fpnp; PO Box 218, Haverfordwest, Pembrokeshire SA61 1WR) Conservation charity dedicated to protecting, conserving and enhancing the national park.

● **Marine Conservation Society** (☎ 01989-566017, 🖳 www.mcsuk.org; 9 Gloucester Rd, Ross-on-Wye, Herefordshire HR9 5BU) Aims to protect Britain's marine environment and its wildlife and promote global marine conservation. Lots of voluntary projects such as beach cleans and species surveys.

● **National Trust in Wales** (☎ 01492-860123, 🖳 www.nationaltrust.org.uk; Trinity Square, Llandudno, Conwy LL30 2DE) Conservation charity that owns and protects countryside and historic buildings such as Cilgerran Castle, near Cardigan and Tudor Merchant's House, Tenby.

● **Royal Society for the Protection of Birds (RSPB)** (☎ 029-2035 3000, 🖳 www.rs pb.org.uk; Wales Headquarters: The RSPB, Sutherland House, Castlebridge, Cowbridge Rd East, Cardiff CF11 9AB)

● **The Wildlife Trust of South & West Wales** (☎ 0166-724100, 🖳 www.welshwild life.org; Nature Centre, Parc Slip, Fountain Rd, Tondu, Bridgend, Mid-Glamorgan CF32 0EH) manages 92 nature reserves. **The Wildlife Trust West Wales** (☎ 01437-765462, 🖳 http://members.aol.com/skokholm/trust.htm; 7 Market St, Haverfordwest, Pembrokeshire SA61 1NF) is the second oldest wildlife trust in the UK and it actively promotes and protects the area's wildlife and well as organizing marine and coastal wildlife-watching events.

● **Woodland Trust** (☎ 01476-581111, 🖳 www.woodland-trust.org.uk; Autumn Park, Dysart Rd, Grantham, Lincs, NG31 6LL) Restores woodland throughout Britain for its amenity, wildlife and landscape value.

● **World Wide Fund for Nature (WWF)** (☎ 01483-426444, 🖳 www.wwf.org.uk) Panda House, Weyside Park, Godalming, Surrey, GU7 1XR. One of the world's largest conservation and campaigning organizations.

● **Friends of the Earth** (🖳 www.foe.co.uk) International network of environmental groups campaigning for a better environment. Also appreciates the value of local environmental issues.

● **Greenpeace** (🖳 www.greenpeace.org) International organization promoting peaceful activism in defence of the environment.

and realizing that every one of us plays an important role within the great web. The natural world is not a separate entity. We are all part of it and should strive to safeguard it rather than work against it. So many of us live in a world that does seem far removed from the real world, cocooned in centrally heated houses and upholstered cars. Rediscovering our place within the natural world is both uplifting on a personal level and important regarding our outlook and approach to life.

Walkers are in a great position to appreciate this, yet some people still find it difficult to shake off the chaos of modern life even when they are in the countryside. When you are out on the coast path don't just look at the view. Slow down and use all your senses. Listen, smell and touch everything you see.

Flora and fauna

REPTILES

The only poisonous snake in Wales is the **adder** (*Vipera berus*) which can be identified by its dark colouring, the zigzagging down its back and a diamond shape on the back of its head. Common on heathland, it can be seen basking in the sun on rocks or on the path during warm spring and summer days. If you see one consider yourself lucky and don't frighten it. Despite their reputation adders are not as fearsome as you might think. Their venom is designed to kill small mammals, not humans and they bite only if provoked. However, in the unlikely event of a bite, stay still and send someone else to get medical attention. Deaths in humans are extremely rare but the bite is unpleasant and can be dangerous to children, the elderly and pets.

The **grass snake** (*Natrix natrix*) is an adept swimmer and is a much longer, slimmer snake with a yellow collar around the neck. It's non-venomous but does emit a foul stench should you attempt to pick one up. It's much better for you and the snake to leave them in peace.

The **common lizard** (*Lacerta vivipara*) is a harmless creature often seen basking in the sun on rocks and stone walls.

MAMMALS

The Pembrokeshire coast is a stronghold for marine mammals and no trip to the region is complete without spotting a **grey seal** (*Halichoerus grypus*). From late August to October the downy white pups can be seen in the breeding colonies hauled up on the rocks. The best places to spot them are around the Skomer Marine Nature Reserve and in Ramsey Sound and your chances of a sighting increase should you take a boat trip to one of the islands. Look out too for schools of **common porpoise** (*Phocoena phocoena*), a small slate-grey dolphin which can be seen breaking the surface as they head up Ramsey Sound, and the **bottle-nosed dolphin** (*Tursiops truncatus*) which can be found in Cardigan Bay.

Further inland in woodland and on farmland, particularly around the Preseli Hills, are a number of common but shy mammals. One of the most difficult to see is the **badger** (*Meles meles*), a sociable animal with a distinctive black-and-white-striped muzzle. Badgers live in family groups in large underground setts coming out to root for worms on the pastureland after sunset. Unfortunately the most common way of seeing them is as a bloody mess on the road: they are one of the most frequent animal road casualties.

The much maligned **fox** (*Vulpes vulpes*) inhabits similar country to the badger. Despite relentless persecution it is a born survivor, even having adapted to life in cities where they are quite tolerant of human presence. In Pembrokeshire the fox is far more wary and any sightings are likely to be brief.

Keep an eye out for one crossing fields or even scavenging on the beach. They are not exclusively nocturnal. In fact where they are least disturbed they are more likely to be active during the day.

The cliff tops are home to the **rabbit** (*Oryctolagus cuniculus*) where their warrens can prove to be quite a safety hazard to the careless walker. They come out both during the day and at night.

The **otter** (*Lutra lutra*) is a rare native species which is slowly increasing in numbers thanks to long-running conservation efforts. It's at home both in salt and fresh water, although here in Pembrokeshire they are more likely to inhabit rivers and lakes. The otter is a good indicator of a healthy unpolluted environment and it's encouraging to see their numbers increasing not only in Wales but across the British Isles. A good place to see an otter is at the Bosherston lily ponds (see Map 11, p89), where a walk at dawn or dusk may reward the patient and quiet watcher with a sighting.

If you are serious about otter watching take binoculars and choose a good vantage point above the lake, making sure the wind is blowing into your face. A calm evening or morning is best as it is easier to spot the wake of a swimming otter on a still lake surface rather then a choppy one.

In the woodlands you may be lucky enough to spot the native **red squirrel** (*Sciurus vulgaris*). Persecuted to extinction in other parts of the British Isles, here in west Wales they are making a comeback thanks in part to the efforts of local conservationists. In some parts of Wales grey squirrels, which are seen to be one of the main causes of the reds' decline, have been trapped. The effect has been a marked increase in red numbers. No one is entirely sure why reds suffer in the presence of greys but it seems clear that the red revival accelerates when greys are removed. Particularly good places to see reds are in the wooded sections on the south coast such as Rhode Wood north of Tenby and in the forested Cwm Gwaun valley (see box pp192-4) in the Preseli Hills.

The **grey squirrel** (*Sciurus carolinensis*) on the other hand was introduced from North America at the turn of the 20th century. Its outstanding success in colonizing Britain is very much to the detriment of other native species including songbirds and, most famously, the aforementioned red squirrel. Greys are bigger and stockier than reds and to many people the reds, with their tufted ears, bushy tails and small beady eyes are the far more attractive of the two.

The **roe deer** (*Capreolus capreolus*) is a small native species of deer that tends to hide in woodland. They can sometimes be seen alone or in pairs on field edges or clearings in the forest but you are more likely to hear its sharp dog-like bark when it smells you coming.

On Ramsey Island there is a famous herd of **red deer** (*Cervus elaphus*), the largest land mammal in Britain. They have adapted successfully to open country due to the loss of their natural habitat of deciduous woodland and can be spotted quite easily on Ramsey's windswept slopes.

At dusk **bats** can be seen hunting for moths and flying insects along hedgerows, over rivers and around street lamps. Bats have had a bad press thanks to Dracula and countless other horror stories but anyone who has seen one up close knows them to be harmless and delightful little creatures. As for

THE ENVIRONMENT & NATURE

their blood-sucking fame, the matchbox-sized species of Britain would not even be able to break your skin with their teeth let alone suck your blood. Their reputation is improving all the time thanks to the work of the many bat conservation groups around the country and all fourteen species in Britain are protected by law. The commonest species in Britain, and likewise in Pembrokeshire, is the **pipistrelle** (*Pipistrellus pipistrellus*).

Some other small but fairly common species which can be found in the scrubland and grassland on the cliff tops include the carnivorous **stoat** (*Mustela erminea*), its smaller cousin the **weasel** (*Mustela nivalis*), the **hedgehog** (*Erinaceus europaeus*) and a number of species of **voles**, **mice** and **shrews**.

> ❏ **The Skomer vole**
> The island of Skomer (see box p134) is famous for its puffins and shearwaters but is also home to a diminutive character perhaps deserving of a little more attention. The Skomer vole (*Clethrionomys glaeolus skomerensis*) is a sub-species of the bank vole. An estimated 20,000 of the little rodents inhabit the island, playing an important role in the diet of the resident short-eared owls. Unique to the island, the Skomer vole is larger than its mainland cousin and is a perfect example of Darwin's evolutionary theory, evolving differing characteristics from its mainland cousin due to its geographic isolation.

BIRDS

Without doubt Pembrokeshire is a hot spot for ornithologists. The cliffs, and more especially the islands, are important breeding grounds for a number of species such as the razorbill which has been adopted as the symbol of the national park authority. Away from the rolling waves other species, adapted to completely different habitats, can be spotted in the woodland, farmland and heathland that covers the cliff tops and valleys.

Islands and cliffs

The islands of Skomer and Skokholm are home to the **manx shearwater** (*Puffinus puffinus*) which lives in huge colonies of thousands, breeding in burrows along the cliff top. They can be identified by their dark upperside and paler underside with slender pointed wings and a fast swerving flight across the surface of the sea. Boat trips (see box p134) at dusk can be taken to watch the spectacular displays as the birds leave their burrows to look for food.

Grassholm Island is one of the world's most important breeding sites for the **gannet** (*Morus bassanus*), a large bird with a wing span of 175cm. They are easily identified by their size and white plumage, with a yellow head and black wing tips. In winter they spend most of their time over the open sea, returning in summer to breed in huge colonies on offshore rocky outcrops such as Grassholm. They catch fish by folding their wings back and diving spectacularly into the water.

The **cormorant** (*Phalacrocorax carbo*) is a prehistoric-looking bird. It can often be seen perched on rocks, its wings outstretched. Unlike other birds their feathers are not oily and water resistant so this is the only way of drying out. Dark in appearance, often with a white patch around the stocky bill, it swims with an out-stretched neck and frequently dives underwater with a little jump as it bobs on the surface. It is commonly seen in estuaries and on more sheltered stretches of water. From the same family as the cormorant is the **shag** (*Phalacrocorax aristotelis*).

The **razorbill** (*Alca torda*) is another auk that breeds on the cliff tops. It is black with a white belly and has a distinctive white stripe across the bill to the eye. Similar in appearance to the razorbill but with a much more slender bill is the **guillemot** (*Uria aalge*). It stands more upright than the razorbill and is less stocky. They nest in huge colonies on cliff-face ledges and are often seen in small groups flying close over the surface of the sea with very fast wing beats.

The **storm petrel** (*Hydrobates pelagicus*) spends most of the time over the open sea. It has an erratic flight pattern often just skimming the surface. It can be identified by the square tail, white rump and a white band on the underside of the wings which contrasts with the dark body. They also have strange tube-like nasal implements on a hooked beak.

Looking something like a medium-sized gull, the **fulmar** (*Fulmarus glacialis*) can also be seen far out to sea but nests on ledges on the cliff face. They vary in appearance from a buff grey to white and can be distinguished from gulls by their gliding flight pattern and occasional, slow, stiff wing beats.

The **kittiwake** (*Rissa tridactyla*) spends the winter out at sea where large flocks follow the fishing boats. In the summer they breed in large colonies on the coastal cliffs. It is a small gull with a short yellow bill and short black legs. It has a white plumage except for the light grey wings with black tips. The tail is distinctively square when in flight.

Cormorant

It's not difficult to tell cormorants and shags apart. The **cormorant** is larger than the shag and has a bigger bill and head. In the breeding season the cormorant has a white patch on its flank. The **shag** is slimmer, has a more uniform dark plumage with a green glossy sheen. It also has a more slender bill and a pronounced tuft on the top of the head. Shags are often seen in flocks on the coast or out to sea, whereas cormorants are usually found in river estuaries and in pairs or alone except when in nesting colonies.

Shag

THE ENVIRONMENT & NATURE

Puffin

The **common tern** (*Sterna hirundo*) is gull-like but smaller. It is generally white but with grey wings and a black crown. Its short legs are red as is its short, pointed bill which usually has a black tip.

There are three species of auk in Pembrokeshire, the most famous and popular of which has to be the **puffin** (*Fratercula arctica*) with its lavishly coloured square bill. Like the manx shearwater, puffins breed in burrows or under boulders. They can often be seen with a bill full of fish on their way back to their burrows. Skomer Island is Puffin Central but remember that they come to the island only during the breeding season (April to early August), spending the winter out at sea. You are far less likely to spot a puffin on the mainland.

The **chough** (*Pyrrhocorax pyrrhocorax*), pronounced 'chuff', is one of the more attractive members of the crow family; slender and elegant in appearance with a deep red curved and pointed bill and legs of the same colour. Choughs are often found in mountainous areas, but in Pembrokeshire they breed on the coast where they can be seen flying acrobatically around the cliffs.

The **peregrine falcon** (*Falco peregrinus*) is a beautiful raptor that can be found nesting on some of the sea cliffs. It is a lean and efficient hunter with slate grey plumage and a white underside with thin black barring. It kills its prey with a spectacular dive known as stooping, in which the bird closes its wings and plummeting from the sky like a small missile, stunning its prey on impact. It's a fantastic sight.

Of the numerous gulls the most common include the **herring gull** (*Larus argentatus*), a large white gull with grey wings tipped with black, a bright yellow bill with a red spot at the end and yellow eyes. It is not a shy bird and can often be seen around harbours where it is something of a scavenger. Some other gulls which you may spot include the **great black-backed gull** (*Larus marinus*) similar to the herring gull but with black wings and the **lesser black-backed gull** (*Larus fuscus*) which is, not surprisingly, smaller.

Herring gull

Great black-backed gull

The **Herring gull** (above) is the most frequently-seen member of the gull family. It has pink legs and feet and a grey upper body. Largest of the gulls is the **great black-backed gull** (left) which has, as the name implies, a black back. It also has pink legs and feet which distinguish it from the **lesser black-backed gull**, which has yellow legs.

THE ENVIRONMENT & NATURE

The **black-headed gull** (*Larus ridibundus*) spends a lot of time feeding in large flocks on farmland close to the coast. It is a slender gull with a distinctive black head and black wing tips.

Beaches and mudflats

A distinctive bird that can often be seen running along the shingle and sandy beaches is the **ringed plover** (*Charadrius hiaticula*). This stocky little bird the size of a thrush has a white belly and brown upper-parts with a pair of characteristic black bands across its face and throat. The legs and bill are both orange.

Similar in size is the **common sandpiper** (*Actitis hypoleucos*), a small bird that can be found on rocky shores. It has white under-parts with a light brown breast and upper-parts. White bars can be seen on the wings when it is in flight.

Also to be found on the beach and often feeding on inland fields is the **oystercatcher** (*Haematopus ostralegus*). It is quite common and easily identified by the distinctive black upper-parts and white belly. It has a sharp stabbing orange bill used for probing the ground when feeding and a distinctive shrill call.

The **lapwing** (*Vanellus vanellus*) with its long legs, short bill and distinctive long head crest also feeds on arable farmland. Sadly, this attractive bird is declining in numbers. The name comes from its lilting flight, frequently changing direction with its large rounded wings. It is also identified by a white belly, black and white head, black throat patch and distinctive dark green wings.

Inhabiting the sand dunes, moors and bogs is the **curlew** (*Numenius arquata*) a brown mottled bird with a very long slender bill which curves downwards. It has an evocative far-reaching call that reflects its name: 'Kooor-lee'. In the winter it groups in large flocks on open ground such as fields and mudflats.

Scrubland and grassland

On open ground you may be lucky enough to see the **short-eared owl** (*Asio flammeus*) which, unlike other owls, often hunts during the day. Skomer is a good place to look out for it. It is quite large with fairly uniform dark streaks and bars over an otherwise golden-brown plumage. The pale face is a typical round owl's face with golden eyes ringed by black eye patches.

A more common sight is the **stonechat** (*Saxicola torquata*), a colourful little bird with a deep orange breast and a black head. Its name comes from its call which sounds like the chink of two stones being knocked together. During the summer months you will see it along the coast path flitting from the top of one gorse bush to another.

The **yellowhammer** (*Emberiza citrinella*), a bunting, is not seen quite so much as the stonechat though it has the same habit of singing atop gorse bushes. It has a distinctive call said to sound like 'a little bit of bread and no cheese' according to those with vivid imaginations, although it's certainly no mynah bird. Less striking in appearance is the **meadow pipit** (*Anthus pratensis*), a rather drab-looking small brown bird. It can be identified by white flashes on the edge of its tail as it flies away. Another small brown bird spotted above grassland is the **skylark** (*Alauda arvensis*). It has a distinctive flight pattern rising directly upwards ever higher singing constantly as it goes. It climbs so high that the relentless twittering can be heard while the bird is nowhere to be seen.

THE ENVIRONMENT & NATURE

Woodland

The **raven** (*Corvus corax*) is so big that it is often mistaken for a buzzard. They have lifelong breeding partners and nest on rocky ledges along the coast and further inland high in the tree tops. In St David's there is a rookery in Cross Square. The raven has all-black plumage, a thick stocky bill and a deep guttural croaking call.

A common raptor that is often heard before being seen is the **buzzard** (*Buteo buteo*), a large broad-winged bird of prey which looks much like a small eagle. It is dark brown in appearance and slightly paler on the underside of its wings. It has a distinctive mewing call and can be spotted soaring ever higher on the air thermals, or sometimes perched on the top of telegraph poles.

Much smaller than the buzzard is the **kestrel** (*Falco tinnunculus*), a small falcon and the most commonly seen bird of prey. It hovers expertly in a fixed spot, even in the strongest of winds, above grassland and road side-verges hunting for mice and voles.

TREES

Before man and his axe got to work there were forests covering 80% of what is now the national park. Sadly this woodland cover has dropped to just 6%, some of which is coniferous plantation. From an ecological perspective the most important forest cover is the ancient semi-natural woodland which covers a mere 1% of the national park area. Twenty of these ancient broadleaved woodlands are designated sites of special scientific interest (SSSI).

On the Pembrokeshire Coast Path most of the woodland is encountered along the southern section from Amroth to Tenby and on the southern side of the Milford Haven estuary. The windswept northern stretches are more barren although many of the small valleys are wooded. Another good place to find ancient broadleaved woodland is the Cwm Gwaun valley in the Preseli Hills. Look out for lichen on the tree trunks as this is a classic indicator of clean air. Over 300 species of lichen can be found in many of the forests.

None of the woodland in Pembrokeshire can be described as completely natural as it has all been managed or altered in some way by man. In the past rural communities coppiced the trees and used the wood from hazel for fencing and thatching. Evidence of charcoal burning is also present and oak was grown along sheltered bays and estuaries to provide wood for shipbuilding.

These practices began to die out at the end of the 19th century when cheap coal began to replace coppiced wood and charcoal as fuel. However, there has been a small revival in recent years by aficionados of traditional countryside ways and conservationists who recognize the benefits of coppicing for a number of species, including the endangered dormouse. In Pembrokeshire coppicing can be seen in several places and is a method of woodland management that has been used by the National Park Authority itself.

Predominant tree species

The dominant species in semi-natural broadleaved woodland is the **sessile oak** (*Quercus petraea*) with good examples around the Daugleddau estuary. The ses-

THE ENVIRONMENT & NATURE

sile oak differs from the English common oak in a number of ways; most notably in having brighter more shapely leaves. The name 'sessile' means 'without stalks' referring to the acorns which grow directly from thin branches. Oak woodland is a diverse habitat and is also home to **downy birch** (*Betula pubescens*), **holly** (*Ilex aquifolium*) and **hazel** (*Corylus avellana*) which has traditionally been used for coppicing.

Ash (with seeds)

The **common ash** (*Fraxinus excelsior*) is well adapted to cope with the salt-laden sea winds and can be found on the limestone rich soils in the south of the county, around the Bosherston lily ponds for example. The **common alder** (*Alnus glutinosa*) is often found alone growing by streams.

Perhaps surprisingly the mighty **beech** (*Fagus sylvatica*) is not native to this part of the country but has established itself wherever there is well-drained soil and is surely one of the most beautiful of the broadleaved trees. Other species to look out for include the **aspen** (*Populus tremula*), **hawthorn** (*Crataegus monogyna*) and **rowan** or mountain ash (*Sorbus aucuparia*) with its slender leaves and red berries.

Hazel (with flowers)

FLOWERS

The coast path is renowned for its wild flowers. Spring is the time to come and see the spectacular displays of colour on the cliff tops while in late summer the heather on the northern slopes turns a vibrant purple.

The coast and cliff-top meadows

The coastline is a harsh environment subjected to strong winds, wind-blown salt and tides. Plants that colonize this niche are hardy and well adapted to the conditions. Many of the cliff-top species such as the pink flowering **thrift** (*Armeria maritima*) and white **sea campion** (*Silene maritima*) turn the cliff tops into a blaze of colour from May to September.

On shingle beaches and dunes you might see the **yellow-horned poppy** (*Glaucium flavum*), but don't think about eating it, it's poisonous. On the cliff top and track sides you might encounter the straggly stems of **fennel** (*Foeniculum vulgare*), a member of the carrot family which grows to over a metre high. Other plants to look for are **spring squill** (*Scilla verna*) and **scurvy-grass** (*Cochlearia officilanis*), and in saltmarshes and estuaries **sea-lavender** (*Limonium vulgare*) and **sea aster** (*Aster tripolium*).

THE ENVIRONMENT & NATURE

Woodland and hedgerows

The **wood anemone** (*Anemone nemorosa*), the **bluebell** (*Hyacinthoides non-scripta*) and the yellow **primrose** (*Primula vulgaris*) flower early in spring, with the bluebell and wood anemone covering woodland floors in a carpet of white and blue. The bluebell and primrose are also common on open cliff tops. **Red campion** (*Silene dioica*), which flowers from late April, can be found in hedgebanks along with **rosebay willowherb** (*Epilobium augustifolium*) which also has the name fireweed owing to its habit of colonizing burnt areas.

In scrubland and on woodland edges you will find **bramble** (*Rubus fruticosus*), a common vigorous shrub, responsible for many a ripped jacket thanks to the sharp thorns and prickles. The blackberry fruits ripen from late summer to autumn. Fairly common in scrubland and on woodland edges is the **dog rose** (*Rosa canina*) which has a large pink flower, the fruits of which are used to make rose-hip syrup.

Other flowering plants to look for in wooded areas and in hedgerows include the tall **foxglove** (*Digitalis purpurea*) with its trumpet-like flowers, **forget-me-not** (*Myosotis arvensis*) with tiny, delicate blue flowers and **cow parsley** (*Anthriscus sylvestris*), a tall member of the carrot family with a large globe of white flowers which often covers roadside verges and hedgebanks.

Heathland and scrubland

Some of the cliff tops, particularly in the north of the region, are carpeted in heather resulting in a spectacular purple display when it comes into flower in late summer. Heathland is an important habitat for butterflies, snakes and lizards. There are good examples of it on the west side of the Dale peninsula, east of Marloes Sands, on the high slopes north of Newport Sands and most notably on the St David's peninsula.

There are three species of heather. The dominant one is **ling** (*Calluna vulgaris*) which has tiny flowers on delicate upright stems. The other two species are **bell heather** (*Erica cinera*) with deep purple bell-shaped flowers and **cross-leaved heath** (*Erica tetralix*) with similarly shaped flowers of a lighter pink, almost white colour. Cross-leaved heath prefers wet and boggy ground. As a consequence, it usually grows away from bell heather which prefers well-drained soils.

Heathland is also the stronghold of **gorse** (*Ulex europeous*), a dark green bush of sharp thorns with spectacular displays of yellow flowers from February through to June. Not a flower but worthy of mention is the less attractive species **bracken** (*Pteridium aquilinum*), a vigorous non-native fern that has invaded many heathland areas to the detriment of native species.

In more overgrown areas where the heath has reverted to scrubland you invariably find **broom** (*Cytisus scoparius*), a big bushy plant with dark green stalk-like leaves and bright yellow flowers. As its name suggests it looks like a big upturned broom and was indeed used for this purpose. It was also believed to have magical powers and was used as a diuretic. On hot days you can hear the seed pods cracking open, spreading the seeds about.

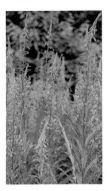

Rosebay Willowherb
Epilobium angustifolium

Common Fumitory
Fumaria officinalis

Thrift (Sea Pink)
Armeria maritima

Lousewort
Pedicularis sylvatica

Bell Heather
Erica cinerea

Heather (Ling)
Calluna vulgaris

Foxglove
Digitalis purpurea

Common Centaury
Centaurium erythraea

Red Campion
Silene dioica

Spear Thistle
Cirsium vulgare

Sea Holly
Eryngium maritimum

Sea Campion
Silene maritima

Herb-Robert
Geranium robertianum

St John's Wort
Hypericum perforatum

Scarlet Pimpernel
Anagallis arvensis

Cornflower
Centaurea cyanus

Bluebell
Endymion non-scriptus

Rowan (tree)
Sorbus aucuparia

Honeysuckle
Lonicera periclymemum

Common Ragwort
Senecio jacobaea

Gorse
Ulex europaeus

Tormentil
Potentilla erecta

Primrose
Primula vulgaris

Evening Primrose
Oenothera erythrosepala

Ransoms (Wild Garlic)
Allium ursinum

Hogweed
Heracleum sphondylium

Yarrow
Achillea millefolium

Common Vetch
Vicia sativa

Old Man's Beard
Clematis vitalba

Germander Speedwell
Veronica chamaedrys

Silverweed
Potentilla anserina

Self-heal
Prunella vulgaris

Violet
Viola riviniana

Meadow Buttercup
Ranunculis acris

Birdsfoot-trefoil
Lotus corniculatus

Cowslip
Primula veris

Dog Rose
Rosa canina

Common Hawthorn
Crataegus monogyna

Ox-eye Daisy
Leucanthemum vulgare

PART 4: ROUTE GUIDE & MAPS

Using this guide

The trail guide and maps have not been divided into rigid daily stages since people walk at different speeds and have different interests. The **route summaries** below describe the trail between significant places and are written as if walking the path from south to north. To enable you to plan your own itinerary **practical information** is presented clearly on the trail maps. This includes walking times for both directions, all places to stay, camp and eat, as well as shops where you can buy supplies. Further service details are given in the text under the entry for each settlement. For an overview of this information see Itineraries, pp26-8.

TRAIL MAPS

Scale and walking times
The trail maps are to a scale of 1:20,000 (1cm = 200m; 3¹/₈ inches = one mile). Walking times are given along the side of each map and the arrow shows the direction to which the time refers. Black triangles indicate the points between which the times have been taken. **See note below on walking times**.

The time-bars are a tool and are not there to judge your walking ability. There are so many variables that affect walking speed, from the weather conditions to how many beers you drank the previous evening. After the first hour or two of walking you will be able to see how your speed relates to the timings on the maps.

Up or down?
The trail is shown as a dotted line. An arrow across the trail indicates the slope; two arrows show that it is steep. Note that the arrow points towards the higher part of the trail. If, for example, you are walking from A (at 80m) to B (at 200m) and the trail between the two is short and steep it would be shown thus: A— — — >> — — – B. Reversed arrow heads indicate a downward gradient.

Accommodation
Apart from in large towns where some selection of places has been necessary, almost every place to stay that is within easy reach of the trail is marked. Details

> ❏ **Important note – walking times**
> Unless otherwise specified, **all times in this book refer only to the time spent walking**. You will need to add 20-30% to allow for rests, photography, checking the map, drinking water etc. When planning the day's hike count on 5-7 hours' actual walking.

of each place are given in the accompanying text. Unless otherwise specified **B&B rates are summer high-season prices per person** assuming two people sharing a room with a separate bathroom. The number and type of rooms are given after each entry: S = single room, T = twin room, D = double room, F = family room (sleeps at least three people).

Other features
Features are marked on the map when pertinent to navigation. In order to avoid cluttering the maps and making them unusable not all features have been marked each time they occur.

The Pembrokeshire Coast Path

KILGETTY (CILGETI) MAP 1
If you are coming by train or coach Kilgetty is the closest stop to the start of the coast path at Amroth three miles (5km) away. Kilgetty is pleasant enough but there is not much to keep you here so it would be best to head straight to the start of the trail proper.

Services
Everything of importance can be found by turning left out of the train station and walking down the main street.

The **tourist information centre** (☎ 01834-814161, 🖥 info@tourismpembroke shire.co.uk; daily 10am-5pm, to 7pm in spring and summer holiday periods) is the last building on the left-hand side. They say that you can call them even outside office hours. Before it is the Co-op **supermarket** (Mon-Sat 8am-10pm, Sun 10am-4pm), which is a good place to get some last-minute supplies, as is the smaller **Bridge Stores** which is where the name suggests it is. There is also a **cash machine** at the Co-op and a **post office** (☎ 01834-812239; Mon-Fri 9am-1pm, 2-5.30pm, Sat 9am-12.30pm) just before it. There is no bank at the next port of call, Amroth. If you are already worried about blisters you should head for the **chemist** near The White Horse.

The **bus stop** for the National Express coach is outside the tourist information centre at the far western end of the village.

Transport
Bear in mind that Kilgetty is a request stop so trains only stop at the **railway station** if you let the driver know before you get on, otherwise you will end up in Tenby, missing the first seven miles (11km) and that's just cheating. Silcox Coaches **bus** services Nos 350 and 351 operate between Tenby, Saundersfoot and Amroth, No 352 between here, Saundersfoot and Tenby, and No 381 between Tenby and Haverfordwest; all services stop near the post office.

If you have come by car, or have a return bus or train ticket from Kilgetty, you could make your way to Cardigan and do the entire coast path in reverse so that you end up back at your departure point at the end of the walk. The best way to do this is take Silcox's No 381 service to Narberth and then Midway Motors' No 430 to Cardigan.

For full details see the public transport map and table, pp39-41.

Where to stay
There are not many places to stay in Kilgetty but if you do decide to spend the first night here rather than at Amroth you could try *Pleasant View* (☎ 01834-814040, 🖥 redford@btinternet.com, Apr-Sep, 1S/7D) with en suite rooms from £27 per person. You'll find it up Ryelands Lane.

Campers should aim for *Ryelands Park Campsite* (☎ 01834-812369, Apr-

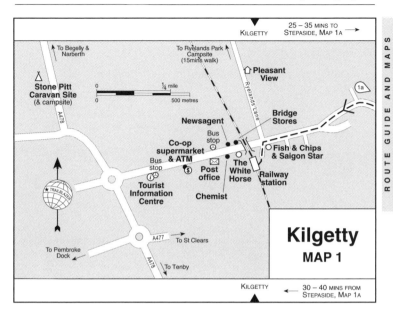

▼
25 – 35 MINS TO
KILGETTY   STEPASIDE, MAP 1A →

↗ To Begelly &
Narberth

To Ryelands Park ↗
Campsite
(15mins walk)

⌂ Pleasant
View

Stone Pitt
Caravan Site
(& campsite)

0   ¼ mile

0   500 metres

Ryelands Lane

1a

Bridge
Stores

A478

Newsagent

Bus
stop

Co-op
supermarket
Bus
stop & ATM

⊙ Fish & Chips
& Saigon Star

✉
Post
office

The
White
Horse

Railway
station

Tourist
Information
Centre

⑤

Chemist

★ TRAILBLAZER

↑

To Pembroke
Dock ↙

A477 → To St Clears

A478

↘ To Tenby

Kilgetty

MAP 1

KILGETTY   ← 30 – 40 MINS FROM
STEPASIDE, MAP 1A

▲

Oct) which can be found about half a mile up Ryelands Lane to the north of the village. Prices are around £5 per person. *Stone Pitt Campsite* (☎ 01834-810110; 🖳 www .walesholidays.co.uk/stonepittcara.html, closed Jan-Feb) in **Begelly** charges £10 for a two-man tent. Unfortunately, it's in the wrong direction for the coast path lying on the main road towards Narberth, about a 15-20 minute walk away.

Better located is *Mill House Camping and Caravan Park* (see Map 1a; ☎ 01834- 812069, 🖳 www.millhousecaravan.co.uk, Mar-Oct) in **Stepaside**. It's geared more towards caravans and those big tents the size of bungalows but they should be able to squeeze in a smaller one. Prices are from

£8.50 a pitch. Book well in advance in the summer. It is on the way towards the start of the coast path about a mile east of Kilgetty.

Where to eat
Next to the exit from the train station is a **fish and chip** shop (☎ 01834-812024; Mon-Thu 4-10pm, Fri/Sat 12-10pm) and the *Saigon Star* ☎ 01834-814100, a Vietnamese takeaway (Wed-Mon 5.30- 10pm). On the other side of the bridge, *The White Horse* by the railway bridge now does food (Tue-Sun noon-2.30pm, 6-8.30pm), including their popular curry nights on Wednesday.

KILGETTY TO AMROTH   MAPS 1, 1a & 1b

These **three miles (5km, 1-1½hrs)** provide a pleasant walk to the coast and the start of the path at Amroth but if you are feeling lazy you can catch the No 350 or 351 bus (see pp39-41). The bus drops you at Amroth Castle, which is now a caravan park, close to the start of the path at New Inn.

ROUTE GUIDE AND MAPS

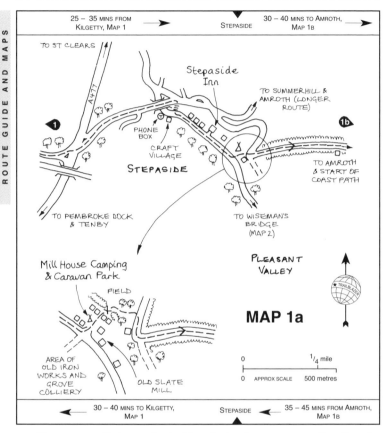

TO ST CLEARS

A477

Stepaside Inn

TO SUMMERHILL & AMROTH (LONGER ROUTE)

1

PHONE BOX

1b

CRAFT VILLAGE

STEPASIDE

TO AMROTH & START OF COAST PATH

TO PEMBROKE DOCK & TENBY

TO WISEMAN'S BRIDGE (MAP 2)

PLEASANT VALLEY

Mill House Camping & Caravan Park

FIELD

TRAILBLAZER

MAP 1a

AREA OF OLD IRON WORKS AND GROVE COLLIERY

OLD SLATE MILL

0   1/4 mile

0   APPROX SCALE   500 metres

If you want to limber up for the big trek ahead you may as well walk to the start of the path by following the lane to **Stepaside**. Take care crossing the main road, the A477. Stepaside received its quirky name thanks, it is said, to Oliver Cromwell who in 1648, while marching to Pembroke, stopped here and told his men to step aside and take their victuals. At Stepaside you should join the little lane through Pleasant Valley to Mill House Camping and Caravan Park where you can see the old slate mill and the iron works, both dating from the mid-19th century. A path takes you through the caravan park and then you join the lane through **Summerhill** to **Amroth**.

You are now on the coast path but unfortunately it officially begins at the northern end of the village, at New Inn. If you want to say you have done the whole path you will have to walk to the start and then come back again the way you have just come.

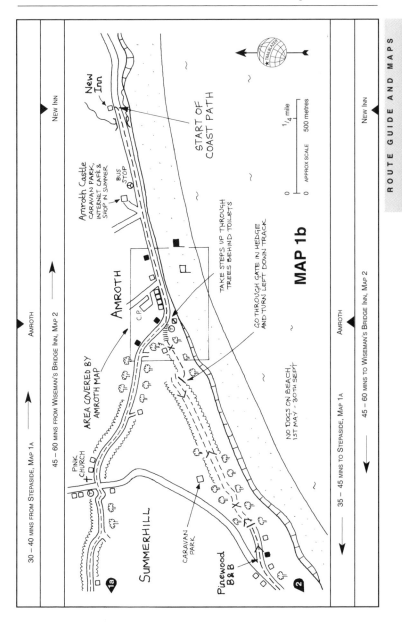

30 – 40 MINS FROM STEPASIDE, MAP 1A   AMROTH ▶

45 – 60 MINS FROM WISEMAN'S BRIDGE INN, MAP 2   ▶ NEW INN ▶

New Inn

START OF COAST PATH

Amroth Castle
CARAVAN PARK,
INTERNET CAFÉ &
SHOP IN SUMMER

BUS STOP

AMROTH

AREA COVERED BY AMROTH MAP

TAKE STEPS UP THROUGH HEDGE BEHIND TOILETS

GO THROUGH GATE IN HEDGE AND TURN LEFT DOWN TRACK

MAP 1b

PINK CHURCH

SUMMERHILL

CARAVAN PARK

Pinewood B & B

NO DOGS ON BEACH,
1ST MAY - 30TH SEPT

0   APPROX SCALE   ¼ mile

0   500 metres

TRAILBLAZER

◀ 1a

2

◀ NEW INN

◀ AMROTH

35 – 45 MINS TO STEPASIDE, MAP 1A

45 – 60 MINS TO WISEMAN'S BRIDGE INN, MAP 2

ROUTE GUIDE AND MAPS

❏ Getting to Amroth by car

If you are coming by car you need to turn off for Stepaside (opposite the turning for Kilgetty). The lane goes down to the village and then goes uphill. About halfway up the hill turn right along a very narrow lane which leads to Summerhill. Go straight over at the crossroads and follow the road downhill to Amroth. The start of the path is at the far eastern end of the village at New Inn but a better place to leave the car is in the free National Park Authority car park. It is just off the seafront road near Amroth Castle and is indicated by a blue 'P' sign.

AMROTH

Amroth is stretched out along a single road facing a pretty beach with forested slopes at either end. It's not a big place but being a popular holiday spot there are a few eating places and two B&Bs.

At the southern end of the village where the coast path leaves the road there is a **toilet** block and a **phone box**. In the summer there is sometimes a small **shop** selling basic supplies through a doorway in the wall by the castle; it also offers **internet access**.

Silcox Coaches' **bus** services Nos 350 and 351 connect Amroth with Kilgetty, Saundersfoot and Tenby, and the No 222 runs between here and Carmarthen; see the public transport map and table, pp39-41, for full details.

Where to stay and eat

Halfway along the seafront road, *Beach Haven Guest House* (☎ 01834-813310, 1S/2T/1F), formerly the post office, charges £30/pp per night. There used to be

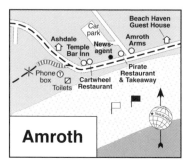

a string of B&Bs on the steep road leading down to the village from Summerhill but these days only *Ashdale* (☎ 01834-813853; 1S/2D/1T) with beds currently around £24 per person, seems to be operating.

If you feel like a break before you've even started, *New Inn* (see Map 1b; ☎ 01834-812368, daily, food served daily 12-8pm) is ideally placed to distract you from the walk. It's a pretty spot with a garden by a stream at the very beginning of the coast path. They have curries from £6.90 or for something less fiery try one of their lunchtime baguettes. It's a good place for a pint but unfortunately they don't do bed and breakfast. It's sometimes closed in winter.

Another popular spot is the *Temple Bar Inn* (☎ 01834-814943; food served 11am-10.30pm), in the centre of the village, a bustling place with meals for about £6-10.

Slightly more expensive and perhaps the classiest place in Amroth, the *Amroth Arms* (☎ 01834-812480, daily, food served Tue-Sun 12-2pm, 6.30-9pm) has Welsh pork and local fish dishes.

The award-winning *Cartwheel Restaurant* (☎ 01834-812100, 🖳 cartwheel amroth@aol.com, Tues-Sat 6pm-late, Sun lunch from noon) displays the Pembrokeshire Produce Mark guaranteeing the food to be of local origin. They specialize in seafood dishes with prawn and crab salad for £11.95 and honey-roast duck at £13.95. After such a strenuous half mile it's worth treating yourself.

For something cheaper try the *Pirate Restaurant and Takeaway* (☎ 01834-812757; daily 9.30am-6pm, to 8.30pm in holidays and high season).

AMROTH TO TENBY   MAPS 1-3, 3a

These first **seven miles (11km, 3hr 10min-4¹/₂hrs)** pass through beautiful and varied scenery, mixing cool cliff-top woodland with small sandy beaches and coves which can be spied through the trees. Don't underestimate this stretch. Although not as rugged as the coastline further north there is enough up and down to make this a tiring introduction especially if you have been slacking in the training!

The path leaves Amroth at its western end where some steps lead up through the trees taking you into a meadow above the cliffs and along a dirt track to **Wiseman's Bridge**. En route you pass *Pinewood* (Map 1b; ☎ 01834-811082, 🖥 www.pinewoodholidaypark.co.uk; Cliff Rd, 2D/1T all en suite) with rooms starting at £25 per person with a £5 single supplement. They also own the neighbouring caravan park but there are no camping facilities.

WISEMAN'S BRIDGE   MAP 2
This is a great spot for a morning break, or lunch if you started from Kilgetty.

The hamlet, which hugs a sandy bay, comprises a scattering of houses, a **phone box**, **public toilets** and, most importantly, *Wiseman's Bridge Inn* (☎ 01834-813236,

🖥 www.wisemansbridgeinn.co.uk; 2T/3D/3F) which has rooms starting at £45 per person or £60 for single occupancy of one of their rooms. It's a good idea to book in advance.

They also have a **campsite** over the road, charging £13/20 for a hard/soft pitch.

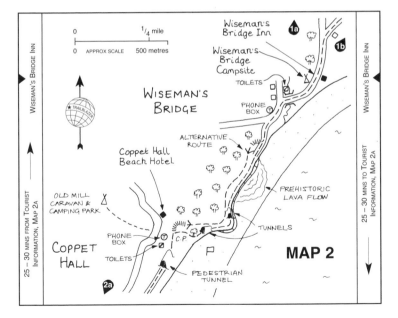

The inn also does good **food** (daily noon-2.30pm, 6-9pm) but they are often very busy in the summer; below the restaurant is an arcade with a pool table.

Silcox's **bus** Nos 350 and 351 call here en route to/from Amroth, Kilgetty and Tenby. For full details about public transport see the map and table, pp39-41.

From here the path follows the route of an old colliery railway passing through two old tunnels. The railway dates from 1834 when coal from the Stepaside colliery was transported by horse-drawn trams and later steam engines to Saundersfoot where it was shipped to the continent. As you walk this stretch look out for the interesting fan-shaped rock formation on the beach. This was produced by wave erosion acting on a fold (anticline in geological terms) in the coal measure strata.

An alternative path passes through shady woodland above the beach to Coppet Hall, where a third tunnel on the other side of the beach car park leads you into the lively seaside town of **Saundersfoot**.

SAUNDERSFOOT   MAP 2a

This is a typical small seaside town pleasantly free of any tackiness. In fact, despite the hustle and bustle, on a summer day Saundersfoot has a rather lazy, even care-free feel to it.

Somewhat overshadowed by the more famous seaside town of Tenby, many see Saundersfoot as a quieter alternative to the commotion of its southern neighbour.

Services

The **tourist information centre** (☎ 01834-813672, ☐ saundersfoot.tic@pembroke shire.gov.uk; Easter to end April, Sep & Oct daily 10am-5pm, May-Aug to 5.30pm) is in a small building by the car park.

There is also a **newsagent**, a small Spar **supermarket** and **post office**, all of which are scattered around the car park by the harbour. If your feet are not suffering from blisters already there are remedies at the **chemist** on The Strand where you can also find a **bank** with a cashpoint.

Silcox's **bus** Nos 350 and 351 connect Saundersfoot with Kilgetty, Amroth, Tenby and Pendine; bus No 381 also stops here. For full details see the public transport map and table, pp39-41.

Where to stay

Unfortunately, there is a distinct lack of cheap accommodation although there is

camping at the *Old Mill Caravan and Camping Park* (☎ 01834-812657) which charges £6.50/pp; no booking is necessary. It is ten minutes from the coast path near Coppet Hall (see Map 2). There is another campsite a mile south of Saundersfoot at *Trevayne Farm* (see Map 4; ☎ 01834-813402, ☐ www.camping-pembrokeshire .co.uk; Apr-Sep); pitches are £4 per person.

In contrast there is plenty of B&B-style accommodation. Before you reach the town, on the other side of the pedestrian tunnel is *Coppet Hall Beach Hotel* (☎ 01834-814467; ☐ www.coppethallbeachhotel.co .uk; 1S/4T or D/3D/3F) with rooms from £40 per person.

In the town you could try *Cliff House* (☎ 01834-813931, ☐ www.smoothhound. co.uk/hotels/cliffhse, Wogan Terrace, 5D). the rooms are en suite and cost from £40 for single occupancy and £30 per person for two sharing. Close by you'll find *Wogan Guest House* (☎ 01834-812473, ☐ www.s-h-sys tems.co.uk/hotels/woganhou.html, Wogan Terrace, 6D), which is 300 years old and is reputed to be the oldest building in the village; prices start at £35 per person. Some rooms are en suite.

The Harbour Light (☎ 01834-813496, ☐ www.harbourlightguesthouse.co.uk, 2 High St, 4D/1T/4F en suite) is a large place with beds from £30 and a £10 single occupancy supplement. On the way out of town,

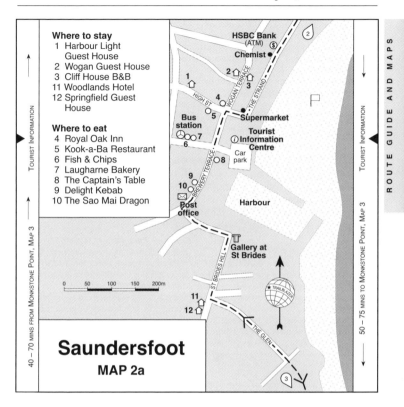

opposite the Glen where you turn off to enter the forest, is **Woodlands Hotel** (☎ 01834-813338, 🖳 www.hotelwoodlands.co.uk; 2S/5D/3F), a smart but cosy place with light, en suite bedrooms that charges £40, or £33 per person for two sharing; next door, **Springfield Guest House** (☎ 01834-810260; 🖳 www.springfieldguesthouse.com; 4D), a smart place with en suite rooms, charges £30 per person, rising to £32.50 in summer, with a £10 suppplement if staying in the room with a four-poster bed.

Where to eat

There are a plethora of eating dens here. A fantastic pub to look out for with friendly staff is the **Royal Oak Inn** (☎ 01834-

812546, 12-2.30pm, 6-9pm) where you can blow your bags on a 10oz pork steak with smoked bacon and stilton for £15.95, or neck a pint of prawns for £6.25. For a more regular pint they have a selection of real ales including their own Royal Oak ale at £2.30. The cosy bar is a good place to unwind after a hard day.

The **Captain's Table** (☎ 01834-812435, food served daily 12-2.30pm, 6.15-9pm) is renowned for its barbecues with live music, held every Tuesday from 6pm in the summer.

Also on Brewery Terrace there is **The Sao Mai Dragon**, a good Vietnamese restaurant (daily 5pm to midnight) which is useful if you arrive late with an empty belly. It has curries from £4.30 and seafood dishes from £4.60. Next to it is the ***Delight Kebab*** (daily noon to midnight) with jacket potatoes, kebabs, and fish and chips at down-to-earth prices. There are a couple of other **fish and chip shops** including one by the bread shop (see column opposite).

Globalization has reached Saundersfoot in the shape of ***Kook-a-ba*** (☎ 01834-813814, daily 6-9.30pm), a good Australian bar and restaurant with 'Long Neck' ostrich and 'Skippy' kangaroo steaks; something to put a spring in your step for £11.95 and £9.95 respectively.

Packed lunches can be bought at the ***Laugharne Bread Shop*** (☎ 01834-844077; daily 9am-4.30pm) where you can get filled baguettes starting at £1.90 for a simple bacon one.

In Rhode Wood south of Saundersfoot keep an eye out for red squirrels. At Monkstone Point you have the option of a ten-minute detour to the wooded headland. The path to the right after the steps leads to Trevayne Farm Camping (see p72). The final stretch takes you through more woodland and fields, and also passes the track to Meadow Farm Campsite (see p78), eventually entering **Tenby** above the immaculate sands of North Beach.

TENBY (DINBYCH Y PYSGOD)
MAP 3a, p77

Dinbych y Pysgod (the Little Fort of the Fishes), as it is known in Welsh, has grown from being just a fishing port to a delightful holiday town.

In many respects it is typical of the great British seaside resort, yet it retains a certain charm and sophistication, having resisted stumbling down the road to cheap tackiness as some other seaside towns have done. Immaculate expanses of sand almost surround the town attracting throngs of holidaymakers in the summer. Colourful houses perch above the harbour and South Beach while the wonderfully

---

❏ Caldey Island

The small island of Caldey (☎ 01834-844453, 🖳 www.caldey-island.co.uk) is clearly visible just south of Tenby. Monks have been on the island for around 1500 years and about 20 monks from the Reformed Cistercian Community live on the island, attending seven services a day in the private monastery. The first service kicks off at 3.15am!

Boat trips (☎ 01834-844453 and ☎ 01834-842296) to the island from Tenby (Easter-Oct, Mon-Fri 10am-5pm, the last boat returns after 5pm, every 20 minutes; also Sat May-Sep). Tickets cost £10 return and are sold at the kiosk by Tenby harbour.

There is a surprising amount to see on the island although tours of the **monastery** itself are available only for men. Everyone is free to explore the island outside the monastery grounds including **St Illtud's Church** and **Old Priory**. There is also a tea room, small museum, post office (with its own official Caldey stamp) and a good bathing beach at Priory Bay. Look out for seals around the lighthouse on the southern tip of the island. Services for the public are held in the island's parish church, **St David's**, at 2.45pm most weekdays.

The resident monks are a dab hand at farming with many of their dairy products on sale in the shop. Perhaps more surprising is their range of perfumes and toiletries, available in the **Perfumery Shop**. All the products are based on local flowers, herbs and even prickly gorse.

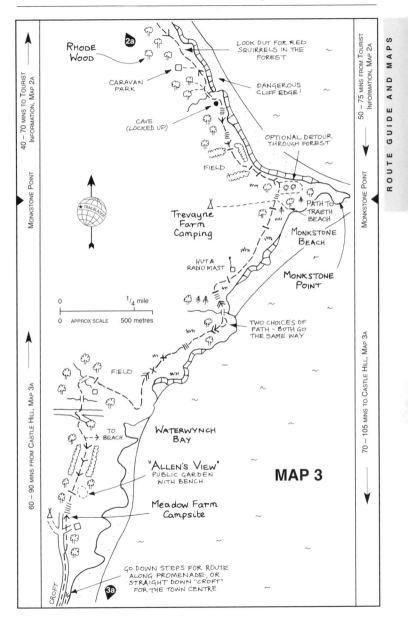

RHODE WOOD

2a

LOOK OUT FOR RED SQUIRRELS IN THE FOREST

CARAVAN PARK

DANGEROUS CLIFF EDGE!

CAVE (LOCKED UP)

OPTIONAL DETOUR THROUGH FOREST

FIELD

★ TRAILBLAZER

Trevayne Farm Camping

PATH TO TRAETH BEACH

MONKSTONE BEACH

HUT & RADIO MAST

MONKSTONE POINT

0   1/4 mile

0   APPROX SCALE   500 metres

TWO CHOICES OF PATH – BOTH GO THE SAME WAY

FIELD

WATERWYNCH BAY

TO BEACH

"ALLEN'S VIEW" PUBLIC GARDEN WITH BENCH

MAP 3

Meadow Farm Campsite

GO DOWN STEPS FOR ROUTE ALONG PROMENADE, OR STRAIGHT DOWN "CROFT" FOR THE TOWN CENTRE

3a

CROFT

40 – 70 MINS TO TOURIST INFORMATION, MAP 2A

MONKSTONE POINT

60 – 90 MINS FROM CASTLE HILL, MAP 3A

50 – 75 MINS FROM TOURIST INFORMATION, MAP 2A

MONKSTONE POINT

70 – 105 MINS TO CASTLE HILL, MAP 3A

TENBY – MAP KEY
Where to stay
1 Sunny Bank Guest House
2 Ivy Bank Guest House
3 Kingsbridge House
4 Weybourne Guest House
5 Lyndale House
6 Sea Breezes
13 Normandie Inn
18 Glenholme Guesthouse
19 Lindholme House

Where to eat
7 Bay of Bengal Indian Restaurant
8 Get Stuffed Pizza
9 Crumbs and Cream Coffee Shop
10 The Sun Inn
11 No. 25 Café & Internet
12 Lamb Inn
13 Normandie Inn
14 Five Arches Tavern
15 Plantagenet Restaurant and Quay
      Room
16 Nana's Trattoria
17 China Town Chinese Restaurant

ROUTE GUIDE AND MAPS

well preserved **mediaeval town walls** hide a maze of crooked streets.

One of the original three gateways and seven of the original twelve towers which make up the town wall still remain. It was probably built in response to attacks on the town in 1187 and 1260. In the 12th century the Normans built a **castle** on the promontory and though there is little left of it today, built into part of it is **Tenby Museum** (☎ 01834-842809, 🖳 www.tenbymuseum.org .uk; daily 10am-5pm, weekdays only in winter; £3, £2.50 concession; Castle Hill) where they have an art gallery and exhibitions covering everything from local maritime and social history to displays on archaeology, geology and natural history. They also trace the history of the town from the tenth century, as well as a 'pirate's cell'. You can even find out if you have any ancestors from the local area by checking out their local family-history researcher.

Look out for the National Trust's **Tudor Merchant's House** (☎ 01834-842279, April-Oct Sun-Tue 11am-5pm, admission £2.50 with discounts for members), an old townhouse tucked into tiny Quay St near the harbour. It dates back to the 15th century and still has the original roof beams and a herb garden.

Tenby itself has plenty to keep you busy for a day, even if that means just wandering the streets or exploring the wonderful beaches. It is also the place to catch the boat over to **Caldey Island** and its monastery (see box p74).

Services

The **tourist information centre** (☎ 01834-842404, 🖳 tenby.tic@pembrokeshire.gov .uk; daily Easter to late May 10am-5pm, late May to end June, Sep & Oct to 5.30pm, July & Aug to 6pm, to 9pm for accommodation booking, Mon-Sat Nov-Easter to 4pm) is down by the entrance to Somerfields **supermarket** on Upper Park Rd.

There's a **post office** (☎ 01834-843213; Mon-Fri 8.30am-5pm; Sat 8.30am-12.30pm) at the northern end of town near the B&Bs on Warren St. Another vital port of call for most people is a **bank** of which there are plenty in the centre, including a branch of HSBC on Tudor Sq, a Barclays behind the church, and an Abbey National a little further north on the High St; all have **cashpoints**. Apart from the ATM in Manorbier, Tenby is the last place you can get money until you reach Pembroke (53 miles/85km away). It is also worth taking into account that many of the pubs and guesthouses along the path to Pembroke do not take credit cards; another good reason to fill your pockets with cash before you leave town.

Another possibly essential stop for many a trekker is the No 25 Café (see p79) which has **Internet facilities**, the first since Amroth and the last until Pembroke.

Neither are there any shops to speak of until you reach Angle so take a good supply of food unless you plan to eat out every night. For camping supplies head for **TYF Outdoor** (☎ 01834-843488, 🖳 www.tyf .com, Mon-Sat 9am-5.30pm, Sun 10am-

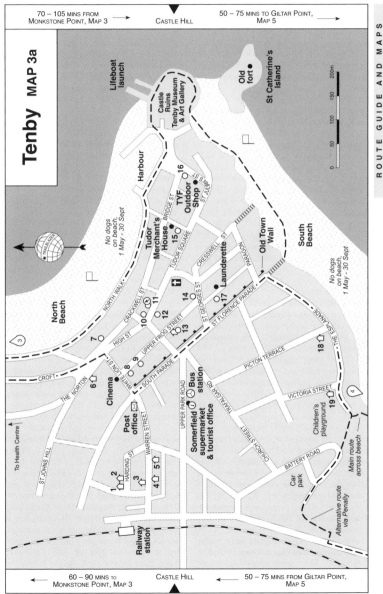

ROUTE GUIDE AND MAPS

Tenby MAP 3a

70 – 105 MINS FROM MONKSTONE POINT, MAP 3 →

CASTLE HILL

50 – 75 MINS TO GILTAR POINT, MAP 5 →

Lifeboat launch

Castle Ruins
Tenby Museum & Art Gallery

Old fort ●

St Catherine's Island

0   50   100   150   200m

Harbour

16
TYF Outdoor Shop

ST JULIAN'S ST

BRIDGE ST

Tudor Merchant's House

15

TUDOR SQUARE

CRESSWELL ST

Launderette

17

Old Town Wall

South Beach

No dogs on beach, 1 May - 30 Sept

TRAILBLAZER

No dogs on beach, 1 May - 30 Sept

North Beach

③

NORTH WALK

CRACKWELL ST

HIGH ST

7

10 11

12

14

ST GEORGES ST

PARAGON

THE CROFT •

ST JOHN'S HILL

THE NORTON

6

Cinema

WHITE LION ST

8 9

UPPER FROG STREET

13

SOUTH PARADE

ST FLORENCE PARADE

THE ESPLANADE

18

PICTON TERRACE

To Health Centre

HARDING ST

WARREN STREET

Post office ✉

1 2
3
4 5

UPPER PARK ROAD

Bus station

Somerfield ⓘ supermarket & tourist office

TRAFALGAR RD

VICTORIA STREET

19

④

Children's playground

Railway station

CHURCH STREET

BATTERY ROAD

Car park

Main route across beach

Alternative route via Penally

60 – 90 MINS TO MONKSTONE POINT, MAP 3 ←

CASTLE HILL

50 – 75 MINS FROM GILTAR POINT, MAP 5 ←

4pm) at 16 St Julian's St. They also organize courses in climbing, canoeing, surfing and coasteering (see box p83). For any medical problems you can always pay a visit to the **health centre** which is in the north of the town on Narberth Rd. There's a **launderette** for your smelly socks just south of St George's St.

For entertainment there's no shortage of **pubs** in the town centre, and a **cinema** on White Lion St as you enter the town.

Transport
The **bus station** is on Upper Park Rd while the **train station** can be found a little further along the same road. Trains run to Pembroke Dock and all the way back to Swansea and London for those who have already had enough. Buses connect Tenby with Amroth (Nos 350/351), Pembroke Dock (Nos 333/358), Kilgetty (No 352), Haverfordwest (No 349) and other places further afield. See the public transport map and table, pp39-41, for full details.

Where to stay
On the path just to the north of town (see Map 3) is *Meadow Farm* (☎ 01834-844829, ✉ meadowfarmcampsite-tenby@hotmail.co .uk, Mar-Oct) charging £6 per person per night (children £4), or £7 with a car.

Like most seaside towns there are countless B&Bs and guesthouses but they do, of course, get very busy at holiday time. As you enter the town from the north, close to North Beach is *Sea Breezes* (☎ 01834-842753, ✉ www.seabreezesonline.co.uk; 18 The Norton, 1D/2D or T), once a large hotel, now a small guesthouse, with beds from £28 per person. There is a cluster of guesthouses around Warren St and Harding St just above the centre of town. *Lyndale House* (☎ 01834-842836, ✉ wardshome@hotmail .com; 3D en suite), on Warren St, has rooms for £30 per person and *Weybourne Guest House* (☎ 01834-843641, ✉ wey bourne@tiscali.co.uk; 14 Warren St, 1T/3F) charges from £30/pp. Slightly more expensive is *Sunny Bank Guest House* (☎ 01834-844034, ✉ www.sunny-bank.co.uk; Harding St, 4D) with en suite rooms from £35 per person (£45 single occupancy), or

it's £38 in a room with a four-poster; the nearby *Ivy Bank Guest House* (☎ 01834-842311, ✉ www.ivybanktenby.co.uk, Harding St; 5D) charges from £35. Finally in this area, *Kingsbridge House* (☎ 01834-844148; 3D/1T/2F) is a spacious Victorian house with rooms from £30 per person.

Close to the town centre is the *Normandie Inn* (☎ 01834-842227, Upper Frog St, 5D/2F) where all the rooms are en suite and cost £35/pp or £45 for single occupancy. Just off The Esplanade is *Glenholme Guesthouse* (☎ 01834-843909, ✉ www .glenholmetenby.co.uk, Picton Terrace, 1S/7D) with rooms for £32 per person; and *Lindholme House* (☎ 01834-843368, 27 Victoria St, 6D) which can be found near the end of The Esplanade by South Beach. It has rooms from £29 per person.

Where to eat
There are some great little restaurants in Tenby, most of them on High St and Tudor Sq or at the top end of Upper Frog St. *Plantagenet Restaurant and Quay Room* (☎ 01834-842350; Quay Room open summer daily 10am-2.30pm, 6pm to late, Plantagenet open summer daily noon-2.30pm, 6pm to late; winter times vary), said to be the oldest house in Tenby, is definitely worth finding. It is on the corner of Tudor Sq with the short and narrow Quay Hill. The menu guarantees local ingredients with the home-made sausages a speciality. In addition to some cracking meat dishes including a divine lamb shank (£17.95) they also serve some great vegetarian food.

Round the corner and down the hill next to the harbour is *Nana's Trattoria* (☎ 01834-844536; Tue-Sun 11am-2.30pm, 6pm-late) with simple Italian food for those who want to load up with carbs before the next leg. Equally cheap but tasty food can be found on the High St at the *Lamb Inn* (☎ 01834-842151; Sun-Thur 11am-5pm, Fri & Sat 11am-8pm; 14 High St) which has a variety of pub food such as jacket potatoes for £3.50 and baguettes from £3.25. Close by is *The Sun Inn* (☎ 01834-845941, 11am-late, food served daily 12-3pm), a bright and cheerful joint with reasonably cheap food including fisherman's pie for

£7, while next door is *No 25 Café* (☎ 01834-842544, daily 9.30am-5pm) with a range of snacks and sandwiches to eat while you're using their internet (see p76).

For more traditional pub grub try the *Normandie Inn* (see opposite, daily 5.30-9.30pm) which does a tasty 8oz rump steak for £6.95, or it's £12.95 for two. They also have live music most nights. Also on Upper Frog St you will find the rustic *Five Arches Tavern* (☎ 01834-842513, daily 12-2pm, 6-8.30pm) with local fish dishes from £7.25.

Those with oriental tastes should head to Crackwell St, just off High St, for the *Bay of Bengal Indian Restaurant* (☎ 01834-843331, daily 5.30-11.30pm).

They have a typically extensive Indian menu. The chicken curry is £6.75 and the wonderful views over the North Beach are totally free. Alternatively there is the *China Town Chinese Restaurant* (☎ 01834-843557, Lower Frog St, Mon-Sat 12-2pm, 5.30pm-midnight, Sun 12.30-2pm, 6-11.30pm) which has the usual array of rice and sweet and sour dishes.

Slightly less sophisticated food can be found at *Get Stuffed Pizza* (☎ 01834-845945, 10 Upper Frog St, daily 5.30-11pm) and next door at the *Crumbs and Cream Coffee Shop* (☎ 01834-842928, daily 10am-4.30pm), a useful stop for a cheap and filling lunch.

TENBY TO MANORBIER BAY   MAPS 4-8

These **ten and a half miles (17km, 3-4¹/₂hrs)** are reasonably straightforward. The scenery is tamer than before but no less interesting. The path leaves Tenby at the end of The Esplanade and drops down onto the vast sands of South Beach. The direct route takes you across the beach to **Giltar Point** in the south. In the unlikely event of an exceptionally high tide or if you are planning on staying in the village of Penally you will need to take the alternative and slightly longer path which follows the track between the railway line and the golf course.

Giltar Point is the first of a number of MoD firing ranges and it is occasionally closed to the public (indicated, as with all the firing ranges, by a red flag flying); there is a number you can call to check the times of firing on the range (☎ 01834-845950). If it is open you can climb the steps up through the high dunes onto the cliff top. When it is closed you must take the detour from the beach through the dunes to **Penally**.

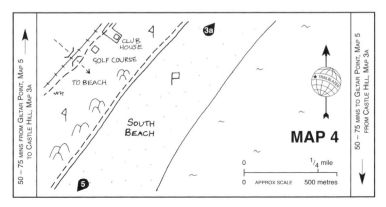

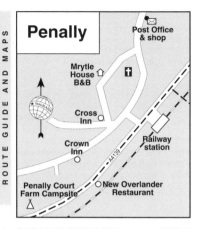

PENALLY (PENALUN)   **MAP 5**

Penally has a pretty church set beside the village green. If you're not staying in Tenby there's more accommodation here and several places to eat. There's also a **post office** (Mon-Fri 8am-5.30pm, Sat 8am-noon) in the centre of the village, which also incorporates a small **shop**.

First's **bus** No 349 stops by The Crown Inn. The **railway station** lies on the main road; there are trains every two hours or so for Pembroke and Pembroke Dock via Manorbier in one direction, and for Swansea via Tenby, Saundersfoot, Kilgetty and Narberth in the other. For details of public transport services see pp39-41.

Where to stay and eat
Should your feet be aching after the first day there are some good places to stay. Campers should head for *Penally Court*

Farm Campsite (☎ 01834-845109, open Apr-Oct) at the western end of the village. Pitches cost around £5 per person.

There are also a number of good B&Bs. In the centre of the village up the lane behind the church is *Myrtle House* (☎ 01834-842508, 1S/5D/1T/1F) where beds are £32 per person. *Brambles Lodge* (☎ 01834-842393, 🖳 www.brambleslodge.co.uk, 1S/3D/2T/1F) can be found in the western corner of Penally, just off the main road. It has standard rooms from £30 single, or en suite in a twin or double from £28 per person.

Wychwood House (☎ 01834-844387, 🖳 www.wychwoodhousebb.co.uk; 1D/2F en suite) at the other end of the village is a very classy place charging affordable rates. Rooms are en suite. Prices are from £30 rising to £35 per person in a four-poster bed. Dinner costs £23; there's no licence so bring your own wine.

There are two pubs in the centre of the village: The *Crown Inn* (food served Mon-Sat 11.30am-2pm, 5.30-9pm; Sun noon-2.30pm, 7-9pm) is a traditional pub with good cheap food. Just around the corner you will find another mouthwatering menu at the *Cross Inn* (☎ 01834-844665, daily 12-2.30pm, 6-8.30pm); they also do breakfasts from 9.30am by arrangement (call in or phone the day before).

On the main A4139 road is the *New Overlander Restaurant* (☎ 01834-842868, daily 9.30am-9pm in summer; winter times vary), a smart little place with a garden and lots of clocks for sale on the walls. Try the Welsh lamb for £6.95. For under £3 the garlic mushrooms are fantastic. They also do breakfasts from £3.95.

From here you must follow the main road a short distance before joining a track that goes under the railway line and back up onto the coast path proper.

(Opposite) Top: Amroth (see p70), the start of the trail. **Bottom**: There are numerous beaches along the coast path and they range from great wide sandy stretches to beautiful secluded beaches such as this one – Barafundle Bay (see p88).

(Overleaf) Top: Looking down on Swanlake Bay (see p85), near Manorbier.
Bottom: Impressive cliff erosion – the Green Bridge of Wales (see p95).
                                                                (All photos © Henry Stedman)

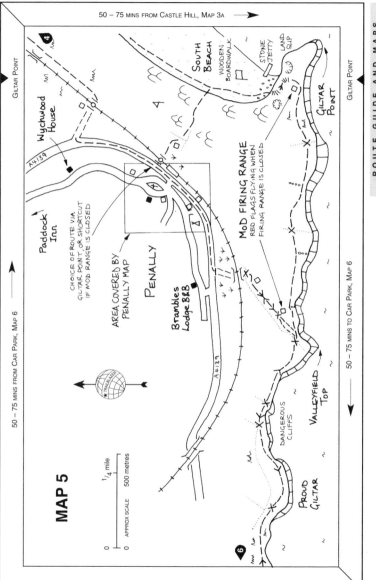

MAP 5

50 – 75 MINS FROM CASTLE HILL, MAP 3A →

GILTAR POINT

GILTAR POINT

SOUTH BEACH

WOODEN BOARDWALK

STONE JETTY

LAND SLIP

GILTAR POINT

4

Wychwood House

A4139

Paddock Inn

50 – 75 MINS FROM CAR PARK, MAP 6 →

CHOICE OF ROUTE VIA
GILTAR POINT, OR SHORTCUT
IF MOD RANGE IS CLOSED

AREA COVERED BY
PENALLY MAP

PENALLY

Brambles Lodge B&B

A4139

MOD FIRING RANGE
RED FLAGS FLYING WHEN
FIRING RANGE IS CLOSED

50 – 75 MINS TO CAR PARK, MAP 6 →

VALLEYFIELD TOP

DANGEROUS CLIFFS

PROUD GILTAR

6

¼ mile
0
APPROX SCALE
0   500 metres

★ TRAILBLAZER

ROUTE GUIDE AND MAPS

The path continues over low grassy cliff tops, passing the pretty sandy bay of Lydstep Haven. At Lydstep there's an optional 20-minute detour to the open headland of Lydstep Point with views along the coast in both directions.

LYDSTEP   MAP 6

Lydstep Haven is dominated by an unattractive caravan park though the village of Lydstep itself is further inland, reached by following the coast path up from the beach and turning right just past the caravan park entrance. It's a small village with just a pub, one B&B and a phone box. The No 349 **bus** from Tenby to Haverfordwest stops by the Tavern; for full details see the public transport map and table, pp39-41.

Rosendale Guesthouse (☎ 01834-870040, 🖳 www.rosendalepembrokeshire .co.uk; 3T/4D) is a good B&B charging from £30 per person (£45 for single use of a double or twin room).

Lydstep Tavern (☎ 01834-871521, daily 12-2.30pm, 6-9pm) is on the bend of the main road with fine local beers and ciders to accompany their home-cooked snacks and bar food.

Budget travellers should head for *Manorbier Youth Hostel* (☎ 0870-770 5954, 🖳 manorbier@yha.org.uk, open all year), a little further along the coast path, some 200 metres from the beach at Skrinkle

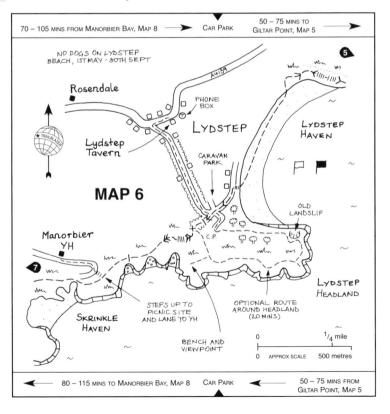

70 – 105 MINS FROM MANORBIER BAY, MAP 8 ➡ CAR PARK   50 – 75 MINS TO GILTAR POINT, MAP 5 ➡

NO DOGS ON LYDSTEP BEACH, 1ST MAY - 30TH SEPT

A4139

Rosendale

PHONE BOX

LYDSTEP

LYDSTEP HAVEN

TRAILBLAZER

Lydstep Tavern

CARAVAN PARK

MAP 6

OLD LANDSLIP

Manorbier YH

C.P.

LYDSTEP HEADLAND

STEPS UP TO PICNIC SITE AND LANE TO YH

OPTIONAL ROUTE AROUND HEADLAND (20 MINS)

SKRINKLE HAVEN

BENCH AND VIEWPOINT

0   ¹/₄ mile

0   APPROX SCALE   500 metres

⬅ 80 – 115 MINS TO MANORBIER BAY, MAP 8   CAR PARK ⬅   50 – 75 MINS FROM GILTAR POINT, MAP 5

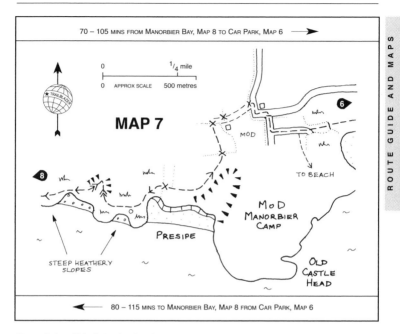

70 – 105 MINS FROM MANORBIER BAY, MAP 8 TO CAR PARK, MAP 6 →

0   1/4 mile
0   APPROX SCALE   500 metres

MAP 7

MOD

6

TO BEACH

8

MoD
MANORBIER
CAMP

PRESIPE

STEEP HEATHERY
SLOPES

OLD
CASTLE
HEAD

← 80 – 115 MINS TO MANORBIER BAY, MAP 8 FROM CAR PARK, MAP 6

Haven. It has 69 beds but is often full in the summer months.

The rather unfortunate sardine-tin appearance of the hostel is thanks to its original use as a 1950s NATO storage building. Thankfully the interior is actually quite habitable now. Prices start at £14 for members, or an en-suite twin (in bunk beds) is £17.50. The hostel is licensed and serves meals.

The cliffs up to **Skrinkle Haven** are impressive but then the path heads inland to avoid another MoD enclosure. The stretch to **Manorbier Bay** follows some beautiful coast, the path contouring steep heathery slopes that drop straight into the sea.

❏ **Coasteering**
Coasteering is a real hands-on approach to exploring the Pembrokeshire coastline but is not a sport that everyone will be familiar with. It involves traversing sheer sea cliffs by scrambling, climbing, jumping off ledges into the churning sea and getting very wet. It makes quite a change from simply walking along the cliff tops and certainly provides more of an adrenaline rush.

For guidance on how to do it properly **TYF** (☎ 01437-721611, 🖳 www.tyf.com), who claim to have invented this fast-growing sport, offer day courses around the cliffs of Lydstep and the St David's peninsula.

ROUTE GUIDE AND MAPS

MANORBIER (MAENORBYR) MAP 8a

Pronounced 'manor-bee-er' this village boasts a windswept sandy beach and an impressive, well-preserved castle (see below). It also has a handful of B&Bs, a **shop** with long opening hours and an **ATM** at the top of the village, as well as a good pub, which is a saving grace on a rainy day.

The No 349 **bus** calls in on its way to and from Tenby and Haverfordwest. **Trains** stop at the railway station every couple of hours but it is a bit inland so not that convenient. For full details see the public transport map and table, pp39-41.

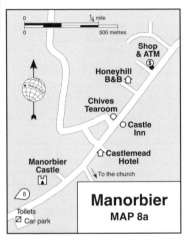

Manorbier
MAP 8a

Where to stay and eat

Castlemead Hotel (☎ 01834-871358; 🖥 www.castlemeadhotel.com; 1S/3T/4D) is the first building on the right as you enter the village by the lane from the beach. This is the most luxurious option and also the most expensive. B&B is from £42/pp. Their restaurant is open to non-residents in the evenings and for lunch on Sundays.

At the far end of the village in the residential area is *Honeyhill B&B* (☎ 01834-871906; Warlows Meadow, 1S/2D) with beds from £25 per person.

For hungry tummies, on the right-hand side past Castlemead Hotel is the *Castle Inn* (☎ 01834-871268, food served daily noon-2.30pm, 6-9pm). It has an extensive menu and a pool table.

On the other side of the road is *Chives Tearoom* (☎ 01834-871709, daily 10am-5pm) with sandwiches from £2.50, baked potatoes from £3.50 and lasagne for £6.50.

A mile and a half (2km) further along the coast path, *Swanlake Bay Farm* (see Map 8 opposite; ☎ 01834-871204, 🖥 www.swanlake-bay.co.uk; 7D) offers B&B from £30 and allow **camping** (costs vary according to the size of the tent but work out at about £3 per person) but there are no facilities. They do have a **tearoom**, however, which is open daily 11am-5.30pm from Easter to the end of September.

❑ Manorbier Castle

History is visible everywhere you go in Pembrokeshire from standing stones and Iron-Age hill-forts to the numerous castles dotted around the countryside.

One of the finest, Manorbier Castle (☎ 01834-871394; 🖥 www.manorbier castle.co.uk) can be visited. The birthplace of Gerald of Wales, a 12th-century scholar who described Manorbier as 'the pleasantest spot in Wales', it stands in a wonderful location close to the beach, just off the coast path. Life-size wax figures and appropriately contemporary music piped throughout much of the building help visitors get a feel for what the castle and its pleasant walled gardens must have been like in Gerald's day. If the castle seems vaguely recognizable, that could be because it has been used as a set in various films including *I Capture the Castle* and the 1989 version of *The Lion, the Witch and the Wardrobe*.

Visitors can explore the turrets and dungeons from Easter to the end of September, daily 10am-6pm. Admission £3.50.

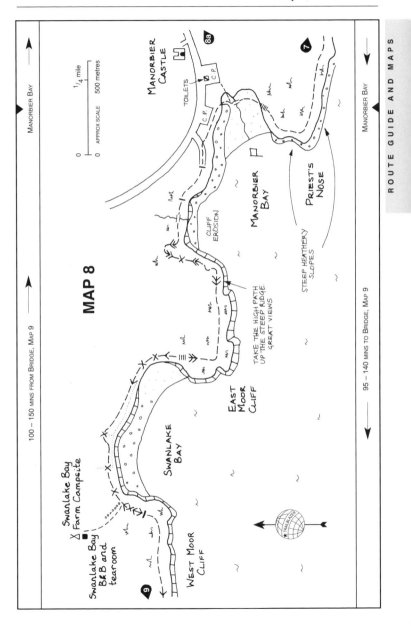

MANORBIER BAY TO FRESHWATER EAST   MAPS 8-9

ROUTE GUIDE AND MAPS

This short section of **four miles (6km, 1¹/₂-2hrs)** takes in two wild windswept headlands which sandwich **Swanlake Bay**, a sandy beach backed by steep slopes and farmland. Short but strenuous accurately describes this section. No sooner do you drop down the side of one steep cliff than you find yourself climbing up another. It can make for slow progress if you have a heavy pack. The broad sands of Freshwater East make a welcome sight.

It is worth bearing in mind that budget accommodation is pretty thin on the ground from here until Pembroke and the same can be said for any other services you may be looking for. Forward planning is essential. Book all your accommodation well in advance especially in the high season.

FRESHWATER EAST   MAP 9

Freshwater East is a peculiar place. A number of houses lie scattered among the wooded slopes above the bay while the steep road up from Trewent Park is lined by yet more homes. In fact there is little here other than houses.

If you are staying here it is worth using the footpath that cuts in to the village just before the coast path drops down to the beach. Otherwise you have to walk down and then back up the steep road to reach the village.

The No 387 and 388 Coastal Cruiser **bus** services call here on the way round the coast via Pembroke Dock, Angle, Hundleton and Stackpole. For further information see pp39-41.

Accommodation, at least B&B accommodation, is decidedly thin on the ground,

though the Georgian country mansion *Port Clew House* (☎ 01646-672800; 🖳 www .portclewhouse.co.uk; 1S/3T/2D/1F) is a grand place boasting en suite only rooms with internet facilities. They also serve great breakfasts. Prices for a one-night stay start at £34, rising to £38 in high season, with discounts for children and those staying longer than a single night.

Closer to the path, half a mile west of Freshwater East, is *East Trewent Farm* (☎ 01646-672127, 🖳 www.easttrewentfarm .co.uk; 1S/2D/2T) with rates from £28 per head.

Well worth the detour from the path, the food at the *Freshwater Inn* (☎ 01646-672828, daily 12-2.30pm, 6-9pm) comes with a wide choice and big helpings including some fine baguettes.

FRESHWATER EAST TO BROAD HAVEN (FOR BOSHERSTON)
MAPS 9-12

The scenery really is spectacular for the next **six and a half miles (10km, 2-3hrs)** to Broad Haven (not to be confused with the village of Broad Haven further north). It begins with more tortuous 'up-and-downs' as the cliffs twist and turn their way west of Freshwater East.

Between Trewent Point and Greenala Point there are some fantastic contorted green cliffs, coves and blowholes lining the coastline. Once past Greenala Point the path follows the high top of a long steep cliff before dropping down to Stackpole Quay.

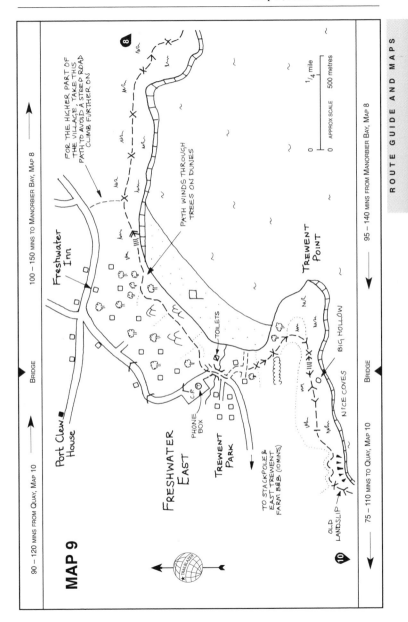

MAP 9

90 – 120 MINS FROM QUAY, MAP 10 ▶ BRIDGE ▶ 100 – 150 MINS TO MANORBIER BAY, MAP 8 ▶

75 – 110 MINS TO QUAY, MAP 10 ◀ BRIDGE ◀ 95 – 140 MINS FROM MANORBIER BAY, MAP 8 ◀

Port Clew House

Freshwater Inn

FOR THE HIGHER PART OF THE VILLAGE, TAKE THIS PATH TO AVOID A STEEP ROAD CLIMB FURTHER ON

PATH WINDS THROUGH TREES ON DUNES

TREWENT POINT

FRESHWATER EAST

TREWENT PARK

PHONE BOX

C.P.

TOILETS

TO STACKPOLE & EAST TREWENT FARM B&B (10MINS)

BIG HOLLOW

NICE COVES

OLD LANDSLIP

0 APPROX SCALE 500 metres

0 ¼ mile

TRAILBLAZER

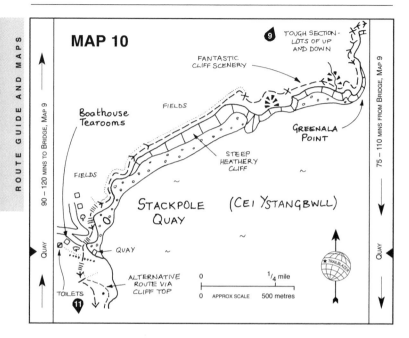

The scenery changes dramatically as you pass **Stackpole Quay**. Leaving the old red sandstone behind, the path moves into carboniferous limestone country where the cliffs drop precipitously into the sea. Flat grassy tops here make the walking easier on the feet.

Barafundle Bay is probably one of the most beautiful beaches along the entire walk with lush woodland dropping down to its southern edge. It's a great spot for a picnic lunch on a nice day. If it's raining you're better off stopping at the *Boathouse Tearooms* (☎ 01646-672058; daily 10.30am-5.30pm, hot food 12-3.30pm, sandwiches 12-4.30pm) at Stackpole Quay; the Coastal Cruiser bus services (see pp40-1) stop at the car park if you have had enough of walking.

The path continues on through Stackpole Warren Nature Reserve, before leading you to the wonderful beach at **Broad Haven**.

There is limited accommodation and food at Bosherston (see p90; 15 to 20 minutes from Broad Haven if walking on the western side of the ponds), which is on the alternative road detour route (see p94). The Coastal Cruiser bus services stop at Broad Haven (see pp40-1).

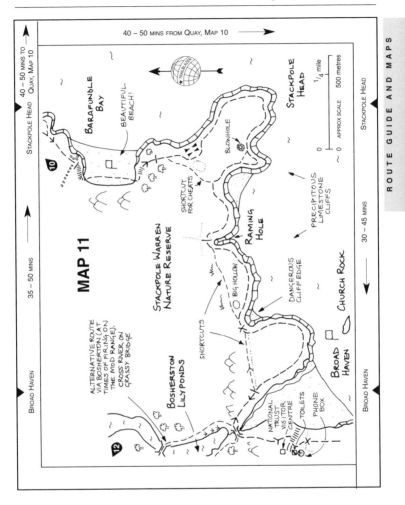

BROAD HAVEN TO CASTLEMARTIN

MAPS 12-15

There is a choice of route here. The route proper continues across the cliff tops through the Castlemartin **MoD firing range**, said to be one of NATO's most important training areas in Europe. Covering 5880 acres it also hides some of the finest limestone cliff scenery in Britain. Unfortunately it is closed to the public when firing is taking place. It is well worth checking the opening times (☎ 01646-662367) since the detour is a monotonous trudge along a boring road.

There are two points where the path may be closed (indicated by a red flag). The first is just above Broad Haven beach and the other is at St Govan's. At both points there are roads which take you to Bosherston and on to the alternative road route described below.

Via Stack Rocks   Maps 12, 13, 14, 15

If the range is open it is **ten miles (16km, 3¹/₄-4hrs)** to Castlemartin, following the jeep track along the flat limestone cliff tops. The cliffs, when you can see them, are spectacular but signs along the track warn you to stick to the path through the firing range. There are many rewards to walking this route as opposed to the road detour, the first of which is at St Govan's.

St Govan's Chapel, sitting just before the sentry box into the MoD range, should not be missed. It's in an extraordinary location hidden down some steep stone steps in a cleft. A tiny stone chapel, cold, dark and empty inside, it is squeezed between sheer rocky cliffs which seem to prevent it from falling into the heaving sea below.

On entering the Castlemartin firing range follow the jeep track across open grassland and scrubland with vertical limestone cliffs to your left all the way to the dead-end road at **Stack Rocks** or Elegug Stacks, two impressive sea stacks sitting a short way offshore. A little further on, past the car park, is the natural arch known as the **Green Bridge of Wales**, a spectacular sight when the waves are crashing around it and the gulls are wheeling above the cliff tops. It's only a three-minute detour from the coast path.

From here you must follow the lane which takes you inland across the firing range to the main B4319 road. There are two options here; turn left for the quicker route along the main road to **Castlemartin** or turn right to follow the country lanes through the villages of **Merrion** and **Warren**. These villages are pretty enough and country lanes are always preferable to main roads but the truth is you really won't miss much if you choose to take the quicker, main road route.

BOSHERSTON   **MAP 12**

If you are taking the road detour either from Broad Haven or St Govan's you will pass through this quaint little village with its photogenic church. Even if you are taking the cliff-top route through the military firing range it is worth making the short detour to the village.

This is partly because it is the only place with any accommodation along this stretch and also because it gives you the opportunity to explore the intricate creeks and woodland of **Bosherston lily ponds**. These peaceful lakes, reed beds and heavily wooded slopes contrast greatly with the crashing waves on the beach. It's a great place to spot wildlife. Otters can sometimes

be seen at dusk if you are quiet and there is plenty of birdlife from coots and moorhens to herons and buzzards.

The No 387/388 Coastal Cruiser **bus** services go via Bosherston on the looping journey between Pembroke Dock and St Govan's Head. See public transport map and table pp39-41 for further details.

The village itself is small and compact with a tiny **shop** and **toilets** on the main street. At the end of the main street is *St Govan's Inn* (☎ 01646-661455, ⌨ tre falen@trefalen.f9.co.uk; food served daily 12-2.30pm and 6.30-9pm; 2T/1D/1F). They do B&B from £35 a night in the smart en suite rooms upstairs (no single supplement). *(cont'd on p94)*

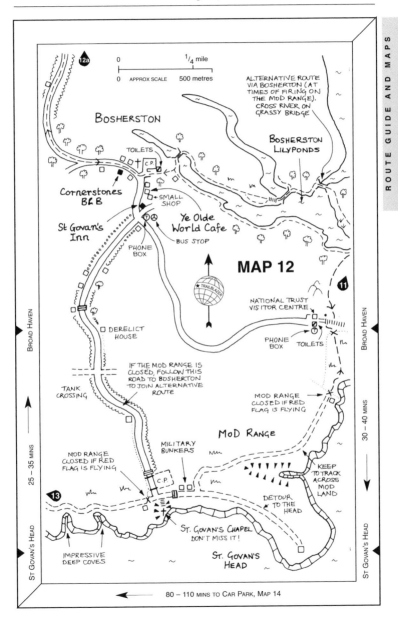

12a

0   1/4 mile

0   APPROX SCALE   500 metres

ALTERNATIVE ROUTE VIA BOSHERTON (AT TIMES OF FIRING ON THE MOD RANGE). CROSS RIVER ON GRASSY BRIDGE

BOSHERSTON

BOSHERSTON LILYPONDS

TOILETS

C.P.

Cornerstones B&B

← SMALL SHOP

Ye Olde World Cafe

St Govan's Inn

BUS STOP

PHONE BOX

MAP 12

★ TRAILBLAZER

NATIONAL TRUST VISITOR CENTRE

DERELICT HOUSE

PHONE BOX   TOILETS

IF THE MOD RANGE IS CLOSED, FOLLOW THIS ROAD TO BOSHERTON TO JOIN ALTERNATIVE ROUTE

BROAD HAVEN

BROAD HAVEN

TANK CROSSING

MOD RANGE CLOSED IF RED FLAG IS FLYING

30 – 40 MINS

25 – 35 MINS

MILITARY BUNKERS

MOD RANGE

MOD RANGE CLOSED IF RED FLAG IS FLYING

C.P.

DETOUR TO THE HEAD

KEEP TO TRACK ACROSS MOD LAND

13

IMPRESSIVE DEEP COVES

ST. GOVAN'S CHAPEL DON'T MISS IT!

ST. GOVAN'S HEAD

ST GOVAN'S HEAD

ST GOVAN'S HEAD

← 80 – 110 MINS TO CAR PARK, MAP 14

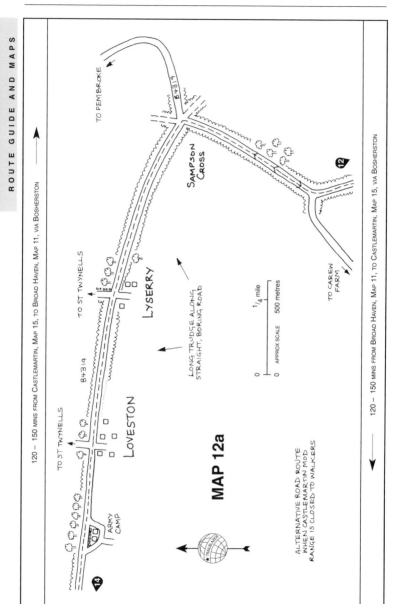

ROUTE GUIDE AND MAPS

120 – 150 MINS FROM CASTLEMARTIN, MAP 15, TO BROAD HAVEN, MAP 11, VIA BOSHERSTON

120 – 150 MINS FROM BROAD HAVEN, MAP 11, TO CASTLEMARTIN, MAP 15, VIA BOSHERSTON

TO PEMBROKE

B4319

SAMPSON CROSS

TO CAREW FARM

TO ST TWYNELLS

LYSERRY

LONG TRUDGE ALONG STRAIGHT, BORING ROAD

¼ mile

500 metres

0 APPROX SCALE

0

B4319

LOVESTON

TO ST TWYNELLS

TO ST TWYNELLS

ARMY CAMP

MAP 12a

ALTERNATIVE ROAD ROUTE WHEN CASTLEMARTIN MOD RANGE IS CLOSED TO WALKERS

TRAILBLAZER

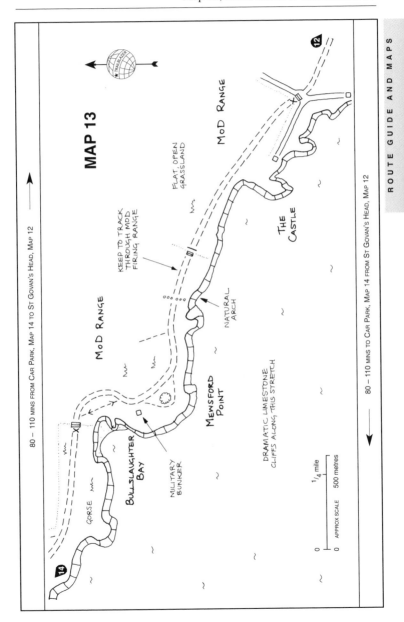

MAP 13

80 – 110 MINS FROM CAR PARK, MAP 14 TO ST GOVAN'S HEAD, MAP 12

80 – 110 MINS TO CAR PARK, MAP 14 FROM ST GOVAN'S HEAD, MAP 12

MoD RANGE

MoD RANGE

KEEP TO TRACK
THROUGH MOD
FIRING RANGE

FLAT, OPEN
GRASSLAND

NATURAL
ARCH

THE
CASTLE

MEWSFORD
POINT

MILITARY
BUNKER

BULLSLAUGHTER
BAY

GORSE

DRAMATIC LIMESTONE
CLIFFS ALONG THIS STRETCH

1/4 mile

APPROX SCALE

0   500 metres

12

14

(cont'd from p90) Opposite the church there is B&B at *Cornerstones* (☎ 01646-661660, 1S/2D/1F) with en suite rooms from £32.50/ pp. Ask for James; if he has no space he can usually direct you to somewhere that does.

There are two places serving food; *St Govan's Inn* (see p90) is a hugely and deservedly popular place with a vast and delicious menu, including curries and lamb shank in rosemary and a red wine jus; while *Bosherton Café* (☎ 01646-661216; daily 9am-7pm) has a wide variety of snacks which you can eat in their big front garden.

Detour route via Bosherston   Maps 12, 12a, 14, 15

If the Castlemartin firing range is closed you must follow the road north via Bosherston. The village of Bosherston and the lily ponds of the same name are the only real highlights if you are going this way. Otherwise these **six and a half miles (10km, 2-2½hrs)** comprise a rather tedious trudge along roads hemmed in by high hedges. If you have the time, it really is worth waiting for the trail through the firing range to reopen.

From Broad Haven, where the main path crosses the stone bridge at the southern tip of the lily ponds, you must follow the path inland up the east bank of the beautiful lake, crossing the three bridges over the arms of the lake and up the steep rocky track to **Bosherston**.

Here the road heads north through farmland to **Sampson Cross** and then along the very straight and boring B4319 road to the turn off for **Merrion** where you rejoin the main coast path.

At Merrion you can continue along the B4319 road which is a bit quicker but slightly more tedious. However, the better route follows the country lanes through Merrion and Warren, where there is a nice church, St Mary's, all the way to Castlemartin.

MERRION & WARREN   MAP 14

Merrion, Warren and Castlemartin (see below) sit along a hilly ridge. Milford Haven estuary is in the distance to the north while to the south is the MoD's vast Castlemartin firing range. All these villages have a laidback friendly feel to them but there is little on offer for the weary walker.

Merrion has a **phone box** and a B&B *The Old Smithy* (01646-661310; 1D/1T or F), a smart and welcoming place charging £28/pp; there is one bathroom for both rooms. Their big back garden is also open to **campers** at £6 per person. The owner will cook an evening meal for about £8.50 if you book in advance.

CASTLEMARTIN (CASTELLMARTIN)
                            MAP 15

Along the road between Warren and Castlemartin the MoD have kindly set aside a 'spectator area' from where you can safely watch the army shooting at things.

On a quieter note there is a tiny **post office** in the village as well as a **phone box**. The only **bus** service coming this way is the Coastal Cruiser (No 387 and No 388); see pp39-41 for full details.

The nearest B&B lies just outside Castlemartin towards Freshwater West, though at least it's a goodie, being one of the more characterful B&Bs on the route. *The Old Rectory* (☎ 01646-661677, 🖳 www .theoldrectoryweb.com; 2D/1T/1F) is a delightful, large old place with many period features; B&B costs £32 per person. The owner, Emma, has ambitions for the place, including the construction of a bunkhouse for trekkers as well as surfers who stay in

ROUTE GUIDE AND MAPS

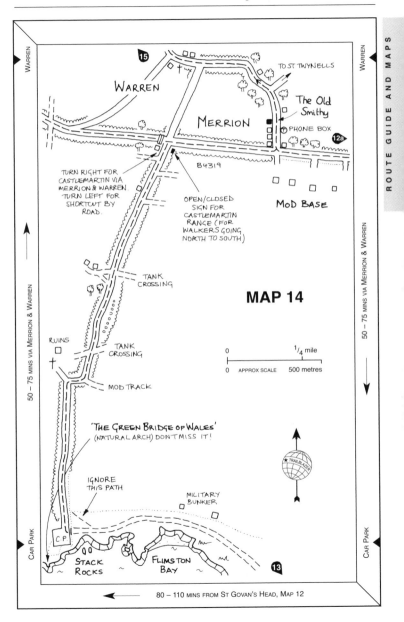

WARREN

WARREN

15

WARREN

MERRION

TO ST TWYNELLS

The Old Smithy

PHONE BOX

12a

B4319

MoD BASE

TURN RIGHT FOR CASTLEMARTIN VIA MERRION & WARREN. TURN LEFT FOR SHORTCUT BY ROAD.

OPEN/CLOSED SIGN FOR CASTLEMARTIN RANGE (FOR WALKERS GOING NORTH TO SOUTH)

TANK CROSSING

MAP 14

RUINS

50 – 75 MINS VIA MERRION & WARREN

50 – 75 MINS VIA MERRION & WARREN

TANK CROSSING

0   1/4 mile

0   APPROX SCALE   500 metres

MOD TRACK

'THE GREEN BRIDGE OF WALES' (NATURAL ARCH) DON'T MISS IT!

TRAILBLAZER

IGNORE THIS PATH

MILITARY BUNKER

CAR PARK

C.P.

STACK ROCKS

FLIMSTON BAY

13

CAR PARK

80 – 110 MINS FROM ST GOVAN'S HEAD, MAP 12

Castlemartin to use the nearby beach of Freshwater West. She can also provide an evening meal (for about £19) of which we have heard good reports; or, if you'd prefer something cheaper, she also offers to run you to the only other place that serves food in the area, the Speculation Inn at Hundleton (see p106), which saves a walk of a good few miles or so each way.

CASTLEMARTIN TO ANGLE

MAPS 15-20

Some beautiful scenery can be found along these **ten and a half miles (17km, 4½-6hrs)** but you must work for it. After the relatively easy walking of the previous section the going once again gets tougher with plenty of ups and downs along the southern side of the Angle peninsula.

Remember to bring plenty of **food and water** as there is nowhere to find any along this stretch until you get to West Angle, only an hour or so from the end.

Things begin easily enough following the lane across farmland and through enormous grassy dunes to the magnificent beach at **Freshwater West**, renowned as being one of Pembrokeshire's finest sweeps of sand. The relentless crashing of the surf makes this a popular haunt for surfers but it is not a safe place for swimming.

At the bridge just past the car park there are two options. You can turn left after the bridge and follow the wonderful beach north or continue along the road which winds its way through high sand dunes. At times the road almost seems to get swallowed up by the shifting sands.

Whichever way you choose the paths meet at the northern end of the beach and climb up above grassy, heathery slopes with wonderful views back across the sands. Although not as high or precipitous as other parts of the coastline this section is beautiful all the same. It is a wild and remote stretch of coast and is probably the least frequented.

You would be foolish to miss it out but you can do exactly that by continuing along the main road north from Freshwater West, taking the first left and next right to bring you onto Angle Bay. Doing this means you have missed out the entire Angle peninsula which may be worth doing if you are behind schedule but is not really recommended.

For those still circumnavigating the Angle peninsula the cliffs become more and more spectacular as you head west, passing the natural arch of **Guttle Hole** and the grassy **Sheep Island**. Look out for the ruins of **East Blockhouse** constructed as a defence building during the reign of Henry VIII.

At **West Angle Bay** *Wavecrest Café* serves large, cheap baguettes (from £2.20); there are **toilets** and a **phone box** and the Coastal Cruiser **buses** stop here (see pp39-41) but there's little else.

Once again there is the option of a shortcut since Angle village is agonizingly close, almost within touching distance along the road leading east. Diehards who want to 'do' the whole path must continue on around the northern half of the peninsula. The consolation is that the walking is less strenuous, pass-

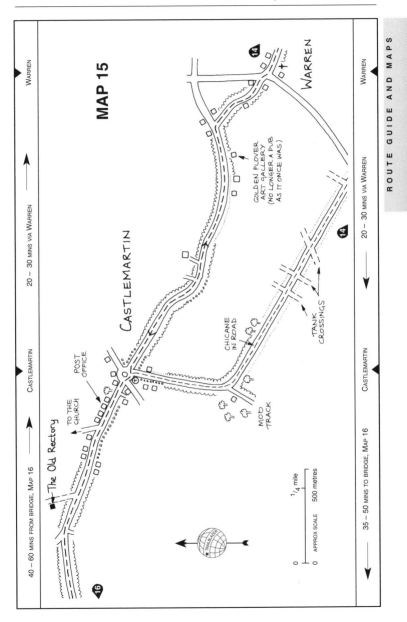

MAP 15

WARREN

CASTLEMARTIN

WARREN

← WARREN

20 – 30 MINS VIA WARREN

CASTLEMARTIN

40 – 60 MINS FROM BRIDGE, MAP 16

The Old Rectory

TO THE CHURCH

POST OFFICE

CHICANE IN ROAD

GOLDEN PLOVER ART GALLERY (NO LONGER A PUB AS IT ONCE WAS)

MOD TRACK

TANK CROSSINGS

20 – 30 MINS VIA WARREN

35 – 50 MINS TO BRIDGE, MAP 16

¼ mile

500 metres

APPROX SCALE

0

0

16

14

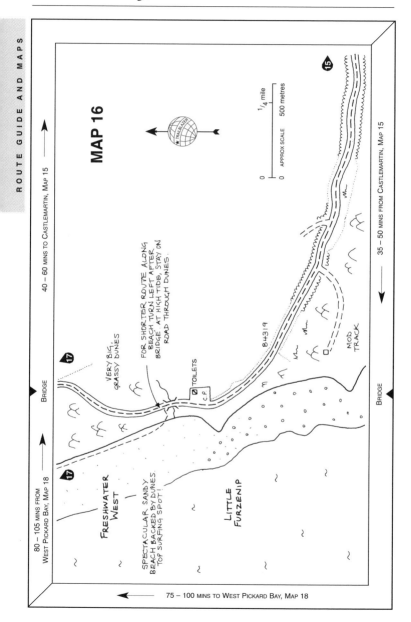

MAP 16

40 – 60 MINS TO CASTLEMARTIN, MAP 15

35 – 50 MINS FROM CASTLEMARTIN, MAP 15

80 – 105 MINS FROM
WEST PICKARD BAY, MAP 18

75 – 100 MINS TO WEST PICKARD BAY, MAP 18

1/4 mile
0
0   APPROX SCALE   500 metres

★ TRAILBLAZER

BRIDGE

BRIDGE

FRESHWATER
WEST

SPECTACULAR SANDY
BEACH BACKED BY DUNES.
TOP SURFING SPOT!

LITTLE
FURZENIP

VERY BIG,
GRASSY DUNES

FOR SHORTER ROUTE ALONG
BEACH TURN LEFT AFTER
BRIDGE AT HIGH TIDE, STAY ON
ROAD THROUGH DUNES.

TOILETS

C.P.

B4319

MOD
TRACK

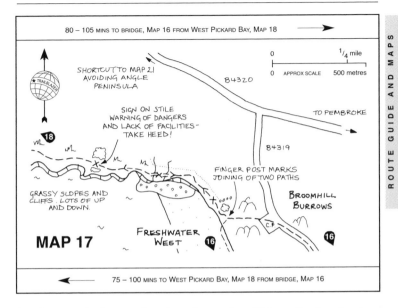

ing above gentle slopes and on through some beautiful woodland on the steep water's edge. To the west, looking very much like Alcatraz, is **Thorne Island** with its 19th-century military defensive building which was once the venue for the World Hopscotch Championships.

There are plans afoot to turn the forbidding fortress into a luxury five-star hotel accessible by cable car from the mainland. It is already being dubbed a hideaway for the rich and famous so expect the room rates to be a little higher than your average B&B. Tired legs will be pleased to reach the village of **Angle**.

ANGLE   MAP 20, p102

Angle is nothing to get too excited about but it is pleasant enough with boats bobbing in the pretty little estuary and some old castle ruins by the stream. Fishing is the main industry and seaweed is also harvested here as it is used as a principal ingredient of the Welsh speciality, laver bread (see box p15).

There is a **post office** and a well-supplied **shop** on the main street opposite the school and some public **toilets** but little else.

For blister sufferers the Coastal Cruiser **buses** stop here; for full information see the public transport map and table, pp39-41.

Campers will find *Castle Farm Campsite* (☎ 01646-641220, Apr-Oct) the perfect spot to pitch at just £2 per person. It's situated in the field to the right just before you cross the bridge into the village.

Regarding accommodation, there are only two options, one of which you'll pass just before you enter the village. The *Old Point House* (☎ 01646-641205; oldpoint houseangle@btopenworld.com; 2T/1D) is an ancient (16th century according to some estimates) place with friendly owners and reasonable rooms. Rustic and eccentric, this place charges £30 per person. The only alternative is the very pleasant and wel-

ROUTE GUIDE AND MAPS

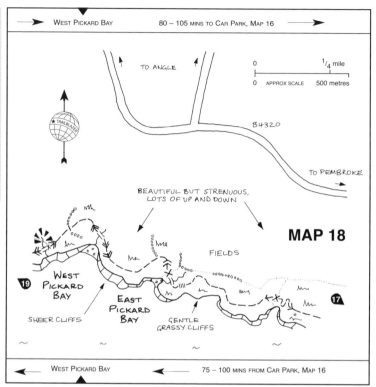

→ WEST PICKARD BAY   80 – 105 MINS TO CAR PARK, MAP 16 →

TO ANGLE

0   1/4 mile

0   APPROX SCALE   500 metres

B4320

TO PEMBROKE

BEAUTIFUL BUT STRENUOUS,
LOTS OF UP AND DOWN

MAP 18

FIELDS

19 WEST
PICKARD
BAY

EAST
PICKARD
BAY

17

SHEER CLIFFS

GENTLE
GRASSY CLIFFS

← WEST PICKARD BAY   ←   75 – 100 MINS FROM CAR PARK, MAP 16

coming **Harding's Hill** (Map 21; ☎ 01646-641232; 2F), a little way out of town though only a short walk up from the coast path. They have only two rooms, each with both a double and single bed in them and charge £30 per person per night (there is no single supplement).

As for food, the **Old Point House** (daily noon-2.30pm, 6.30-9pm; closed Tues in winter) has great grub and probably the best chips in Pembrokeshire. The gulls are pretty fond of them too so be on your guard if you are eating in the garden. The chowder is a delicious starter (£4.75) and, maintaining the fishy theme, the 'trio', a medley of three fish (£12.75), is fresh and fine.

ANGLE TO HUNDLETON   MAPS 20-25

The sad truth is that after such wonderful coastal scenery things really do go downhill from here until Sandy Haven, just under 30 miles (48km) away. Many people choose to catch the bus to Herbrandston, or even as far as Dale, to avoid the oil refineries and urban sprawl that blights the Milford Haven estuary.

(cont'd on p106)

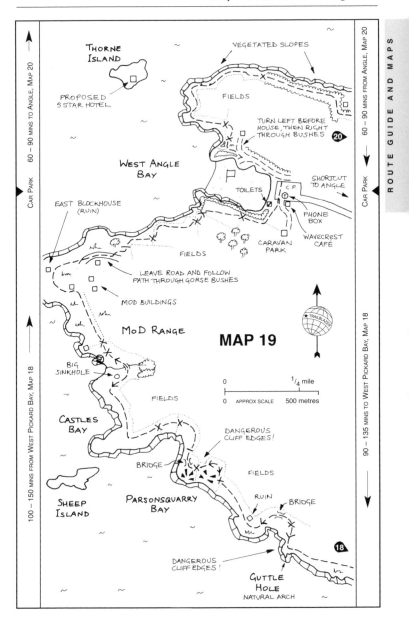

THORNE ISLAND

PROPOSED 5 STAR HOTEL

VEGETATED SLOPES

FIELDS

TURN LEFT BEFORE HOUSE, THEN RIGHT THROUGH BUSHES **20**

WEST ANGLE BAY

SHORTCUT TO ANGLE

TOILETS

C P

PHONE BOX

EAST BLOCKHOUSE (RUIN)

FIELDS

CARAVAN PARK

WAVECREST CAFÉ

LEAVE ROAD AND FOLLOW PATH THROUGH GORSE BUSHES

MOD BUILDINGS

MoD RANGE

MAP 19

★ TRAILBLAZER

0   1/4 mile

0   APPROX SCALE   500 metres

BIG SINKHOLE

FIELDS

CASTLES BAY

BRIDGE

DANGEROUS CLIFF EDGES!

FIELDS

RUIN   BRIDGE

SHEEP ISLAND

PARSONSQUARRY BAY

18

DANGEROUS CLIFF EDGES!

GUTTLE HOLE
NATURAL ARCH

60 – 90 MINS TO ANGLE, MAP 20 ↑

CAR PARK ►

100 – 150 MINS FROM WEST PICKARD BAY, MAP 18 ↑

60 – 90 MINS FROM ANGLE, MAP 20 ↓

◄ CAR PARK

90 – 135 MINS TO WEST PICKARD BAY, MAP 18 ↓

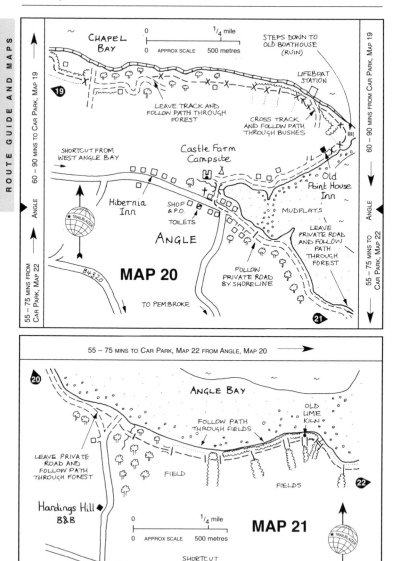

MAP 20

CHAPEL BAY

0 — 1/4 mile
0 — 500 metres
APPROX SCALE

STEPS DOWN TO OLD BOATHOUSE (RUIN)

LIFEBOAT STATION

LEAVE TRACK AND FOLLOW PATH THROUGH FOREST

CROSS TRACK AND FOLLOW PATH THROUGH BUSHES

19

60 – 90 MINS TO CAR PARK, MAP 19

60 – 90 MINS FROM CAR PARK, MAP 19

ANGLE

ANGLE

55 – 75 MINS FROM CAR PARK, MAP 22

55 – 75 MINS TO CAR PARK, MAP 22

SHORTCUT FROM WEST ANGLE BAY

Castle Farm Campsite

Old Point House Inn

Hibernia Inn

SHOP & P.O.

TOILETS

ANGLE

MUDFLATS

LEAVE PRIVATE ROAD AND FOLLOW PATH THROUGH FOREST

FOLLOW PRIVATE ROAD BY SHORELINE

B4320

TO PEMBROKE

TRAILBLAZER

21

MAP 21

55 – 75 MINS TO CAR PARK, MAP 22 FROM ANGLE, MAP 20 →

20

ANGLE BAY

OLD LIME KILN

FOLLOW PATH THROUGH FIELDS

LEAVE PRIVATE ROAD AND FOLLOW PATH THROUGH FOREST

FIELD

FIELDS

22

Hardings Hill B&B

0 — 1/4 mile
0 — 500 metres
APPROX SCALE

TRAILBLAZER

SHORTCUT FROM MAP 17

← 55 – 75 MINS TO ANGLE, MAP 20 FROM CAR PARK, MAP 22

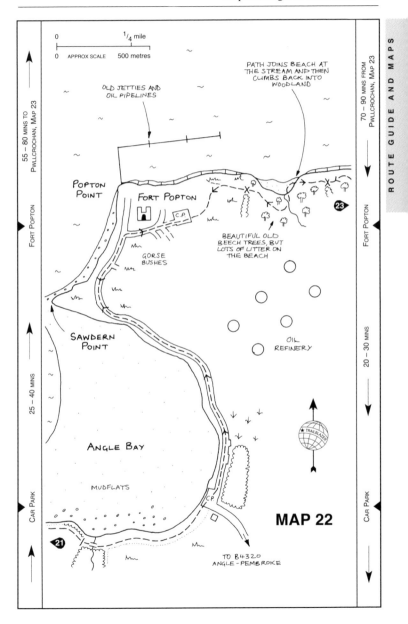

0   ¼ mile

0   APPROX SCALE   500 metres

55 – 80 MINS TO PWLLCROCHAN, MAP 23

70 – 90 MINS FROM PWLLCROCHAN, MAP 23

FORT POPTON

FORT POPTON

OLD JETTIES AND OIL PIPELINES

PATH JOINS BEACH AT THE STREAM AND THEN CLIMBS BACK INTO WOODLAND

POPTON POINT

FORT POPTON

C.P.

23

BEAUTIFUL OLD BEECH TREES, BUT LOTS OF LITTER ON THE BEACH

GORSE BUSHES

SAWDERN POINT

OIL REFINERY

20 – 30 MINS

25 – 40 MINS

TRAILBLAZER

ANGLE BAY

MUDFLATS

C.P.

MAP 22

CAR PARK

CAR PARK

21

TO B4320 ANGLE–PEMBROKE

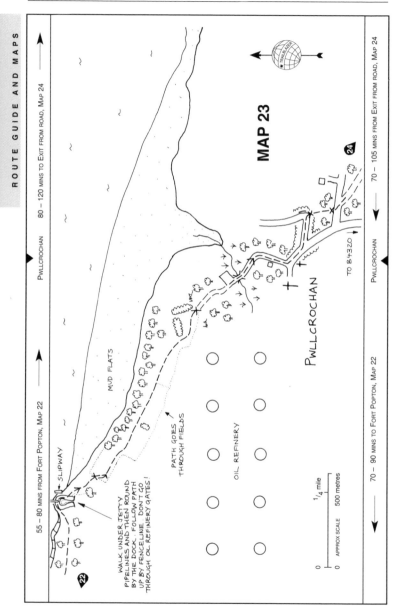

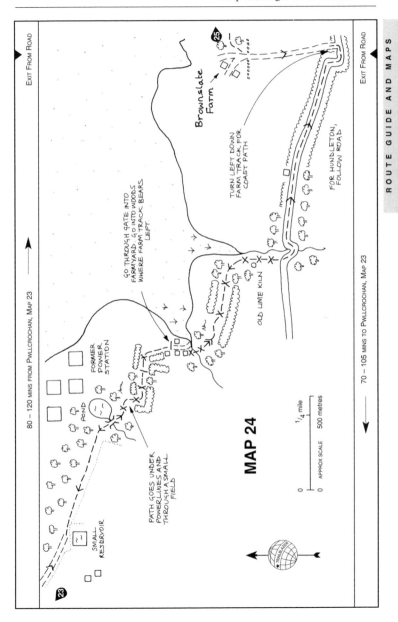

EXIT FROM ROAD

EXIT FROM ROAD

80 – 120 MINS FROM PWLLCROCHAN, MAP 23

70 – 105 MINS TO PWLLCROCHAN, MAP 23

Brownslate Farm

25

TURN LEFT DOWN FARM TRACK FOR COAST PATH

FOR HUNDLETON, FOLLOW ROAD

GO THROUGH GATE INTO FARMYARD. GO INTO WOODS WHERE FARM TRACK BEARS LEFT

OLD LIME KILN

FORMER POWER STATION

POND

PATH GOES UNDER POWERLINES AND THROUGH A SMALL FIELD

SMALL RESERVOIR

23

MAP 24

1/4 mile

500 metres

0

0

APPROX SCALE

TRAILBLAZER

(cont'd from p100) No doubt it was once a beautiful harbour, described by Nelson as one of the world's finest but sadly it has been very spoilt. If you can happily skip this bit and still hold your head up high when you get home the Coastal Cruiser runs between Angle, Hundleton and Pembroke Dock. However, services are infrequent; see the public transport map and table, pp39-41).

These **nine miles (14km, 3-4¹/₂hrs)** begin pleasantly following the shoreline of **Angle Bay** through some nice woodland and fields. However, on the way to Fort Popton on the other side of the bay the first of two oil refineries looms above you belching out acrid fumes.

To be fair the path does its best to avoid any possible eye contact with this blot on the landscape passing through some beautiful old oak and beech woodland wherever it can, but at times it is impossible not to notice it. The stench of crude oil is certainly hard to miss. The path crosses farmland and then joins a small lane before passing the churches at **Pwllcrochan**.

Having left the delights of the oil refinery you now have the old power station site to walk around. Again the path does well to hide in the woodland but even so the scenery is nothing compared to what has gone before or is to come further ahead.

Leaving the power station site, the path continues across farmland passing the two creeks (locally known as 'pills') at Goldborough mudflats and joins the Goldborough Rd, a country lane that climbs steeply up to the village of **Hundleton**.

The coast path actually heads down the farm track to Brownslate Farm a few hundred metres short of the village.

HUNDLETON   MAP 25

Hundleton has little to offer and it is probably better to carry on to Pembroke which isn't far away.

The post office has disappeared but the **phone box** and **bus stop** (for the Coastal Cruiser services; see pp39-41) can be found in the centre next to the green.

The only place to stay in the centre of the village is *Highgate Inn Hotel* (☎ 01646-685904, 🖳 lewissandie@aol.com, 2D/4T). The beds are a rather pricey £32.50 per person.

Heading east along the B4320 road to Pembroke is the charming, ivy-clad *Bowett Farmhouse* (☎ 01646-683473, 🖳 www .bowettfarmhouse.co.uk; 1S/1D/1T or D),

set on a 250-acre dairy farm, with B&B accommodation from £32.50/pp. It is easiest to reach it from Quoits Mill which is further along the coast path from Hundleton.

You can eat at *Highgate Inn Hotel*; meals are served all day in summer from noon onwards, and from 12 to 2.30pm and from 6.30 to 9.30pm in winter, the three-course Sunday lunch is £9.95.

Alternatively, one mile away, there's the *Speculation Inn* (☎ 01646-661306); the menu here is limited but unusual (with rabbit pie and pigeon pie both featuring; £6.95 for either) and the portions are generous. Food is served daily noon-3pm and 6-8pm.

HUNDLETON TO HAZELBEACH   MAPS 25-29

If you survived the last section you may as well keep going. It's **ten and a half miles (17km, 3¹/₂-4¹/₂hrs)** to Hazelbeach on the other side of the Milford Haven

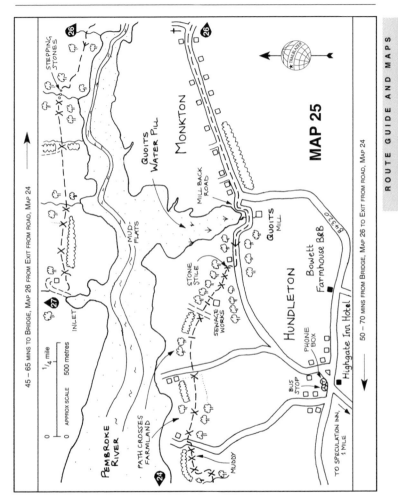

estuary. This may not be the most stimulating stretch of the coast path but there are some pleasant bits.

From Brownslate Farm the path continues across fields to **Quoits Mill** before passing through the housing estate of Monkton. The road then drops down into Pembroke with the impressive and well-preserved **Pembroke Castle** the first thing you see.

ROUTE GUIDE AND MAPS

PEMBROKE – MAP KEY

Where to stay
3 Lion Hotel
5 Old King's Arms Hotel
6 Middlegate Hotel
14 Beech House
15 Woodbine B&B
16 Coach House Hotel
19 Old Cross Saws Inn
20 Penfro B&B
22 High Noon Guest House

Where to eat
1 Haven Christian Coffee Shop
2 Eleven

4 Pembroke Carvery and Chinese
   Takeaway
5 Old King's Arms Hotel
7 Rowlies
8 Double Dragon Chinese
9 Jay's Sandwich Shop
10 Monsoon Tandoori Takeaway
11 Kebabs & pizzas
12 Middlegate
13 Brown's Snack Bar
17 Top of the Town
18 Royal Oak
19 Old Cross Saws Inn
21 Hope Inn

PEMBROKE (PENFRO)   MAP 26

Pembroke, birthplace of Henry VII (1457-1509), is steeped in history and comes as a pleasant surprise. Stretched out along one long street on top of a ridge by the river, there are plenty of pubs and places to stay.

The 900-year-old Norman **castle** (see box below) is the focal point of the town, standing guard over the river and well worth a visit. Down on Commons Rd you can see the remains of **Gun Tower** and **Gazebo Tower**; mediaeval defensive towers which formed part of the old town wall.

Next to them is a 200-year-old **lime kiln**, one of many scattered along the Pembrokeshire coast. (The lime was scattered on the fields to 'sweeten' the acidic soil round here, with some going into the local buildings as mortar.)

Services

Pembroke Visitor Centre (☎ 01646-622388, 🖳 pembroke.tic@pembrokeshire.gov.uk; daily Easter to June, Sep & Oct 10am-5pm, July & Aug to 5.30pm) is on Commons Rd.

There are a number of **banks** as well as a **post office**, plenty of **shops** including **Mendus Pharmacy** and a **Somerfield supermarket**.

There are also a couple of places offering **internet access**: Dragon's Alley (☎ 01646-621456; Tue, Thur-Sat 10am-6pm, Wed 10am-9pm), next to HSBC and Henry's Gift Shop, both of which charge £1 for 15 minutes. These, and indeed almost everything else of interest to the trekker, can be found on Main St.

❏ Pembroke Castle

The mighty Pembroke Castle (☎ 01646-681510; 🖳 www.pembroke-castle.co.uk, open 9.30am-6pm Apr-Sep, 10am-5pm Mar & Oct, 10am-4pm Nov-Feb; admission £3.50), birthplace of Henry VII, is a picture-book, turreted castle overlooking the town and the river estuary. It is one of many Norman castles in Pembrokeshire built in the 11th century to keep the Welsh at bay and can proudly claim to be the only one that never fell to the Welsh.

It has been the scene of many a bloody battle; most famously in 1648 during the civil war. The local mayor John Poyer caused consternation in parliament when he switched his allegiances, deciding to support the king. A rather annoyed Oliver Cromwell marched over, blew up the town walls and took Poyer prisoner.

During the summer there are a number of organized events within the castle walls, including falconry and archery displays, battle re-enactments and Shakespeare plays.

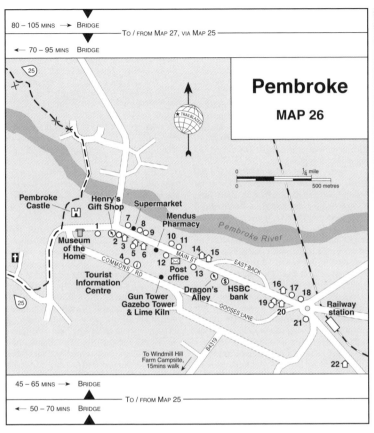

Pembroke

MAP 26

80 – 105 MINS → BRIDGE

To / FROM MAP 27, VIA MAP 25

← 70 – 95 MINS BRIDGE

★ TRAILBLAZER

0   ¼ mile

0   500 metres

Pembroke Castle

Henry's Gift Shop

Supermarket

Mendus Pharmacy

Pembroke River

Museum of the Home

Tourist Information Centre

Gun Tower
Gazebo Tower
& Lime Kiln

MAIN ST

COMMONS RD

Post office

Dragon's Alley

HSBC bank

GOOSES LANE

EAST BACK

Railway station

To Windmill Hill Farm Campsite, 15mins walk

B4319

45 – 65 MINS → BRIDGE

To / FROM MAP 25

← 50 – 70 MINS BRIDGE

Transport

Bus Nos 356, 358, 387 & 388 depart from in front of Somerfield supermarket and outside the castle on Main St. The **train station** is at the far end of the town past the roundabout on Station Rd.

There are regular services to Pembroke Dock or back to Tenby, Kilgetty and Swansea for connections elsewhere. See the public transport map and table, pp39-41, for further details.

Where to stay

There are plenty of places to spend the night. Campers will have to head up the steep B4319 road for about half a mile where you will find *Windmill Hill Farm Campsite* (☎ 01646-682392, open all year) with prices starting from £3.50 per person.

Near the station is the very comfortable and friendly *High Noon Guest House* (☎ 01646-683736, 🖳 www.highnoon.co.uk, Lower Lamphey Rd, 3S/1T/3D/2F), which has been operating since 1958! Beds start from £24.50 per person.

There are several places on Main St including the amazingly good-value *Beech House* (☎ 01646-683740, 78 Main St, 1S/1T/1D/1F), a fine B&B boasting comfy rooms, a pool room and a great breakfast... and all for the hostel-type price of £17.50 per person – or a tenner for kids! Next door is the more expensive but still reasonable-value *Woodbine B&B* (☎ 01646-686338; 3D), where rooms with either en suite or private bathroom cost £30 per person, or £35 for single occupancy.

At the eastern end of Main St is the *Old Cross Saws Inn* (☎ 01646-682475; victor rees@btconnect.com; 6T) with B&B from £28/pp, while very nearby is *Penfro B&B* (☎ 01646-682753, 🖳 www.penfro.co.uk; 3D), a Grade 2 listed Georgian mansion dating back to 1760 with big high-ceiling rooms and a large back garden. The rooms are highly individual. Rates depend on which room you stay in but start at £30 per person and rise to £40 for the largest.

A little further on, opposite the now defunct petrol station, is the smart but expensive *Coach House Hotel* (☎ 01646-684602, 🖳 www.coachhouse-hotel.co.uk) with 15 en suite rooms. Prices start from £37.50/pp. The *Old King's Arms Hotel* (☎ 01646-683611, 🖳 www.oldkingsarmshotel.co.uk; Main St, 13S/4D/1T) is Pembroke's oldest hotel, dating back to the 15th century. It's a quite luxurious place with satellite TV in every room, each of which is en suite. Expect to pay £40 single, or £35 per person in a double or twin.

Close to are two more upmarket hotels: *Middlegate Hotel* (☎ 01646-622442, 🖳 www.themiddlegate.co.uk, 41-43 Main St; 3S/3D/3T) charges £29 per person, and the *Lion Hotel* (☎ 01646-684501, 5S/2T/4F) with en suite rooms costs from £28 for a single, £27.50 per person for two sharing.

Where to eat

There is a wide variety of choice for food in Pembroke: *Eleven* (☎ 01646-681400; Mon-Thu 9am-6pm, Fri-Sat 9am-9pm, Sun 9am-

5pm) is a cheerful place serving a variety of meals including a tasty sweet chilli chicken stir fry. They also have a late bar at weekends. Almost opposite, *Rowlies* (☎ 01646-686172, Mon-Sat 9am-9pm) claims to serve the best all-day breakfast (£3.50) in town.

Not surprisingly, many of the pubs and hotels do food. The *Old King's Arms Hotel* (☎ 01646-683611; see column opposite; lunch noon-2.30pm, evenings Mon-Sat 7-10pm, Sun 7-8.30pm) has a good restaurant in a rustic, dimly lit room with a variety of dishes including duckling at £14.75 and steaks at £17.45. At the other end of Main St is the Coach House Hotel (see column opposite) with an expensive à la carte menu in their award-winning *Griffins Bistro* (daily 7.30-9am, 12-2pm, 7-9.30pm).

Also along Main St you'll find *Brown's Snack Bar* (☎ 01646-682419; Mon-Sat 9am-5pm, open Sun in August only 9am-5pm), a Pembroke institution that's been serving locals since 1928; the décor is more 1970s but the food is fine and the service friendly. Most remarkable of all, however, are the staff: Constance 'Connie' Brown opened the shop with her husband and, at the time of writing, was still working in the kitchen! She was awarded the MBE in 2006 and celebrated her 100th birthday in August 2007. *Jay's Sandwich Shop* (☎ 01646-683838; Mon-Fri 7am-3.30pm, Sat 8am-3.30pm) is a good spot to get a packed lunch for the day and has several vegetarian options. Meanwhile there are a number of cafés and coffee shops, the best perhaps being the simple *Haven Christian Coffee Shop* (☎ 01646-685469; Mon-Fri 10am-3pm) opposite the castle – a no-frills place but one with a great outdoor seating area out back. Also on Main St, the *Middlegate* (☎ 01646-622442; daily 9.15am-2.45pm, to 6pm in summer) is OK for lunch, with eggs, chips and beans costing just £2.60. At the road's eastern end, the *Old Cross Saws Inn* (☎ 01646-682475; noon-2pm, 5.30-7.30pm) does standard pub food and also shows the football.

There are also a number of fast-food outlets along Main St including *Double

Dragon Chinese (☎ 01646-622425; Sun-Thur 12-2pm, daily 5-11pm) near Somerfield, a **kebab-cum-pizza house** and the **Monsoon Tandoori Takeaway** (☎ 01646-687766; daily 5-11pm) next door, and *Top of the Town* (☎ 01646-622332, Mon-Sat 10am-10pm), a well-regarded chippy, at the street's eastern end. There's also the **Pembroke Carvery and Chinese Takeaway** (☎ 01646-686224; daily 12-2pm, 5.30-9.30pm), a large restaurant on Commons Rd, with typical Chinese fare and English food to eat in or take away.

Good places for a pint include the *Royal Oak* (☎ 01646-682537; bar open daily 11am-11pm) and the *Hope Inn* (☎ 01646-621102; bar open daily 11am-11pm) both of which are at the far eastern end of Main St by the roundabout.

THE DAUGLEDDAU AND THE LANDSKER BORDERLANDS

The one part of the national park that is completely by-passed by the coast path, thanks to the Cleddau Bridge, is the Daugleddau estuary. This is a shame because it is also one of the most beautiful and quietest parts. In stark contrast to the rest of the coastline there are no dramatic cliffs or crashing waves. Instead the intricate creeks and waterways are sheltered by heavily wooded banks, offering peaceful walks far from the rest of the crowds who flock to the coast.

This part of Pembrokeshire is known as the Landsker Borderlands. The invisible Landsker Line separates the Welsh-speaking north of Pembrokeshire from the southern half where the Norman influence is predominant. Along this invisible line are a number of Norman castles and fortresses, one of which can be seen at Carew on the banks of the estuary east of Pembroke. To this day southern Pembrokeshire has a distinctly English feel to it earning itself the unofficial title of 'Little England Beyond Wales'.

Walks

Unfortunately, circumnavigating the entire estuary is a little complicated since the western side is distinctly lacking in rights of way. Most of it would have to be walked on roads, many of which are not even that close to the estuary. It is best to explore the eastern side by following part of the Landsker Borderlands Trail and starting your walk from Cresswell Quay.

Important! It is paramount that you check the tide tables for the following walks since the path at Garron Pill and the stepping stones at Cresswell Quay are submerged at high tide. Aim to reach Garron Pill as the tide is falling so that you have time to reach the crossing at Cresswell Quay before it comes back in.

A long walk via Landshipping
If your feet are not too tired from the coast path you could try the long circular walk from Cresswell Quay, up the lane to Martletwy and on to Landshipping Quay. From here the Landsker Borderlands Trail can be followed back along the shoreline passing the pretty village of Lawrenny on the way. This walk is 13¹/₂ miles (22km) and takes about 6 hours.

A short walk via Garron Pill and Lawrenny (see map p113)
A shorter **six-and-a-half-mile (10km, 2³/₄-3¹/₄hrs)** walk is described here for coast-path walkers who are looking for an easy day. (Note the times below are cumulative.)

ROUTE GUIDE AND MAPS

From **Cresswell Quay** head north up the left-hand lane. After crossing Cresswell Bridge take the first left up a steep hill through woodland. Follow this lane bordered by hedges. Ignore the left turn and go straight over at the crossroads where there is a letterbox. The lane drops down through woodland to reach another set of crossroads. Turn left here to reach **Garron Pill** estuary (1-1¹/₄hrs).

At the car park by the estuary walk directly onto the mudflats and after five minutes look out for the less than obvious path cutting up into the shore-side forest and over a stile. Follow the path through woodland, past a shed and south along the wooded shoreline of the main Daugleddau estuary; the heather and oak trees here have been stunted by the prevailing wind. Across the water is the white tower of **Benton Castle** poking through the trees.

The path then crosses a stile and comes out on a track which you follow through the boatyard and onto the road at **Lawrenny Quay** (1¹/₄-1³/₄hrs). Between 1780 and 1860 Lawrenny Quay was an important shipbuilding site. Follow the lane past the Lawrenny Arms Hotel. After ten minutes the path leaves the road on the right-hand side just before reaching the village of **Lawrenny**. It's worth popping up to the village to see the pretty Norman church. On the other side of the estuary, by the way, is the privately owned Benton Castle.

Back on the path, hop over the stone wall and cross the wooden boardwalk through the reed bed. The path follows the edge of the field, passes a marshy inlet and then continues through more fields, crossing a number of stiles before reaching a farm track next to woodland. Go up the farm track and turn right following the hedgerow before crossing a stile into the woods. Another stile takes you back into another field.

Follow the edge of the woodland and then bear left following another hedgerow. Cross through a small field to reach a farm track. Leave the track at the sharp left-hand bend and follow the steps down through some beautiful woodland to reach the stepping stones across the Cresswell River and back to **Cresswell Quay** (2³/₄-3¹/₄hrs).

By now you deserve some liquid refreshment in the wonderfully traditional *Cresselly Arms* (☎ 01646-651210; bar open daily 12-3pm, 5-11pm) where you can also get a roast lunch on Sunday but otherwise they do not serve food.

● **Transport** Cresswell Quay is on Silcox Coaches' Route No 361 (Pembroke Dock to Tenby); see pp39-41 for further information. Cresswell Quay is about six miles (10km) from Pembroke so you could get a taxi if you have a bit of spare cash. To return to the coast path catch the bus to Pembroke Dock or back to Tenby, Kilgetty or Saundersfoot.

● **Accommodation** Rather than catching a bus back to the coast path the same day you could spend the night locally. In Cresswell Quay *Cresswell House* (☎ 01646-651435, ▣ www.cresswellhouse.co.uk, 2D/1T en suite) has rooms from £35 per person.

In Lawrenny there are en suite rooms from £30 at *Knowles Farm* (☎ 01834-891221, ▣ www.lawrenny.org.uk, 3D).

From Pembroke the path passes through woodland and farmland before dropping steeply down Treowen Rd and Pembroke St to **Pembroke Dock**.

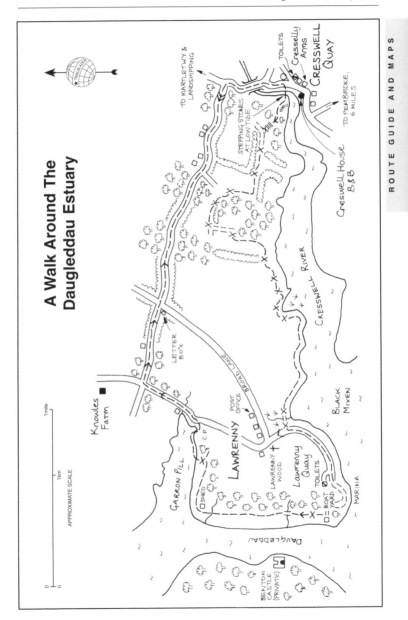

A Walk Around The Daugleddau Estuary

1mile

1km

APPROXIMATE SCALE

Knowles Farm

GARRON PILL

Daugleddau

BENTON CASTLE (PRIVATE)

SHED

C.P.

LAWRENNY

LAWRENNY WOOD

POST OFFICE

BROAD LANE

LETTER BOX

LAWRENNY QUAY

TOILETS

BOAT YARD

MARINA

BLACK MIXEN

CRESSWELL RIVER

STEPPING STONES AT LOW TIDE

TO MARTLETWY & LANDSHIPPING

TOILETS

Cresselly Arms

CRESSWELL QUAY

TO PEMBROKE, 6 MILES

Creswell House B&B

PEMBROKE DOCK (DOC PENFRO)
MAP 27

Pembroke Dock won't win any beauty contests but study it a little closer and you will find it is a place with a short but interesting history.

The town sprung up quite suddenly in the early 1800s when the Royal Navy came to the tiny hamlet of Paterchurch, built a dockyard and then started constructing ships. In 1814 the first terraced row (**Front St**) was built to house the workers. The coast path runs along the road. A number of defensive fortifications sprang up to protect the town.

One of the two **Martello Towers** can be seen off Front St. These days the oil industry provides most of the employment and the Irish ferry terminal keeps a steady flow of visitors going through the town.

Services

There is a **tourist information centre** (☎ 01646-622753, 🖳 pembrokedock.tic@pembrokeshire.gov.uk, Easter-Oct daily 10.30am-2.30pm) in the ferry terminal.

As you would expect there are also a number of **shops** in town, though the place is not quite the shoppers' paradise you might have been hoping for. There are three **banks** with cashpoints and a **post office** (☎ 01646-621202; Mon-Fri 9am-5.30pm, Sat 9am-12.30pm) near each other on Dimond St; all the shops and best places to eat are here as well.

Pembroke Dock is not short of big **superstores**: Asda is across the road after leaving Front St, Kwiksave and Lidl lie just to the north while Tesco can be found off London Rd.

Near Tesco is Pembrokeshire Outdoors, a convenient place to pick up **camping/backpacking equipment**. On Water St, near Asda, there is a **health centre**.

Transport

There are three **bus stops**, one outside Tesco, one on Laws St and the other on Albion Sq, which is not square at all but decidedly road-shaped. Most services (Nos 333, 349, 356, 361, 387 & 388) stop on Laws St; check in advance for the other stops. For the **train station** walk to the far eastern end of Dimond St. This is the terminus of the line from Swansea; services arrive/depart every couple of hours, less frequently on Sunday. See the public transport map and table, pp39-41, for full details.

Adventurous types might want to take a day trip to Rosslare in Ireland. Passenger-only fares are around £20 each way. Contact **Irish Ferries** (see p41) for details and bookings.

Where to stay

The first place you come to is ***Roxana Guest House*** (☎ 01646-683116; 2S/1T/3F) on Victoria Rd just off Treowen Rd; rates start from £30 per person.

At the bottom of the hill on Pembroke St is the ***Dolphin Hotel*** (☎ 01646-685581; 9T). It's not in the nicest part of town but the rooms are en suite (£20 per person, £5 single supplement) and they boast the best breakfasts in town.

On London Rd, following the coast path on the way out of Pembroke Dock, there are a number of places to stay. The ***Welshman's Arms*** (☎ 01646-685643; 23 London Rd; 2S/6T or D) charges from £20 per person but they do not provide breakfast.

Sleepover Rooms (2S/2D/2T) is under new management and at the time of writing was undergoing some changes (including the installation of a phone!). Nevertheless, it should still provide some of the cheapest accommodation in town, with B&B per person at around £15-20 in non en suite rooms.

At the other end of the scale, the most luxurious option is ***Cleddau Bridge Hotel*** (☎ 01646-685961, 🖳 www.cleddauhotel.co.uk; 40 rooms all en suite), on Essex Rd (see map 28, p117), with single rooms for £66 or double/twin rooms for £42.50/pp for two sharing; discounts are available for stays of longer than two nights. Take the left turn at the roundabout just before the toll booth on the bridge and be sure to wipe your feet on entering.

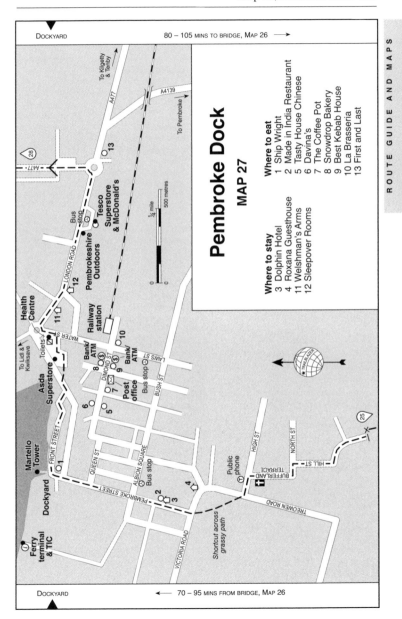

Pembroke Dock

MAP 27

Where to stay
3 Dolphin Hotel
4 Roxana Guesthouse
11 Welshman's Arms
12 Sleepover Rooms

Where to eat
1 Ship Wright
2 Made in India Restaurant
5 Tasty House Chinese
6 Davina's
7 The Coffee Pot
8 Snowdrop Bakery
9 Best Kebab House
10 La Brasseria
13 First and Last

DOCKYARD   80 – 105 MINS TO BRIDGE, MAP 26 →

← 70 – 95 MINS FROM BRIDGE, MAP 26   DOCKYARD

Where to eat

For a curry head for the *Made In India Restaurant* (☎ 01646-681821, Mon-Fri 5.30pm-midnight, Sat to 1am, Sun to 10pm; 9 Pembroke St) and for Chinese/Cantonese try *Tasty House* (☎ 01646-686132, Tue-Sun 5-11pm, 28 Queen St).

Best Kebab House (☎ 01646-686149; Mon-Sat to midnight, Sun to 11pm), on Dimond St, is good for late-night hunger; there's a branch of *McDonald's* near Tesco.

On Dimond St there is a good café, *The Coffee Pot* (☎ 01646-622314; Mon-Fri 9am-5pm, Sat 10am-5pm) with great toasties, and a reasonable bakery, *Snowdrop* (☎ 01646-683373, Mon-Sat 8am-4.30pm).

Along the same road you will find *Davina's* (☎ 01646-682974; Mon-Wed 10am-3pm, Thur-Sat 10am-4pm, Sun noon-3pm) with some reasonably priced and quite unusual dishes including Pembrokeshire trout served with almonds and cream (£8.95).

Rivalling Davina's for exotic fare is *La Brasseria* (☎ 01646-687643, daily 9am-5pm) which, in addition to standard all-day breakfasts (£4.50) and baguettes (£3.95), offers such treats as chicken Gitano (chicken cooked in brandy and served with figs, apricots and cream; £8.95).

On the corner of Front St, right on the official coast path, the *Ship Wright* (☎ 01646-682090, food served daily 12-1.45pm, 6.30-8.30pm) was crowned Pembrokeshire Pub of the Year for 2006 by the *Western Telegraph* for their fine atmosphere and good food. They are also favourites to keep the crown in 2007. Front St used to be home to a number of old taverns that served as drinking dens for the dockyard workers back in the early 1800s. The Ship Wright is the only survivor.

Heading out of town, the *First and Last* (☎ 01646-682687) pub is next to the roundabout where the road heads north to the Cleddau Bridge. It is the first and last pub, hence the name, on this side of Milford Haven harbour. It's open all day for toasties, serves lunch daily from noon to 2.30pm but no food in the evening, and has some great real ales.

After negotiating the streets of Pembroke Dock you must cross the **Cleddau Toll Bridge**. Don't worry; environmentally friendly walkers go for free! It also takes them much longer to cross than it does the motorists so they can really savour the experience.

Immediately you reach the end of the bridge, the path doubles back on your left to take you along the top of the wooded slope. The path eventually brings you to to the top of the quiet town of Neyland, from where it's a straightforward march along the shoreline road through the village of Llanstadwell to Hazelbeach.

NEYLAND   MAP 28

Having crossed the Cleddau toll bridge and left the delights of Pembroke Dock behind you, Neyland is nothing to get excited about, being only marginally less ugly than Pembroke Dock and certainly less interesting.

The modern marina is the only attractive part of the town – and the path avoids that! From the big car park at the end of the marina village you can follow the main street up the hill for five minutes to reach the **post office** and a **small supermarket**.

If you are looking for a bed you are probably better off back in Pembroke Dock as there is little choice here.

First's No 349 **bus** service and Silcox's No 356 stop here; see pp39-41 for further information.

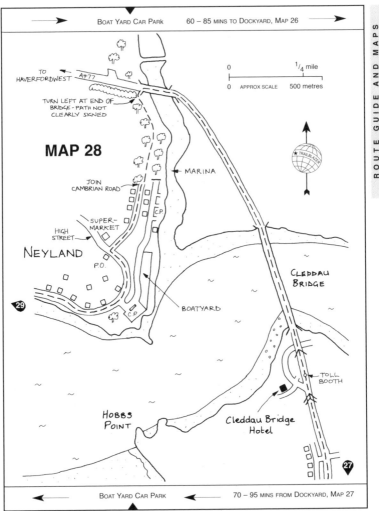

BOAT YARD CAR PARK   60 – 85 MINS TO DOCKYARD, MAP 26

TO HAVERFORDWEST   A477

TURN LEFT AT END OF
BRIDGE - PATH NOT
CLEARLY SIGNED

MAP 28

JOIN
CAMBRIAN ROAD

MARINA

C.P.

SUPER-
MARKET

HIGH
STREET

NEYLAND

P.O.

29

0   ¼ mile
0   APPROX SCALE   500 metres

★ TRAILBLAZER

CLEDDAU
BRIDGE

BOATYARD

C.P.

TOLL
BOOTH

HOBBS
POINT

Cleddau Bridge
Hotel

27

BOAT YARD CAR PARK   70 – 95 MINS FROM DOCKYARD, MAP 27

ROUTE GUIDE AND MAPS

HAZELBEACH   MAP 29

The only bus service passing through here is Silcox's No 356; see pp39-41 for further information. *Ferry House Inn* (☎ 01646-600270, 🖳 www.smoothhound.co.uk/ho tels/ferryinn.html, 1S/1D/2T/2F) has B&B at £39 (single) and £29.50 per person for two

sharing. It is also the best place to get food (daily 12-2pm & Mon-Sat 6-9pm), served in a nice conservatory with harbour views, albeit including the refinery and power station. Despite this, Hazelbeach is a lot prettier than Neyland.

HAZELBEACH TO SANDY HAVEN   MAPS 29-34

After nigh on 20 miles (30km) negotiating oil refineries, power stations and conurbations, the bad news is that there is more of the same for the next **eight and a half miles (14km, 2³/₄-4hrs)** to Sandy Haven. The good news is that the good stuff begins again from Sandy Haven.

The coast path heads up a small lane beside the Ferry House Inn, passing through fields and woodland. You may be surprised to realize that there is a second vast oil refinery to the right. To be fair to the refinery and/or the path designers, they do seem to be doing their best, too, to shield you from the worst of the industrial eyesores, though occasionally it fails, such as when you come to an ugly red bridge over the oil pipelines. There's also the earthworks caused by the excavations necessary for the laying of the LNG pipes (see box p123) that have to be negotiated.

As the excavations progress, expect the path to be altered too; as such, the path may vary its route from the one on map 30, p120. Eventually, however, you should come to the path leading to Venn Farm and then follow the farm track to the main B4325 road.

From here, the official path takes you along a twisting road with some dangerous blind bends and no pavement. It can be hair-raising but unfortunately as yet the authorities have not been able to organize a better alternative.

There is a superior route that involves taking a left down Blackbridge Drive, followed by another left down past some garages and several rather grand houses to the Black Bridge. Unfortunately, this has yet to get official sanction and permission from the landowners. However you get to the bridge, once you're there it's just a case of climbing up the opposite bank and so on into...

MILFORD HAVEN   MAP 31, p121
(ABERDAUGLEDDAU)

The town of Milford Haven, named after the harbour on which it lies, is a relatively modern place. It dates back to 1790 when it was settled by a group of American whalers who provided whale oil for London's street lamps.

The town later became an important fishing port and although fishing is still of importance here, it is now the nearby pipeline constructions and the refineries,

supplemented by a little tourism, that brings in the money.

For a greater insight into the town's history visit the small **Milford Haven Museum** (☎ 01646-694496, Easter to Oct, Mon-Sat 11am-5pm; admission £1.50) by the dockyard.

Also in the docks is a working **seal hospital** (see Map 32, p124) built into an oil refinery storage tank. A sign outside usually tells you whether any seals are resident; visitors are welcome.

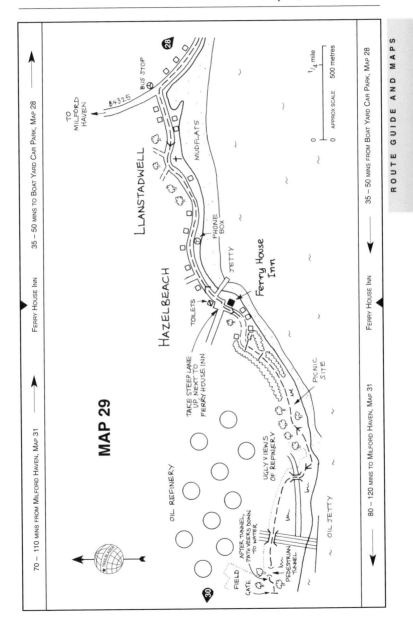

70 – 110 MINS FROM MILFORD HAVEN, MAP 31

FERRY HOUSE INN

35 – 50 MINS TO BOAT YARD CAR PARK, MAP 28

MAP 29

TAKE STEEP LANE
UP NEXT TO
FERRY HOUSE INN

HAZELBEACH

LLANSTADWELL

TO
MILFORD
HAVEN

B4325

BUS STOP

28

MUDFLATS

PHONE
BOX

TOILETS

JETTY

Ferry House Inn

OIL REFINERY

UGLY VIEWS
OF REFINERY

PICNIC
SITE

FIELD

AFTER TUNNEL,
PATH VEERS DOWN
TO WATER

GATE

PEDESTRIAN
TUNNEL

OIL JETTY

30

0   ¼ mile
APPROX SCALE
0   500 metres

80 – 120 MINS TO MILFORD HAVEN, MAP 31

FERRY HOUSE INN

35 – 50 MINS FROM BOAT YARD CAR PARK, MAP 28

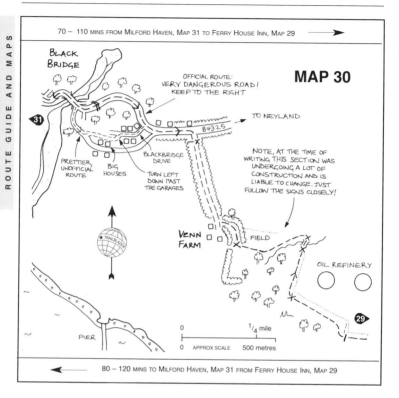

BLACK BRIDGE

OFFICIAL ROUTE:
VERY DANGEROUS ROAD!
KEEP TO THE RIGHT

MAP 30

31

TO NEYLAND

B4325

NOTE, AT THE TIME OF
WRITING THIS SECTION WAS
UNDERGOING A LOT OF
CONSTRUCTION AND IS
LIABLE TO CHANGE. JUST
FOLLOW THE SIGNS CLOSELY!

PRETTIER,
UNOFFICIAL
ROUTE

BIG
HOUSES

BLACKBRIDGE
DRIVE

TURN LEFT
DOWN PAST
THE GARAGES

★ TRAILBLAZER

VENN
FARM

FIELD

OIL REFINERY

29

0   ¼ mile

0   APPROX SCALE   500 metres

PIER

The enormous harbour, lauded by both Vice-Admiral Horatio Nelson and Daniel Defoe (author of *Robinson Crusoe*), is one of the natural wonders of the British Isles but has sadly been exploited by the oil giants as anyone who has walked from Angle can testify. Only two of the original four terminals remain in operation but the jetties and pipelines still scar the coastline.

However, the harbour is now undergoing some sort of renovation project and is home to a number of new facilities, including the Charthouse Restaurant (see p122), in the old sail loft, and the **Waterfront Gallery** (☎ 01646-695699; Mon-Sat 10am-5pm), a not-for-profit showcase of the best in local art.

Services

Milford Haven is the last of the big towns around the estuary. From here there is little chance of getting any provisions until Broad Haven, about 30 miles (48km) away, although there are small shops-cum-post offices at Dale and Marloes (the former open mornings only). The next cash machine is also at Marloes (in the pub) with another at Broad Haven.

Charles St is where you'll find most of the shops and services including: the **tourist information centre** (☎ 01646-690866, ✉ milfordhaven.tic@pembroke shire.gov.uk; at No 94, Apr-Oct Mon-Sat 10am-4pm) and the main **post office** (☎ 01646-690103; Mon & Thur 8.30am-5.30pm, Tue & Wed 9am-5.30pm, Sat 9am-

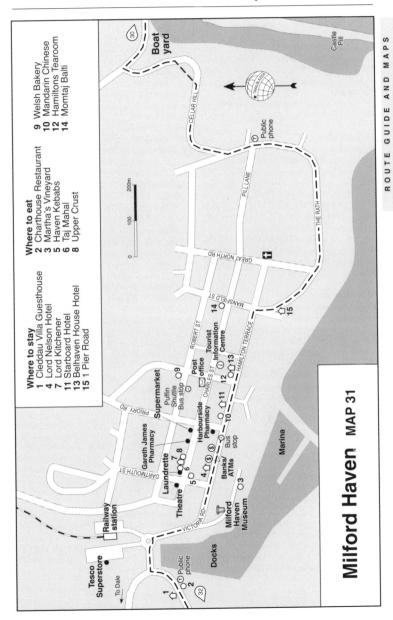

Milford Haven MAP 31

Where to stay
1 Cleddau Villa Guesthouse
4 Lord Nelson Hotel
7 Lord Kitchener
11 Starboard Hotel
13 Belhaven House Hotel
15 1 Pier Road

Where to eat
2 Charthouse Restaurant
3 Martha's Vineyard
5 Haven Kebabs
6 Taj Mahal
8 Upper Crust
9 Welsh Bakery
10 Mandarin Chinese
12 Hamiltons Tearoom
14 Momtaj Balti

ROUTE GUIDE AND MAPS

2pm). You will find the **laundrette** (Mon-Sat 8am-5.30pm, last wash 4.30pm) at No 17, a Kwiksave **supermarket**, and Gareth James **pharmacy** (at No 47); another pharmacy, Harbourside, is on Hamilton Terrace, as well as the majority of **banks**, most with **cashpoints**.

There's also a big Tesco **superstore** in the retail park by the docks.

Transport
Opposite Tesco is the **train station** with services to Haverfordwest; there are also trains to Swansea and London. Silcox's No 356 **bus** service to Pembroke stops on Charles St, Hamilton Terrace and outside Tesco. The No 300 service goes round town and to Herbrandston, and First's No 302 service goes to Haverfordwest.

The **Puffin Shuttle** departs from Robert St (outside Lord Nelson Hotel); for further information see public transport map and table, pp39-41.

Where to stay
Where the coast path enters the main part of town there's bed and breakfast for £20 per person (though with no en suite rooms) at *1 Pier Rd* (☎ 01646-694531, 1S/1T/2D) just off The Rath; it's strictly non-smokers only.

Belhaven House Hotel (☎ 01646-695983, 29 Hamilton Terrace; 3S/2T/4D) charges £38.50 for a single, or £25-35 per person for two sharing. Also on Hamilton Terrace is *Lord Nelson Hotel* (☎ 01646-695341) with 32 en suite rooms at £55 for a single, doubles at £75, and family rooms at £90 and *Starboard Hotel* (☎ 01646-692439; 4S/3T/1F), 21 Hamilton Terrace, which has rooms for £25 per person.

On Charles St, *Lord Kitchener* (☎ 01646-692741; 1S/2T/1F) charges £25 per head.

After passing the dockyard into **Hakin** you'll find *Cleddau Villa Guesthouse* (see Map 32, p124; ☎ 01646-690313; 4D) at 21 St Annes Rd, with good-value accommodation at £20 per person.

Where to eat
For Indian food head to *Momtaj Balti* (☎ 01646-690880; Sun-Thur 6.30-10.30pm, Fri/Sat to 11.30pm) at the eastern end of Charles St.

Alternatively, just down the road from the Torch Theatre (undergoing renovations at the time of writing) is the *Taj Mahal* (☎ 01646-698998; Sun-Thur 5pm-midnight, Fri & Sat to 1am).

Opposite, for fast food there's *Haven Kebabs* (☎ 01646-694747), open similar hours. There's also the *Mandarin Chinese* (☎ 01646-693336, 20 Hamilton Terrace, 5-10.30pm, closed Tue) for chicken fried rice and the like.

During the day the *Welsh Bakery* (☎ 01646-695183; Mon-Fri 8am-4.30pm, Sat 8.30am-4pm), on Robert St, does a roaring trade with its good-value no-nonsense menu; sarnis cost from £2 and buns start at just 33p.

Slightly smarter but smaller, *Hamiltons Tearoom* (☎ 01646-693667, Mon-Fri 10.30am-4.30m, Sat 11am-4pm), 26 Hamilton Terrace, and there's *Upper Crust* (☎ 01646-697713; food served Mon-Sat 7.30am-5pm) on Charles St.

Further west of the main town centre, there's fish & chips at the *Hake Inn* (Map 32, p124; ☎ 01646-690075; Mon-Sat 12-2pm, 5-9pm). on St Anne's Rd in Hakin, while down by the dockyard is the swish *Martha's Vineyard* (☎ 01646-697083, ⌨ www.marthasmilfordmarina.co.uk/; daily 12-2pm, 6-9.15pm) with a smart upstairs bar and restaurant where all food is guaranteed to be of local origin. The food is fine and fancy without being pretentious; the tuna steak, grilled and served on a bed of white cabbage and horseradish, costs £12.95. It's popular with locals so book in advance.

Charthouse Restaurant (☎ 01646-690098; daily 12-2pm, 6.30-8.30pm) by the docks near Tesco specializes in fish dishes and, while it can't quite match the food or ambience at Martha's, is still well worth checking out.

❏ LNG at Milford Haven

Never the prettiest part of the coast path, throughout 2006 the section around Milford Haven was subjected to some pretty extensive development caused by the construction of two new Liquid Natural Gas (LNG) terminals. The terminals were necessary as, following years of plenty, in 2006 Britain became a net importer of gas for the first time as its own sources ran dry.

The gas arrives by ship in liquid form as this reduces its volume, making the entire process economically viable. Upon arrival, the cargo is transferred into LNG storage tanks and converted back into gaseous form, after which it is pumped through the country using the existing network. When the Milford Haven LNG plants come on stream, 30% of the entire country's gas requirements will be imported in this way. The terminals will join the two operational refineries and an oil terminal that already exist in the area.

Whilst the economic benefits are manifold not everyone is entirely happy with the new development, and there have been concerns raised about both the environmental impact of such extensive construction, and the safety of the residents who call this area their home. To back up their argument they point to claims by James Fay, a professor at Massachusetts Institute of Technology, that an LNG spill could endanger 20,000 lives. However, the developers argue, how much environmental impact can one have on an area that used to have five oil refineries? Furthermore, with each delivery of gas arriving in a double-hulled ship that will be heavily protected, and with extensive systems already in place guarding the existing refineries and terminals, fears about the security of the operation should also be allayed.

The question for walkers, however, is how much of impact all this development going to have on the coast path? At the time of walking, the changes to the path brought about by all the ongoing construction were surprisingly minimal and indeed there were only a few places where the construction was actually visible; the authorities did a good job in shielding walkers from the ugliest sections.

The greatest impact so far has been on the region's accommodation: with so many workers having relocated temporarily to this area of Pembrokeshire to help with the construction, it can sometimes be very difficult to find a bed for the night. Hopefully, by the time you read this, the workers will have returned home and the situation will have returned to normal but, if not, book early if you want to stay in a B&B between Pembroke and Milford Haven.

You'll be pleased to hear that **Milford Haven** and the housing estate of **Hakin** are the last of the big urban areas that you have to walk through. The scenery improves a little once past **Gelliswick Bay** as you follow a concrete path through trees and scrubland and past the enormous liquid natural gas terminal (see box above) being constructed up the slopes.

Thankfully, the path once again does its best to shield you from the worst of the industrial scenery, though the pretty beach of **Sandy Haven** is still a very welcome sight. Ahead you can see the harbour opening out with the Angle peninsula on the left and the Dale peninsula on the right.

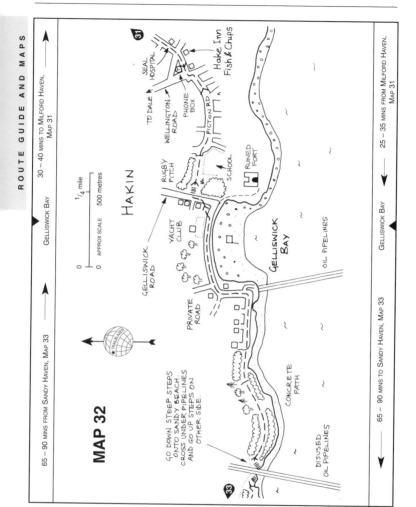

MAP 32

GELLISWICK BAY

30 – 40 MINS TO MILFORD HAVEN, MAP 31

25 – 35 MINS FROM MILFORD HAVEN, MAP 31

65 – 90 MINS FROM SANDY HAVEN, MAP 33

65 – 90 MINS TO SANDY HAVEN, MAP 33

GELLISWICK BAY

ROUTE GUIDE AND MAPS

HAKIN

GELLISWICK BAY

¹/₄ mile

0

500 metres

0   APPROX SCALE

GO DOWN STEEP STEPS ONTO SANDY BEACH. CROSS UNDER PIPELINES AND GO UP STEPS ON OTHER SIDE.

CONCRETE PATH

DISUSED OIL PIPELINES

OIL PIPELINES

PRIVATE ROAD

GELLISWICK ROAD

YACHT CLUB

RUGBY PITCH

SCHOOL

RUINED FORT

TO DALE

WELLINGTON ROAD

PICTON RD

PHONE BOX

SEAL HOSPITAL

Hake Inn Fish & Chips

TRAILBLAZER

HERBRANDSTON   **MAP 33**
Herbrandston lies on the high-tide detour
route and is only a short distance from the
main coast path at Sandy Haven.

This quiet little village can be reached
by following the lane up from Sandy Haven
campsite (see p126). It has a **post office** (☎
01646-692203), incorporating a small **shop**

(Mon-Fri 8am-1pm, 2-6pm, Sat 8am-1pm,
Sun 9am-12.30pm), in the centre of the village by the church hall, and a good pub
where you can sit and wait for the tide to go
out, rather than taking the long-winded
alternative route.

The very useful **Puffin Shuttle bus**,
which serves all the coastal villages as far

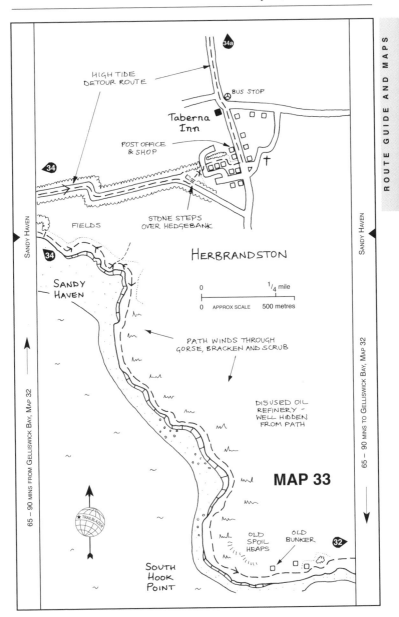

HIGH TIDE
DETOUR ROUTE

34a

BUS STOP

Taberna
Inn

POST OFFICE
& SHOP

34

STONE STEPS
OVER HEDGEBANK

SANDY HAVEN

FIELDS

HERBRANDSTON

34

SANDY
HAVEN

0   1/4 mile

0   APPROX SCALE   500 metres

PATH WINDS THROUGH
GORSE, BRACKEN AND SCRUB

DISUSED OIL
REFINERY –
WELL HIDDEN
FROM PATH

MAP 33

★ TRAILBLAZER

OLD
SPOIL
HEAPS

OLD
BUNKER

32

SOUTH
HOOK
POINT

SANDY HAVEN

65 – 90 MINS FROM GELLISWICK BAY, MAP 32

65 – 90 MINS TO GELLISWICK BAY, MAP 32

as St David's, stops on the main road opposite the Taberna Inn. See the public transport map and table, pp39-41, for full details.

The *Taberna Inn* (☎ 01646-693498; food served daily 12-2pm, 6-9pm; 1S/1D/1F) is a very friendly place to stay

SANDY HAVEN   MAP 34
East bank   Sandy Haven is a beautiful spot with a sandy beach and a long creek, or 'pill', stretching inland. Right on the coast path is the *Sandy Haven Caravan and Camping Park* (☎ 01646-698844, 🖳 www .sandyhavencampingpark.co.uk; Apr-Sep) with pitches from £5.50 per person.

West bank   Just up the lane from Sandy Haven, *Skerryback Farm* (☎ 01646-

and eat – with real ale – boasting an interesting menu with many of the ingredients farmed or caught locally. The pub is open daily 12noon-11pm; the single room costs £30 and for two sharing a room the rate is £22.50/pp.

636598, 🖳 www.pfh.co.uk/skerryback, 2D or T) has B&B from £30 (with a £5 single supplement).

Further from the trail, *Bicton Farm* (☎ 01646-636215, 1S/2D/1T) charges from £30 per person in the doubles (both en suite) or £25 in the other rooms. Rumour has it that they have been known to give residents a lift to and from the Brook Inn, St Ishmaels (see p128), for an evening meal.

SANDY HAVEN TO DALE   **MAPS 34-37**

These **five and a half miles (9km, 2-3hrs)** are quite easy going and, although not spectacular, the scenery is a vast improvement on the industrial landscape around Pembroke Dock and Milford Haven.

The cliffs at the beginning of this section are quite low compared to the rest of the coastline so there is nothing too strenuous. If you have timed it right you will be able to cross the stepping stones across **Sandy Haven Pill** at low tide (see box below). If, however, you find yourself faced with a barrier of water at high tide you will have to take the long road detour described below.

HIGH TIDE DETOUR AT SANDY HAVEN (VIA RICKESTON BRIDGE)
MAPS 34, 33, 34a & 34
This detour will add an extra **four miles (6km, 1½hrs)** to your day. From the campsite at Sandy Haven follow the lane up the hill. Just after the second right-hand bend there is a stone stile and steps on the left which takes you into a

---

❏ **Warning – high-tide obstacles**
It is worth giving advance warning here of two significant obstacles on the next section. The inlet at Sandy Haven and the estuary at The Gann near Dale, four miles (6km) further west, can both be crossed at low tide but at high tide the crossing points are completely submerged necessitating lengthy detours along roads. The trick is to cross the stepping stones at Sandy Haven as the tide is going out. In this way you have time to reach the next crossing near Dale before the tide has had time to come back in. For example, if low tide is at 2pm you should be able to cross at 1pm. The tide won't have cut off the next crossing near Dale until about 6pm giving you plenty of time to reach it. Tide times are posted all over the place, in shops, on noticeboards and in the national park's annual newspaper *Coast to Coast*.

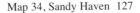

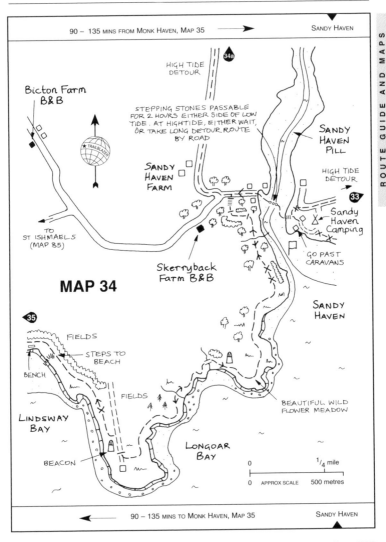

ROUTE GUIDE AND MAPS

small field where a few horses often graze. Cross the field, over another stile and cross the road, following the path behind a line of houses. This brings you out into the centre of **Herbrandston**.

Turn left and go past the Taberna Inn and follow the road north down the hill over Clay Bridge to **Rickeston Bridge**. Ignore the turn-offs to the right

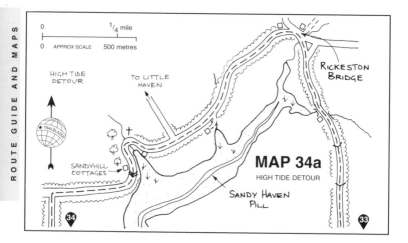

and follow the road round to the left to the **cottages** at Sandyhill. Climb the steep hill and take the next left. Just after passing Sandy Haven Farm turn left towards Sandy Haven. The coast path proper leaves the road on your right up some steps through woodland.

Once across the stepping stones the path takes you into some waterside woodland. It continues along the edge of a number of fields above low cliffs passing the ugly beacon above **Butts Bay**.

The scenery becomes more spectacular around **Lindsway Bay**, a lovely sandy beach protected by steep cliffs on all sides. The quickest way to St Ishmael's is to follow the public footpath from Lindsway Bay (look out for a bench by the coast path marking the trail to the village). The route from Monk Haven is slightly longer unless you are coming from Musselwick.

ST ISHMAEL'S (LLANISMEL) MAP 35
St Ishmael's is a pretty village with a friendly pub.

The **Puffin Shuttle bus** stops by Brook Inn; see public transport map and table, pp39-41, for details.

The **post office** is up the hill at the northern end of the village.

There are no B&Bs in the village but *Brook Inn* (☎ 01646-636277, food served daily 12noon-11pm), a friendly little pub, has quite an extensive menu and a good choice of real ales including their own Brook Inn Ale.

At **Watch House Point** there are old military bunkers and lookout buildings which can provide very welcome shelter in wet weather. The coast path carries on, past the remains of a curious Victorian watchtower, to **Monk Haven**, a pretty little wooded valley with an impressive castle-like wall guarding the bay. It also provides another access point to St Ishmael's.

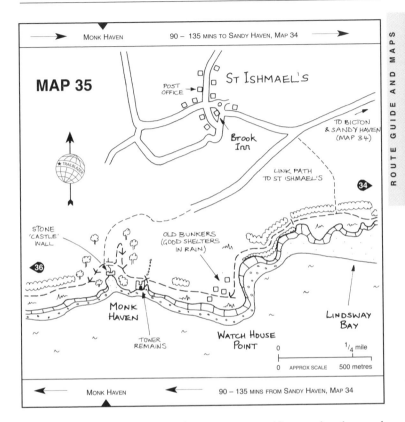

The path now follows gentle slopes overgrown with gorse, hawthorn and bracken to the farm buildings at **Musselwick**. From the small raised pond in the farmyard the path cuts down through shady trees to the stony beach. When there are exceptionally high tides the beach route is impassable and you will have to follow the short detour up the farm track from the raised pond following the fence line round to The Gann.

If you've come by any route save the high tide one, the next obstacle is the plank crossing of the creek at **The Gann**. As with Sandy Haven you will need to have checked the tide times as the crossing is only possible at low tide (see box p126). At high tide you must take the detour route by the road (described below). Once over the other side the path takes you across the shingle beach to the road and down to the village of **Dale**.

ROUTE GUIDE AND MAPS

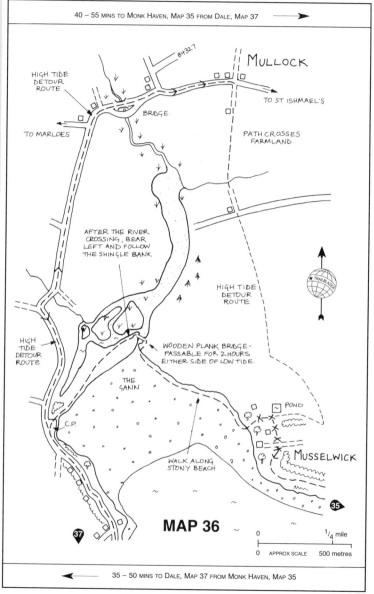

40 – 55 MINS TO MONK HAVEN, MAP 35 FROM DALE, MAP 37

MULLOCK

HIGH TIDE DETOUR ROUTE

B4327

TO ST ISHMAEL'S

BRIDGE

TO MARLOES

PATH CROSSES FARMLAND

AFTER THE RIVER CROSSING, BEAR LEFT AND FOLLOW THE SHINGLE BANK.

HIGH TIDE DETOUR ROUTE

HIGH TIDE DETOUR ROUTE

WOODEN PLANK BRIDGE - PASSABLE FOR 2 HOURS EITHER SIDE OF LOW TIDE.

THE GANN

C.P.

POND

MUSSELWICK

WALK ALONG STONY BEACH

35

MAP 36

0   1/4 mile
0   APPROX SCALE   500 metres

37

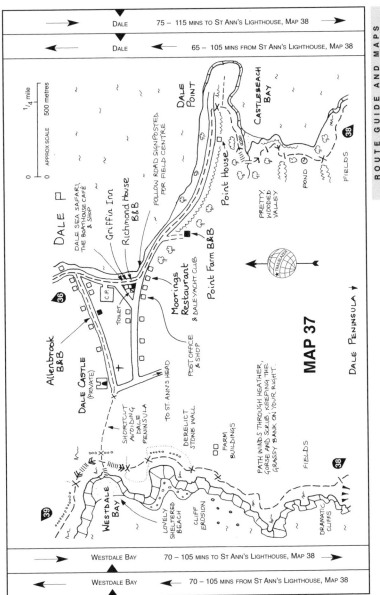

DALE → 75 – 115 MINS TO ST ANN'S LIGHTHOUSE, MAP 38 →

← DALE ← 65 – 105 MINS FROM ST ANN'S LIGHTHOUSE, MAP 38

¼ mile

500 metres

APPROX SCALE

0

0

DALE POINT

CASTLEBEACH BAY

FOLLOW ROAD SIGNPOSTED FOR FIELD CENTRE

38

DALE

DALE SEA SAFARI, THE BOATHOUSE CAFÉ & SHOP

Griffin Inn

Richmond House B&B

Point House

PRETTY WOODED VALLEY

POND

FIELDS

Point Farm B&B

Moorings Restaurant & DALE YACHT CLUB

36

TRAILBLAZER

Allenbrook B&B

Dale Castle (PRIVATE)

TOILET

C.P.

POST OFFICE & SHOP

TO ST ANN'S HEAD

SHORTCUT AVOIDING DALE PENINSULA

DERELICT STONE WALL

MAP 37

DALE PENINSULA

FARM BUILDINGS

PATH WINDS THROUGH HEATHER, GORSE AND SCRUB, KEEPING THE GRASSY BANK ON YOUR RIGHT.

FIELDS

39

WESTDALE BAY

LOVELY SHELTERED BEACH

CLIFF EROSION

DRAMATIC CLIFFS

38

→ WESTDALE BAY 70 – 105 MINS TO ST ANN'S LIGHTHOUSE, MAP 38 →

← WESTDALE BAY ← 70 – 105 MINS FROM ST ANN'S LIGHTHOUSE, MAP 38

HIGH-TIDE DETOUR (VIA MULLOCK BRIDGE) MAP 36

This second detour, around The Gann estuary near Dale, will add a further **two and a half miles (4km, 1hr)** to your day. Turning off the trail at Musselwick, follow the signposted track east, turning north at the first opportunity to continue on to Slatehill Farm. Negotiating the path through the farm buildings, you carry on heading north and, with Whiteholme's Farm on your left, cross the farmland to the road at **Mullock Farm**.

From here walk down the lane joining the B4327 road just before **Mullock Bridge**. After the bridge simply follow the road all the way to Dale, rejoining the coast path proper at the car park by the estuary.

DALE MAP 37, p131

Dale is a small village but it's alive with tourists in the summer months. Sitting on the neck of the Dale peninsula, it overlooks a sheltered bay popular with water-sports enthusiasts.

If you want to have a go you can try everything from surfing and sailing to canoeing and coasteering (see box p83) at **West Wales Wind Surf and Sailing** (☎ 01646-636642; ☐ www.surfdale.co.uk; see box p148). They offer tuition for beginners as well as equipment hire. You can also book tickets here for the Dale Sea Safari operated by **Dale Sailing** (☎ 01646-603123, ☐ www.dale-sailing.co.uk/boat_trips.asp).

There is a small **shop** at the **post office** which can be found just around the corner from The Griffin Inn. It's open only Monday to Friday 9.15am to noon. Another **shop** can be found at Dale Boat House.

The **Puffin Shuttle bus** stops here; see the public transport map and table, pp39-41, for details.

Where to stay and eat

There are few places to stay so booking in advance is recommended.

Richmond House B&B (☎ 07974-925009; 8S/2D/1T) has **bunkhouse** accommodation for £20 (unusually this includes breakfast) or en suite double and twin rooms for £30 per person, with a £5 single-occupancy supplement.

Along the road towards Dale Castle is *Allenbrook* (☎ 01646-636254, ☐ www.allenbrook-dale.co.uk, 1S/2T/1D), a fairly grand country house, which charges from £35 per person in its smart rooms, some of which are en suite and some have a private bathroom.

Point Farm (☎ 01646-636541; ☐ www.pointfarm.info; 1S/1D/1F), just beyond the village, comes recommended by several path walkers for its homely rooms and excellent hospitality. Not a working farm, it is nevertheless a beautifully restored Victorian farmhouse and each room comes with its own private bathroom. Room rates start at £35/pp. Laundry service, packed lunches and luggage/guest transport are also provided for a fee.

The *Griffin Inn* (☎ 01646-636227) is the only pub. They do food throughout the year (daily 12.30-2pm, Mon-Sat 6-8.30pm) and the bar is open Mon-Fri 12-3pm, 5-11pm, Sat/Sun 12noon-11pm with extended opening hours during the summer months). You can't miss it, sitting at the southern end of the village overlooking the water. The menu is limited but there are some tasty dishes, including locally caught prawns served by the pint.

Close by is the *Moorings Restaurant* (☎ 01646-636362, ☎ 07792-592922, Thur-Sat 6pm to late, open for Sun lunch from 12.30pm) situated in Dale Yacht Club, once again specializing in locally caught seafood.

Snacks are available at *The Boathouse Café* which is open in the summer only.

DALE TO MUSSELWICK SANDS (FOR MARLOES)   MAPS 37-41

This beautiful section is **12 miles (19km, 5-6hrs)** so it is tempting to shorten it by missing out the Dale peninsula. If you follow the official path around the peninsula it is five and a half miles (9km, 2¼hrs) to Westdale Bay. If you take the shortcut it is less than a mile (1km, 15 mins). Purists will want to do the whole thing and will be well rewarded since there is some beautiful scenery to enjoy. The peninsula protects Milford Haven harbour from the worst the Atlantic can throw at it. The eastern side is a mixture of gentle cliffs, small wooded valleys and pretty bays while the wind battered western side is characterized by high, rugged cliffs.

From Dale Yacht Club at the southern end of the village the route follows the lane to Point House and then on across farmland before dropping down to a pretty little bay surrounded by woodland.

Just past **Watwick Point** and its ugly beacon is the lovely **Watwick Bay**, then more farmland and low cliffs. At **Mill Bay** there is a stone on the field's edge commemorating the landing of Henry Tudor and his 55 ships and 4000 men from France, on 7 August 1485, after 14 years in exile. From Mill Bay Henry marched east where he got the better of Richard III in the Battle of Bosworth on 22 August 1485. He then became Henry VII, founder of the Tudor dynasty.

St Ann's lighthouse, which is now a set of holiday homes, marks the northern lip of the Milford Haven harbour. North from here the cliffs are precipitous and in places are crumbling into the sea so take great care. The path passes through scrubland and heathland along the level cliff top, eventually dropping steeply to pretty **Westdale Bay**. People do swim here but it is not the safest place for a dip since there are strong undercurrents as the big warning sign indicates.

The path skirts an old disused aerodrome, rapidly becoming overrun with gorse and bracken, before arriving high above the great sweep of **Marloes Sands**, one of the finest beaches in Pembrokeshire. The islands of Gateholm, Grassholm and Skomer can all be seen on the western horizon.

Hostellers should look out for a path above **Raggle Rocks** which leads to the youth hostel (see p138; five minutes from the coast path). The coast path continues on an easy course above some spectacular cliffs with twisted, folded rock dropping into the heaving sea below. This part of the coast is a marine nature reserve and with the proximity of some important breeding islands is a great place to spot seabirds. At **Martin's Haven** there is a National Trust visitor centre with information about the wildlife of the area. Just to the north of the centre, within the wall, is a stone engraved with a ring-cross design dating from somewhere between the 7th and 9th centuries; you'll see further examples of these at the lapidarium of the cathedral at St David's (see p156).

From Martin's Haven you can take a boat trip to Skomer, where you have an even greater chance of spotting wildlife, particularly puffins (see box p134).

The path then follows the fairly level cliff top to **Musselwick Sands**, another wonderful sandy beach with sheer cliffs all around. En route you pass both West Hook Farm Campsite and East Hook Farm Campsite and B&B (see p138)

Skomer, Skokholm and Grassholm islands

Lying to the west of the Marloes peninsula are three barren islands brought to life by the thousands of sea birds which breed on the sheer cliffs. All of them can be visited quite easily with guided walks available on Skomer and Skokholm.

Skomer, a national nature reserve, with its coastline peppered with caves and blowholes, is the largest of the three and is closest to the mainland. It also has the widest variety of bird species of all the islands with razorbills, guillemots, kittiwakes, storm petrels, fulmars, shags and cormorants festooning the cliffs. The puffins and manx shearwaters breed in burrows on the cliff tops with pictures from one of the burrows relayed to a monitor in the island centre. There are 160,000 manx shearwaters making up 40% of the world's population. There are also peregrine falcons and short-eared owls which can often be seen during the daytime.

If you prefer the odd mammal or two there are grey seals on the rocky shoreline while porpoises and dolphins can often be spotted from the boat to the island. There are also plenty of rabbits and some other small mammals, most notably the Skomer vole, a sub-species of bank vole, unique to the island. For the botanist the island is carpeted in bluebells, heather, thrift and sea campion, creating a riot of colour in the spring. For further details about the flora and fauna see pp56-64.

Skokholm, to the south, is smaller but no less noisy with the relentless chatter of seabirds. There are about 35,000 pairs of manx shearwater that breed on Skokholm. You can land on the island but can't wander around as you please. You must join one of the guided walks organized by the Wildlife Trust of South and West Wales who manage the island. Skokholm is also the only island where you can stay overnight; for details, call the Wildlife Trust of South and West Wales on ☎ 01239-621600.

Grassholm, an RSPB reserve, is a rocky outcrop 11 miles (7km) from the mainland. It's Britain's only gannetry, home to 30,000 pairs of gannets in the summer breeding season when it can be hard to see the rock for the gannets.

Although you can't land on the island you can take a boat trip around it. **Dale Sailing** (see p132) sail to Skomer from Martin's Haven on the *Dale Princess*. It costs £8 per person for the boat trip and an additional £6 to land (Easter to Oct, Tue-Sun 10am, 11am, 12pm). No bookings are necessary. Once a month in summer they also sail to Skomer and Skokholm from Martin's Haven (£25 for boat and landing). Bookings must be made through West Wales Wind Surf and Sailing. They also offer a 2-hour trip around Grassholm (daily 12.30pm; £25) for which bookings must be made through Dale Sailing.

but access to both is only possible along the road (see Map 40, p137). At the southern end of the bay next to a picnic bench there is a path leading down to the beach and another one heading inland to the village of Marloes.

MARLOES   MAP 41, p139

Marloes, around half a mile inland from the path, is not an especially attractive village although the strange **clocktower** is quite interesting, looking as though it needs to be on top of something like a town hall rather than sitting solemnly in a small field by the side of the road. The main church is also very pretty and worth a look.

There is a **post office** and **shop** (Mon-Fri 8.45am-1pm, 2.30-5.30pm, Sat 8.45am-1pm, Sun 9am-1pm) as well as a **phone box** opposite the pub. The **Puffin Shuttle bus** stops outside the Lobster Pot Inn; see public transport map and table, pp39-41, for details. *(cont'd on p138)*

ROUTE GUIDE AND MAPS

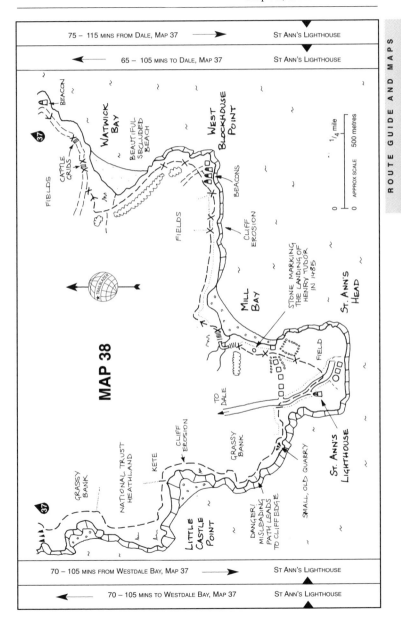

75 – 115 MINS FROM DALE, MAP 37 ⟶ ST ANN'S LIGHTHOUSE

⟵ 65 – 105 MINS TO DALE, MAP 37 ST ANN'S LIGHTHOUSE

MAP 38

BEACON

WATWICK BAY

BEAUTIFUL SECLUDED BEACH

WEST BLOCKHOUSE POINT

CATTLE GRIDS

FIELDS

BEACONS

FIELDS

CLIFF EROSION

STONE MARKING THE LANDING OF HENRY TUDOR IN 1485

MILL BAY

St. ANN'S HEAD

FIELD

TO DALE

KETE

CLIFF EROSION

GRASSY BANK

NATIONAL TRUST HEATHLAND

GRASSY BANK

St. ANN'S LIGHTHOUSE

SMALL, OLD QUARRY

GRASSY BANK

DANGER! MISLEADING PATH LEADS TO CLIFF EDGE

LITTLE CASTLE POINT

¼ mile

500 metres

APPROX SCALE

0

0

70 – 105 MINS FROM WESTDALE BAY, MAP 37 ⟶ ST ANN'S LIGHTHOUSE

⟵ 70 – 105 MINS TO WESTDALE BAY, MAP 37 ST ANN'S LIGHTHOUSE

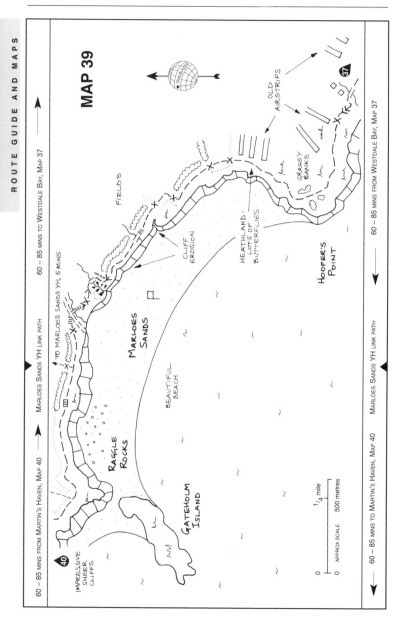

MAP 39

60 – 85 MINS FROM MARTIN'S HAVEN, MAP 40 ⟶   MARLOES SANDS YH LINK PATH   60 – 85 MINS TO WESTDALE BAY, MAP 37 ⟶

60 – 85 MINS TO MARTIN'S HAVEN, MAP 40 ⟶   MARLOES SANDS YH LINK PATH   60 – 85 MINS FROM WESTDALE BAY, MAP 37 ⟶

TRAILBLAZER

OLD AIRSTRIPS

GRASSY BANKS

HOOPER'S POINT

HEATHLAND – LOTS OF BUTTERFLIES

FIELDS

CLIFF EROSION

TO MARLOES SANDS YH, 5 MINS

MARLOES SANDS

BEAUTIFUL BEACH

RAGGLE ROCKS

GATEHOLM ISLAND

IMPRESSIVE SHEER CLIFFS

1/4 mile

0

0   APPROX SCALE   500 metres

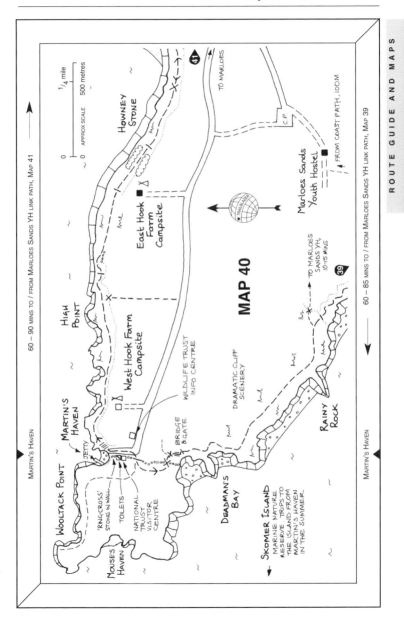

MARTIN'S HAVEN

60 – 90 MINS TO / FROM MARLOES SANDS YH LINK PATH, MAP 41

WOOLTACK POINT

MARTIN'S HAVEN

'RING-CROSS' STONE IN WALL

TOILETS

NATIONAL TRUST VISITOR CENTRE

MOUSE'S HAVEN

JETTY

DEADMAN'S BAY

SKOMER ISLAND
MARINE NATURE RESERVE. TRIPS TO THE ISLAND FROM MARTIN'S HAVEN IN THE SUMMER.

RAINY ROCK

HIGH POINT

WEST HOOK FARM CAMPSITE

WILDLIFE TRUST INFO CENTRE

DRAMATIC CLIFF SCENERY

BRIDGE & GATE

MAP 40

TO MARLOES SANDS YH, 10–15 MINS

39

HOWNEY STONE

EAST HOOK FARM CAMPSITE

41

TO MARLOES

C.P.

MARLOES SANDS YOUTH HOSTEL

FROM COAST PATH, 100M

APPROX SCALE

0   1/4 mile
0   500 metres

MARTIN'S HAVEN

60 – 85 MINS TO / FROM MARLOES SANDS YH LINK PATH, MAP 39

(cont'd from p134) **Marloes Sands Youth Hostel** (see Map 40; ☎ 0870-770 5958 for information, ☎ 0870-770 8868 for bookings) has 26 beds at £9.50 for members and is a self-catering-only property. It is not actually in the village and rather than coming from Musselwick Sands it is much easier to reach it from Marloes Sands (see Map 39; a five-minute walk) where a signpost points the way from the coast path.

Also outside the village itself, a mile and a half (2km) before Musselwick Sands near Martin's Haven (see Map 40), there is camping from £4/pp at **West Hook Farm** (☎ 01646-636424; Apr-Oct) and also at **East Hook Farm** (☎ 01646-636291, Apr-Oct) where a pitch costs £4 per person.

In the village on Glebe Lane there's the highly commended, pink-painted **Foxdale** (☎ 01646-636243, 🖳 www.foxdaleguesthouse.co.uk; 3D/1T) which offers B&B accommodation at £28 in the twin room (which has its own bathroom outside

the room) and up to £30 per person in the en suite doubles; they also offer **camping** (Apr-Sep) for £4.75 per person.

Opposite the post office is the homely **Albion House B&B** (☎ 01646-636365; 1S/1D/1T/1F) with rooms, some en suite, from £25 to £30 per person. At the **Clock House** (☎ 01646-636527; 🖳 www.clockhousemarloes.co.uk; 2S/4D/1T) B&B costs £28 per person or £33 en suite. They also have a good selection of snacks in the café (daily 11am-5pm, and are open to 7.30pm for evening meals in high summer) and at the time of writing planned to start serving evening meals at other times too.

The social centre of the village is undoubtedly the **Lobster Pot Inn** (☎ 01646-636233, 8am-5pm, 6-9.30pm; 1D/2F), which also does B&B with en suite rooms from £25 per person. They have a good menu, including vegetarian food and Welsh beer (the bar is open daily 11am-11pm).

MUSSELWICK SANDS TO BROAD HAVEN   MAPS 41-45

It is **eight and a half miles** (14km, 3¹/₂-4¹/₂hrs) from the link path for Marloes village to Broad Haven following the easy path above the cliffs. The next port of call is **St Brides Haven (Sainffraid)** a sheltered little bay where you will find toilets, a phone box, a church and a cluster of houses but little else. The extravagant-looking castle across the fields is actually the stately home of the St Brides estate.

The next stretch continues along easy-to-follow cliff tops. Once past **Mill Haven** things get a little tougher. The cliffs grow higher and the path rollercoasters its way up and down, passing **Brandy Bay**, a tiny little cove sheltered by frighteningly sheer cliffs. Take care here as the path is very close to the edge. Eventually the path settles down above high, vegetated cliffs at **Ticklas Point**. You can now see the immense sweep of St Brides Bay with Ramsey Island in the far distance.

Once past the mighty **Borough Head** with its 75-metre (246ft) slopes dropping steeply into the sea, the path enters some beautiful forest of oak, beech and pine which cling to the steep cliff side. Howelston Farm Campsite (see p142) is off the first road to the right after joining the road. The pretty village of **Little Haven** is a bit further on down the hill. From here it's a steep climb up the road out over the hill into **Broad Haven**, its bigger sister village.

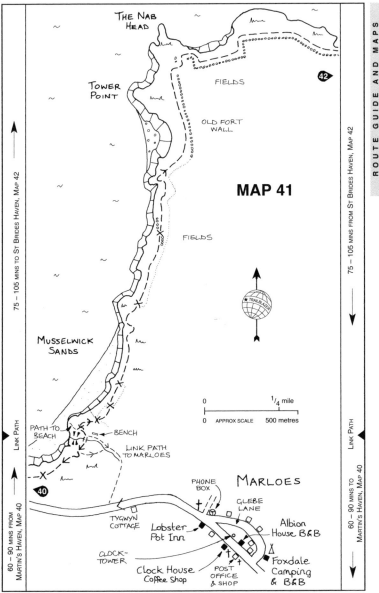

THE NAB HEAD

TOWER POINT

FIELDS

42

OLD FORT WALL

MAP 41

FIELDS

★ TRAILBLAZER

MUSSELWICK SANDS

0   1/4 mile

0   APPROX SCALE   500 metres

PATH TO BEACH

BENCH

LINK PATH TO MARLOES

40

MARLOES

PHONE BOX

GLEBE LANE

TYGWYN COTTAGE

Lobster Pot Inn

Albion House B&B

CLOCK-TOWER

Clock House Coffee Shop

POST OFFICE & SHOP

Foxdale Camping & B&B

75 – 105 MINS TO ST BRIDES HAVEN, MAP 42

75 – 105 MINS FROM ST BRIDES HAVEN, MAP 42

LINK PATH

LINK PATH

60 – 90 MINS FROM MARTIN'S HAVEN, MAP 40

60 – 90 MINS TO MARTIN'S HAVEN, MAP 40

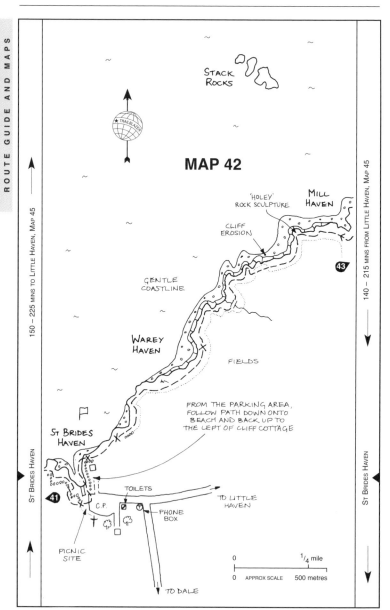

★ TRAILBLAZER

STACK ROCKS

MAP 42

'HOLEY' ROCK SCULPTURE

MILL HAVEN

CLIFF EROSION

43

GENTLE COASTLINE

WAREY HAVEN

FIELDS

FROM THE PARKING AREA, FOLLOW PATH DOWN ONTO BEACH AND BACK UP TO THE LEFT OF CLIFF COTTAGE

ST BRIDES HAVEN

41

C.P.

TOILETS

TO LITTLE HAVEN

PHONE BOX

PICNIC SITE

150 – 225 MINS TO LITTLE HAVEN, MAP 45

140 – 215 MINS FROM LITTLE HAVEN, MAP 45

ST BRIDES HAVEN

ST BRIDES HAVEN

TO DALE

0   1/4 mile
0   APPROX SCALE   500 metres

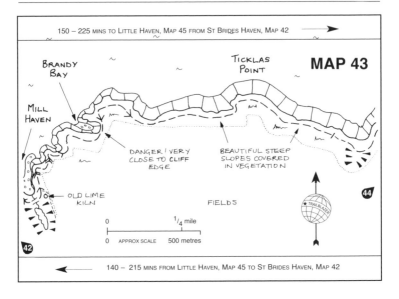

TICKLAS
POINT

MAP 43

BRANDY
BAY

MILL
HAVEN

DANGER ! VERY
CLOSE TO CLIFF
EDGE

BEAUTIFUL STEEP
SLOPES COVERED
IN VEGETATION

OLD LIME
KILN

FIELDS

44

42

0
¹/₄ mile

0   APPROX SCALE   500 metres

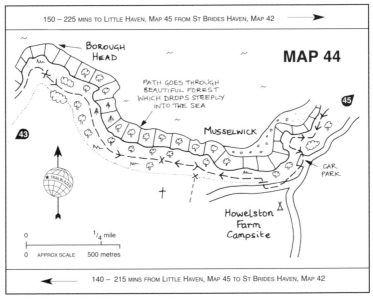

BOROUGH
HEAD

MAP 44

PATH GOES THROUGH
BEAUTIFUL FOREST
WHICH DROPS STEEPLY
INTO THE SEA

45

MUSSELWICK

43

CAR
PARK

Howelston
Farm
Campsite

0
¹/₄ mile

0   APPROX SCALE   500 metres

LITTLE HAVEN (ABER BACH)
MAP 45

Squeezed between two steep hillsides around a tiny cove, Little Haven is a lovely place. It may be smaller than Broad Haven over the hill but is far more appealing and has a good number of pubs to distract the exhausted walker.

Services

By turning right as you come into the village from the south you will find the **post office** and a small **shop**. For anything else of importance you will be better off carrying on to Broad Haven which is only ten minutes away over the hill.

The **Puffin Shuttle bus** stops by Castle Hotel; see pp39-41 for details.

Where to stay

For camping try *Howelston Farm* (see Map 44; ☎ 01437-781818, Mar-Nov) where a pitch costs £6 per person.

Down in the centre of the village, near the post office, is *St Brides Inn* (☎ 01437-781266, 🖳 ghjones333@aol.com, 1T/1D/1F) with en suite rooms from £30/pp. *Castle Hotel* (☎ 01437-781445, 🖳 www.castlelittlehaven.co.uk; 1D/1T) has en suite rooms with views of the coast from £37.50 per person (£55 single occupancy). The **post office** (☎ 01437-781233) also has a self-contained flat that, if it's vacant, is available for rent for a night.

Further up Settlands Hill is *Haven Fort Hotel* (☎ 01437-781401, Apr-Oct; 2S/10D/3F) which charges £35 per person. Further along this road and actually closer to Broad Haven is *Atlantic View* (☎ 01437-781589, 🖳 www.atlantic-view.co.uk, 2T/3D) with all rooms either en suite or with private bath-

room and prices from £34 per person. It also has a small **campsite**; pitches from £6 per tent plus £2 per head.

Finally, for possibly the best location in either of the havens, *Atlantic Sunset* (☎ 01437-781999; 3D all en suite) sits on top of the hill between the two. All the rooms have extensive views over the sea; prices start from £35 per person per night.

Where to eat

St Brides Inn (☎ 01437-781266) has good food on offer daily (noon-2pm, 6-9pm) with the menu changing regularly; they do barbecues in the summer. The bar itself is open Sun-Fri 11am-3pm, 6-11pm and all day on Saturday. The post office on St Bride's Rd has a small **tearoom** (☎ 01437-781233, daily 9am-5pm) where everything on the menu comes from local suppliers. They sell everything from sandwiches to hot meals and an all-day breakfast; they also claim to have the largest cappuccinos in the area.

The *Swan Inn* (☎ 01437-781860; food served Tue-Sun 12-2.30pm, Tue-Sat 6-9pm) was being restored to reflect its original character when we last visited but has now reopened. It sits overlooking the small bay and is the first pub you see as you come in from the coast path; the bar is open daily 11am-3pm, 5-11pm.

The *Castle Hotel* (see column opposite; food served daily noon-2pm, 6-9pm) has an extensive menu and a nice beer garden where you can watch the waves crashing on the small beach.

Away from the beach is the *Nest Bistro* (☎ 01437-781728, 🖳 thenestbistro@hotmail.com; Mon-Sat 7pm to late, from 5.30pm on certain evenings), a quality fish restaurant. Booking is advised.

BROAD HAVEN (ABER LLYDAN)
MAP 45

The wonderful beach is the highlight here. The village itself would not win any beauty contests but it has a nice air about it all the same. Popular with holidaymakers who come for the endless expanse of sand, you may well be tempted to take a dip to soothe those aching feet.

The small **supermarket** (daily 8am-

9pm) on the seafront is probably the only place you will need since it also incorporates the **post office** (Mon, Tue, Thur & Fri 9am-1pm, 2-5.30pm, Wed & Sat 9am-12.30pm) and has a Link **cash machine** too.

The supermarket also has an array of **first-aid bits** and bobs which may be useful for anyone suffering from blisters. The next cash machine, chemist and shop are not until St David's, 17 miles (27km) away,

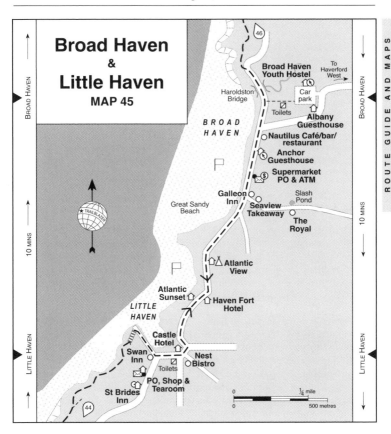

Broad Haven
&
Little Haven
MAP 45

46

BROAD HAVEN
Youth Hostel

To
Haverford
West

Haroldston
Bridge

Car
park

Toilets

*BROAD
HAVEN*

Albany
Guesthouse

Nautilus Café/bar/
restaurant

Anchor
Guesthouse

Supermarket
PO & ATM

Galleon
Inn

Slash
Pond

Great Sandy
Beach

Seaview
Takeaway

The
Royal

TRAIL BLAZER

Atlantic
View

Atlantic
Sunset

Haven Fort
Hotel

*LITTLE
HAVEN*

Castle
Hotel

Swan
Inn

Nest
Bistro

Toilets

PO, Shop &
Tearoom

St Brides
Inn

44

0   ¼ mile

0   500 metres

BROAD HAVEN

10 MINS

LITTLE HAVEN

BROAD HAVEN

10 MINS

LITTLE HAVEN

ROUTE GUIDE AND MAPS

though there is a small shop at Solva.

There is an expensive (£5/hr) **internet** terminal at Broad Haven Youth Hostel. Slightly better value is the wi-fi service provided by the Anchor Guesthouse (see column opposite), at 50p for 10 minutes.

The **Puffin Shuttle bus** stops here; see public transport map and table, pp39-41, for details.

Where to stay
Broad Haven Youth Hostel (info ☎ 0870-770 5728, bookings ☎ 0870-770 8868, ☐ broadhaven@yha.org.uk) has space for 77. The rate for members is £14 per person.

The hostel is licensed and serves meals. Nearby, backing onto the car park, is *Albany Guesthouse* (☎ 01437-781051, ☐ www.albanyguesthouse.co.uk, 27 Milmoor Way; 1D/2D or T) charging £30 per head.

Anchor Guesthouse (☎ 01437-781476, ☐ www.anchorguesthouse.co.uk; 1S/3T/2D/1F, all en suite) is a large place on the seafront. Rates are £40 per person in high season.

Where to eat
The *Galleon Inn* (☎ 01437-781152, food served daily 12-2.30pm, 6-9pm) is the most popular spot with an extensive menu and a

particular slant on eastern dishes. It also has a good selection of real ales; the bar is open daily 11am-11pm. It's the first pub you see as you drop down into the village.

The *Royal* (☎ 01437-781249; food served Thur-Sat from 6pm, also Sat & Sun lunch from 12.30pm) serves a variety of staple meals including lasagnes, curries and roasts; the bar is open Mon-Fri 12-2pm, 5-11pm and Sat/Sun 12-11pm. The pub is opposite the Slash Pond, an old culm pit originally opened in 1859.

For cheaper, quicker fare look behind The Galleon Inn for the *Seaview Takeaway* which serves fish and chips. The smartest

place in town, however, is the new *Nautilus* (☎ 01437-781844, 🖳 www.nautilusbroad haven.co.uk; daily, tea/ coffee 11am-4pm, lunches 12-4pm but to 3pm on Sunday, the bistro is open 6.30-9pm) on the front. Decorated by over 20 local craftsmen, the bistro serves delicious, largely organic and locally sourced food, including braised Pembrokeshire beef shallots in a rich Guinness gravy (£7.95) or some delicious mussels (£12.50); lunch fare (around £3.95) includes paninis and savoury pancakes. Slightly – but only slightly – more expensive than pub food, this is nevertheless great value indeed; go on, spoil yourself!

BROAD HAVEN TO NEWGALE   MAPS 45-49

This short stretch of **seven miles (11km, 2^1/$_2$-3^1/$_4$hrs)** follows easy ground over low cliffs, passing a number of intimate little coves before arriving at the wonderful Newgale Sands, two miles (3km) of uninterrupted sand battered by Atlantic rollers. From Broad Haven the cliffs get steadily higher as you head north with the easy-to-follow path running through scrubland. At the rocky outcrops known as **Haroldston Chins** there's a great bench (dedicated to Paul Blick, one of the men who helped to found the coast path and its first warden); if the weather's fine, there's no better place to stop for a while. The route then turns inland to join the road around *Druidstone Villa* (☎ 01437-781221; 🖳 www.druidstone.co.uk; 2S/8D/1F), an excellent place to stay, where a bed costs from £35 to £70 per person. They also have a bar and restaurant open to non-residents (booking essential for the latter; daily 12.30-2.30pm, 7.30-9.30pm). Just past the villa look out for **The Roundhouse**. Tours of this 'eco-friendly' little building are by arrangement only; contact Druidstone Villa if you're interested.

There is a lovely beach at **Druidstone Haven** which tends to stay reasonably quiet since most people head for the beaches either side at Broad Haven and Newgale. From Druidstone Haven the path climbs over the top of an enormous grassy sand dune and then continues along the cliff top. Much of this section is falling into the sea with large land slips and erosion cutting into the coast path. Watch out for diversions and sudden drops.

NOLTON HAVEN   MAP 47, p146
Nolton Haven is an enchanting little cove and hamlet and a good spot to have lunch, especially if it's raining. There is a rather good pub here, the *Mariner's Inn* (☎ 01437-710469, 1S/6T/1F), which does B&B from £26 per person. The bar is open

daily 12-3pm, 6-11pm and they also do very good food from Indian to seafood (daily 12.30-2.15pm, 6.30-8.30pm). Fish and chips are £6.25 and the excellent jacket potatoes start from £3.30. The **Puffin Shuttle bus** stops here by the car park; see pp39-41 for details.

(Opposite) Top: Looking over the sumptuous sands of Broad Haven. **Bottom:** Surfing at Newgale (see p148). The beach is over two miles long. (Photos © Henry Stedman).

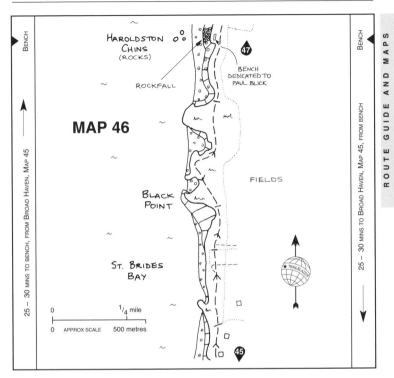

MAP 46

HAROLDSTON
CHINS
(ROCKS)

ROCKFALL

47

BENCH
DEDICATED TO
PAUL BLICK

BLACK
POINT

FIELDS

ST. BRIDES
BAY

0   ¹/₄ mile

0   APPROX SCALE   500 metres

TRAILBLAZER

45

BENCH

BENCH

25 – 30 MINS TO BENCH, FROM BROAD HAVEN, MAP 45

25 – 30 MINS TO BROAD HAVEN, MAP 45, FROM BENCH

ROUTE GUIDE AND MAPS

From Nolton Haven the path climbs steeply above high grassy slopes with views of **Newgale Sands** ahead. At the southern end of this immense beach you will find a disused mine still with the old red-brick chimney and spoil heaps. Coal was exported from Nolton Haven by sea for 25 years before the mine closed at the turn of the 20th century.

At the mine you have a choice. You can clamber down the rather precarious path to the beach, or head up the steep slope to continue along the heathery cliff top. Both routes have their merits. The beach is spectacular with nearly two miles (3km) of straight walking. The cliff route gives you the chance to admire the beach from up high and you still have the chance to walk along the top half of the beach once you climb down from the high ground. If planning to camp at South Wood Cottage (see p148) the cliff route may be better.

If you choose to walk along the beach, bear in mind that loose, dry sand is a pain to walk on. Furthermore, about a third of the way along the cliff juts right out,

(Opposite) Top: Pembroke Castle (see p108), built in the 11th century to control the Welsh. **Bottom**: Horses graze on windswept St David's Head. (Photos © Henry Stedman).

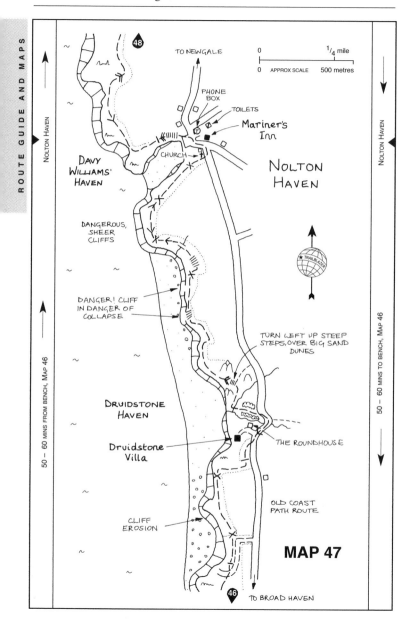

TO NEWGALE

48

NOLTON HAVEN

PHONE BOX

TOILETS

Mariner's Inn

CHURCH

DAVY WILLIAMS' HAVEN

NOLTON HAVEN

DANGEROUS, SHEER CLIFFS

DANGER! CLIFF IN DANGER OF COLLAPSE

TURN LEFT UP STEEP STEPS, OVER BIG SAND DUNES

TRAILBLAZER

DRUIDSTONE HAVEN

Druidstone Villa

THE ROUNDHOUSE

OLD COAST PATH ROUTE

CLIFF EROSION

MAP 47

46

TO BROAD HAVEN

0   ¼ mile

0   APPROX SCALE   500 metres

50 – 60 MINS FROM BENCH, MAP 46

50 – 60 MINS TO BENCH, MAP 46

NOLTON HAVEN

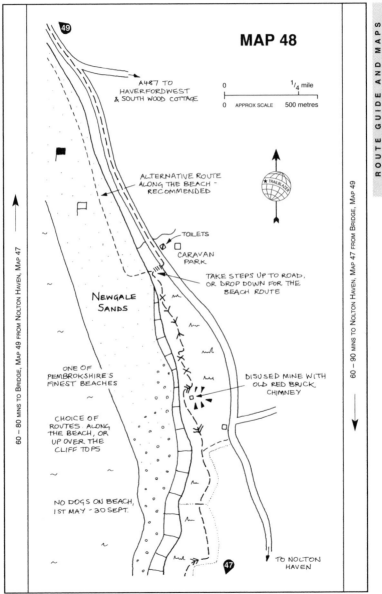

ROUTE GUIDE AND MAPS

ROUTE GUIDE AND MAPS

49

MAP 48

A487 TO
HAVERFORDWEST
& SOUTH WOOD COTTAGE

0   1/4 mile

0   APPROX SCALE   500 metres

ALTERNATIVE ROUTE
ALONG THE BEACH -
RECOMMENDED

TRAILBLAZER

TOILETS

CARAVAN
PARK

TAKE STEPS UP TO ROAD,
OR DROP DOWN FOR THE
BEACH ROUTE

NEWGALE
SANDS

ONE OF
PEMBROKSHIRE'S
FINEST BEACHES

DISUSED MINE WITH
OLD RED BRICK
CHIMNEY

CHOICE OF
ROUTES. ALONG
THE BEACH, OR
UP OVER THE
CLIFF TOPS

NO DOGS ON BEACH,
1ST MAY - 30 SEPT.

47

TO NOLTON
HAVEN

60 – 80 MINS TO BRIDGE, MAP 49 FROM NOLTON HAVEN, MAP 47

60 – 90 MINS TO NOLTON HAVEN, MAP 47 FROM BRIDGE, MAP 49

which could prove tricky to negotiate if the tide's in. As it is close on two miles (3km) of walking it's a good idea to walk close to the sea where the sand is damper and firmer. The village of **Newgale** lies at the far northern end of the beach.

NEWGALE (NÎWGWL)   MAP 49

This is one of the most popular spots for surfers which is not surprising considering it has two miles of immaculate beach continually pounded by Atlantic surf. The village itself is just a collection of houses stretched along the northern end of the beach and up the hill.

Services

There is a **phone box** next to the Duke of Edinburgh pub on the seafront. If you want to try your hand at surfing, tuition is available as well as wetsuit and board hire from **Newsurf** (see box below). They also have **hot showers** for their customers.

The **Puffin Shuttle bus** stops here as does Richards Brothers/Acorn No 411 service; see public transport map and table, pp39-41, for details.

Where to stay and eat

Behind the Duke of Edinburgh is *Newgale Camping Site* (☎ 01437-710253, 🖳 www .newgalecampingsite.co.uk; Mar-Oct) which charges £5 per person; they don't take bookings.

Newgale YMCA (Map 49a, p150; ☎ 01437-720959, 🖳 info@newgaleymca.co .uk, 46 beds), about 45 minutes to an hour from the coast path, two miles (3km) north of Newgale, was the first hostel in the YHA

to be awarded five stars but it is is now in partnership with YMCA Wales.

For most of the year it only accepts group bookings but from June to August individuals can stay here (£14.95/11.95 adult/child for self-catering; £18.85/15.85 for B&B, and £28.60/25.60 for B&B, an evening meal and a packed lunch).

They also offer a large number of outdoor activities, both land and water based, from £35 per half day.

To find it, continue along the coast path from Newgale to the small but deep valley of Cwm Mawr. Here you need to leave the coast path by following the public footpath up to the main A487 road at Penycwm. Cross the road and follow the lane to Rhydygele (signposted for Newgale YMCA). Turn left at Rhydygele and after 200 yards turn left again to reach the hostel.

Some distance back from the seafront road on Woodhill Rise is *South Wood Cottage* (off Map 48, p147; ☎ 01437-710620; 1D) which charges £27.50 per person in its only room.

For a substantial meal try the *Duke of Edinburgh* (☎ 01437-720586, daily noon-3pm, 6-9pm), the pub on the front.

Sands Café (☎ 01437-729222, 9.30am-5pm daily) has a variety of snacks, sandwiches and all-day breakfasts; it's the blue building on the corner across the bridge.

❏ Surfing

Some of the best surfing in Britain can be found at places like Broad Haven and Newgale as the uninterrupted swell from the Atlantic comes rolling in. Even if you have never caught a wave before there are a number of patient instructors who will try to get you standing up on that board in the space of a day.

Newsurf (☎ 01437-721398, 🖳 www.newsurf.co.uk), at Newgale filling station, specializes in surfing tuition and surfboard and wetsuit hire. **West Wales Wind Surf and Sailing** (see p132) in Dale offers half-day courses in surfing, windsurfing, canoeing and sailing with equipment hire too.

Alternatively try **TYF** (🖳 www.tyf.com), which has branches in St David's (see p157) and Tenby (see p76). They also have equipment for hire and offer safe tuition in windsurfing, canoeing, sailing and coasteering (see box p83).

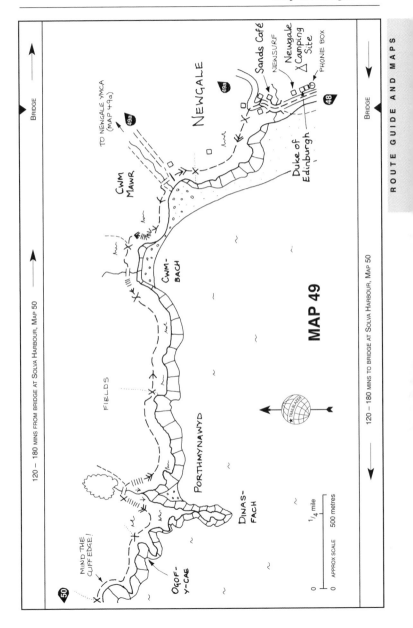

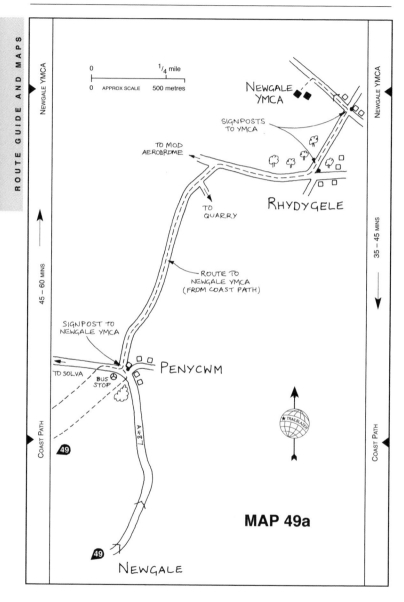

ROUTE GUIDE AND MAPS

NEWGALE YMCA

0   ¼ mile

0   APPROX SCALE   500 metres

NEWGALE
YMCA

SIGNPOSTS
TO YMCA

TO MOD
AERODROME

RHYDYGELE

TO
QUARRY

NEWGALE YMCA

35 – 45 MINS

45 – 60 MINS

ROUTE TO
NEWGALE YMCA
(FROM COAST PATH)

SIGNPOST TO
NEWGALE YMCA

TO SOLVA

BUS
STOP

PENYCWM

★ TRAILBLAZER

COAST PATH

COAST PATH

49

A487

MAP 49a

49

NEWGALE

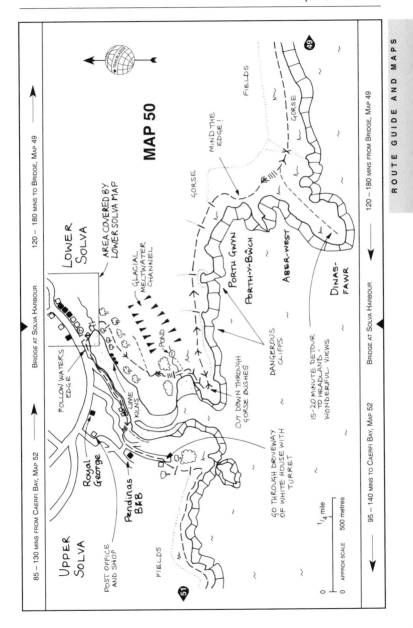

NEWGALE TO CAERFAI BAY (FOR ST DAVID'S)   MAPS 49-52

These **nine miles** (**14km, 3½-4½hrs**) begin with some very strenuous terrain just north of Newgale but become somewhat less arduous once past Solva.

From Newgale the path climbs up a very steep hillside and then drops all the way down the other side into **Cwm Mawr**, a small, deep valley. For Newgale YMCA (see p148) follow the public path up the valley to the road.

Those sticking to the coast path continue over some more tough cliffs, the path eventually settling down somewhat following a high cliff top before dropping into another small valley and passing the rocky promontory of **Dinas-Fach**.

The scenery is quite magnificent along this stretch and at **Dinas-Fawr** you can take the short detour to the end of the headland for great views along the coast. Ahead you can see the southern tip of Ramsey Island while back the way you came are the high cliffs that you have just come over and the sweeping sands at Newgale. Add 15 to 20 minutes to your time if you choose to explore the Dinas-Fawr headland. Follow the line of the cliffs all the way to Solva Harbour and the beautiful village of **Solva**.

SOLVA (SOLFACH)

Solva is probably the prettiest village on the coast path. It is worth keeping a couple of hours spare to stop for lunch here or, even better, to spend the night.

The lower village is a line of painted houses tucked below the steep hillside that leads to the little harbour. The claustrophobic nature of this part is due to its situation. It sits in an old **glacial meltwater channel** formed some 10,000 years ago at the end of the last ice age. Melting ice sent torrents of water towards the sea carving out deep gorges. There are many examples of this in Pembrokeshire, often with a small bay or cove at the end, but the one at Solva is one of the finest. In fact there are two here: the second, the southern one, is crossed on the way to the village along the main coast path.

Next to the harbour there are some well-preserved **lime kilns** which can be seen at many of the coves and inlets along the coast.

Services

The prettiest part of the village is Lower Solva which has most of the eating places. There is also a **phone box** and some public **toilets**. There's no tourist office, though the village does boast its own website which is very useful: 🖳 www.solva.net.

The **Puffin Shuttle bus** stops here as does Richards Brothers/Acorn No 411 service; see pp39-41 for details.

Upper Solva, meanwhile, has the **post office** and a small **shop** all in one.

Where to stay

Campers should continue past the village along the coast path for another mile where there is cheap camping at *Naw Ffynnon Campsite* (see Map 51, p154; ☎ 01437-721809). It is set back from the coast so there is a short detour to reach it from the coast path. As an example of their prices, a tent plus two people will cost £8.

In **Lower Solva** there is B&B at *Gamlyn* (☎ 01437-721542, 17 Y Gribin; 1S/1T/1D) which is just off Main St by the river. Beds are from £29 per person.

Alternatively, *Calebs Cottage* (☎ 01437-721737; 🖳 debbiedaniels@beeb .net; 7 Main St, 1S/2D) has rooms for £29.50 per person during the week, or £27.50 if staying for more than one night.

The *Old Printing House* (☎ 01437-721603, 20 Main St, 1T/2D) is a comfortable and very friendly B&B with rooms from £27.50 per person.

A little further up the street at No 10, *Williams' Accommodation* (☎ 01437-729000, 🖳 www.williamsofsolva.com; 4D) is a smart Georgian house with large,

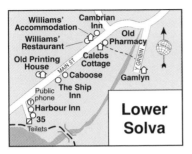

en suite rooms, and period furniture including 'superkingsized' beds. All this doesn't come cheap, however, with rooms starting at £35/pp.

In **Upper Solva** (Map 50, p151) the *Royal George* (☎ 01437-720002, 13 High St, 1T/2D/1F) offers en suite B&B for £35/pp. *Pendinas B&B* (☎ 01437-721283, 💻 www.pendinas.co.uk, 2S/2D) has single rooms (that aren't en suite) at £25, and doubles (that are) at £27. It can be found by leaving the path where it joins the track above the harbour. Access is on St Brides View, not the road the path goes along.

Where to eat
In **Lower Solva** *Harbour Inn* (☎ 01437-720013, food daily 12-3pm, 6-9pm) is where its name suggests. It's a lovely spot with tables out by the river and good bar food as well as some great local seafood and a carvery Sunday lunch. Next door, and actually the first place you come to in the village, is the smart new *35* (☎ 01437-729236; daily 11am-5pm), serving sandwiches and simple meals.

The *Old Printing House* (see opposite) has a smart restaurant in the 'olde worlde' vein. Open daily, all day from April to October only, they do good home-cooked food and are very proud of their herbal teas. All the food is guaranteed to be of local origin.

Virtually opposite, *Caboose* (☎ 01437-720503, daily 10.30am-4pm, to 6pm in summer; 11 Main St) a colourful place with a good vegetarian and gluten-free selection and its own riverside garden; the kedgeree (£6.95) is particularly tasty and they make their own preserves and chutneys.

A little further along the street is the *Old Pharmacy* (☎ 01437-720005; 💻 www .theoldpharmacy.co.uk, 5 Main St, daily 5.30pm to late). A blackboard outside crows about its recommendations in every *Good Food Guide* since 1999; these are deserved and it serves some great local seafood dishes including crab and lobster as well as some tasty vegetarian options. *Williams' Restaurant* (☎ 01437-720802; 💻 www.williamsofsolva.com, 12 Main St, open Wed-Sat from 7pm) is housed in an old warehouse and serves a wide variety of high-quality food.

Up by the bridge is the *Cambrian Inn* (☎ 01437-721210, food served daily 8am-10pm, extended opening hours in summer) with good food including some excellent roast lamb and beef, both sourced locally. It's often very popular so it's worth booking in advance.

In **Upper Solva** there's some great – and cheaper – food at the *Royal George* (see Map 50, p151; ☎ 01437-720002, daily 6-9pm, Sat/Sun also 12-2pm), particularly recommended is the sea bass, which at £10.95 was one of the best-value fish dishes on the route.

From Solva the rest of this stage is quite straightforward, following the obvious path along the cliff edge. The cliffs become less high but no less spectacular as you approach **Caerbwdi Bay** passing through slopes of bracken, around a low headland to **Caerfai Bay**. Take care of the low but precipitous cliffs immediately to the left.

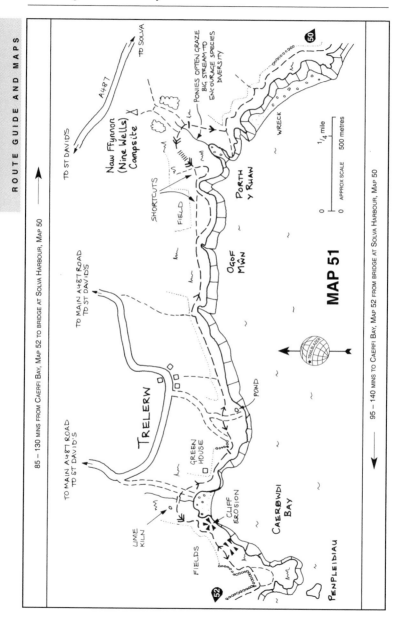

MAP 51

85 – 130 MINS FROM CAERFI BAY, MAP 52 TO BRIDGE AT SOLVA HARBOUR, MAP 50

95 – 140 MINS TO CAERFAI BAY, MAP 52 FROM BRIDGE AT SOLVA HARBOUR, MAP 50

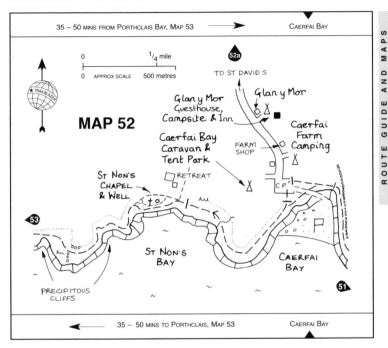

ROUTE GUIDE AND MAPS

CAERFAI BAY   MAP 52
This is the best access point for St David's, only a mile from the coast path. If you need money, more food or new socks St David's is your last chance before Fishguard, 40 miles (64km) away; it's a highlight of the walk and a worthwhile diversion in any case.

Campers are spoilt for choice at caerfai Bay. The biggest of the three campsites is the *Caerfai Bay Caravan and Tent Park* (☎ 01437-720274, 🖥 www.caerfaibay.co.uk; Mar-Nov). It has a camping ground with showers and a laundrette. Prices start at £12.50 in high season plus £4.25 per extra adult. On the other side of the lane and a lit-

tle further up the hill is *Caerfai Farm* (☎ 01437-720548, 🖥 www.cawscaerfai.co.uk; June-Sep) with its own campsite (£6.50/pp) as well as a **farm shop** selling their organic products including delicious cheese and a limited stock of other foods.

A little further on *Glan y Mor Guesthouse & Campsite* (☎ 01437-721788, 🖥 www.glan-y-mor.co.uk, 3D/3F en suite) has doubles from £30/pp, while family rooms are £70 for two sharing (with any extra people charged at £25). The camping pitches are from £8 plus £4 per person. They also have a **bar** and **restaurant** open daily 12noon to late.

❏ **Important note – walking times**
Unless otherwise specified, **all times in this book refer only to the time spent walking**. You will need to add 20-30% to allow for rests, photography, checking the map, drinking water etc. When planning the day's hike count on 5-7 hours' actual walking.

ROUTE GUIDE AND MAPS

ST DAVID'S (TYDDEWI)   MAP 52a

St David's is the smallest city in Britain, qualifying for this grand status thanks to its wonderful cathedral; to come here and not visit **St David's Cathedral** (see box below) is like going to Paris and not seeing the Eiffel Tower. Guided tours (☎ 01437-720691) are available.

To call St David's a city seems to paint an unfair picture of the place. It is really somewhere between a big village and a small town with a definite lazy air pervading the sleepy lanes. In the quieter months the croaking of the ravens in the trees in Cross Sq can sometimes be the only sign of life. Summer is a different matter as hundreds come to this remote pilgrimage site.

You can book a boat trip around the RSPB reserve of Ramsey Island or take a trip to see whales and dolphins with

---

❏ St David and the cathedral

St David was one of a number of Celtic saints from the 6th century and is now the patron saint of Wales. He was born at St Non's (a village named after his mother), where the chapel and the holy well (see Map 52, p155) can be seen just off the coast path to the south of the city. As a missionary his influence was such that the city which now bears his name became an important pilgrimage site and still is to this day.

The cathedral was built on the site of St David's monastery and you can still see a casket in the Holy Trinity Chapel which is purported to contain the bones of both St Justinian and St David himself. The cathedral has had a turbulent history. During the 10th and 11th centuries the Vikings regularly raided it and even killed two of the serving bishops in 999 and again in 1080.

The present-day cathedral came into being in 1181 but was all but destroyed by parliamentary soldiers in 1648. Over the years it has been restored to more than its former glory with the 12th-century nave the oldest part of the building. The fantastic 16th-century Irish oak ceiling is testament to the earthquake of 1247 which caused the western wall of the nave to lean outwards.

Entrance to the cathedral is gained via the **Porth y Twr**, the 14th-century gateway which sits at the top of the steps above the cathedral. The current bells of the cathedral, which were hung in the 1930s, are somewhat surprisingly found here, because it was feared the cathedral tower could collapse with the weight if they were hung there.

One of the original mediaeval bells can still be seen in the permanent **exhibition** (Mon-Sat 8am-6pm, Sun 12.45-5.45pm; £1), also in the gateway, while through another of the gateway's doors is the **Lapidarium**, housing a number of stone treasures including another example of a ring-cross stone, similar to the one that stands in the wall by the National Trust office at Martin's Haven (see p133).

Round the back of the cathedral are the remains of the **Bishop's Palace** (☎ 01437-720517; daily 9.30am-6pm; £2.90 adults, £2.50 concessions). Largely constructed by Bishop Henry de Gower (1328-47), the palace, with its arcaded parapets, state rooms and an impressive Great Hall complete with intact wheel window, speaks eloquently of the wealth and luxury that the early bishops enjoyed – a far cry, it must be said, from the frugal lifestyle of St David himself!

It is well worth trying to catch the atmospheric sound of the bells ringing out across the dell. The local bell ringers practise their pealing on Wednesdays and Fridays between 7.45 and 9pm. For something even more moving try getting a ticket for the Cathedral Festival of Classical Music which is held over a ten-day period at the end of May and beginning of June each year. The acoustics of the building make for an unforgettable concert.

❑ **Ramsey Island**

Ramsey Island is the most northerly of the Pembrokeshire Islands and is another important wildlife reserve managed by the RSPB. It is a vital seal breeding area. The fluffy, white and grey seal pups can be seen in late summer and autumn on the rocky beaches around the island. Like the other islands further south there are thousands of seabirds breeding on the cliffs including puffins and manx shearwaters. In Ramsey Sound you can take a boat ride over 'The Bitches', an unusual phenomenon where the confluence of two currents creates churning rapids in the middle of the sea.

Thousand Islands Expeditions (☎ 01437-721721, 🖥 www.thousandislands .co.uk) offer a number of trips from exploration of the sea caves in a jet boat to fishing for mackerel and pollack. They also land on the island and run wildlife excursions; prices start from £15, with discounts for RSPB members.

Voyages of Discovery (☎ 01437-721911, freephone 0800-854367, 🖥 www .ramseyisland.co.uk) offer trips around the island for £22, or a longer voyage to North Bishop Island to view the puffin colonies and watch the shearwaters migrating. Or you can take their North Coast Explorer that takes you around the northern shores of Pembrokeshire – it's a great way to explore many of the coves and beaches that are inaccessible when walking on the coat path. They also run a popular whale and dolphin watch. Departures are from St Justinian's (see Map 54, p163).

Voyages of Discovery or with **Thousand Islands Expeditions**, who actually land on the island. For more information on Ramsey Island and boat trips there see box above.

Services

As mentioned before, once past St David's you won't find another shop or bank until Fishguard (40 miles, 64km away) so think carefully about what you will need for the next few days.

The **tourist information centre** (TIC; ☎ 01437-720392, 🖥 enquiries@stdavids .pembrokeshire.org.uk; daily 9.30am-5.30pm) is also the new **National Park Information Centre**. If you are coming up the lane from Caerfai Bay you will see the rather impressive glass-fronted TIC on the left where the lane joins the main road entering St David's. There are also public **toilets** and **phone boxes** here.

Cross Sq is the hub of the city. There are a number of **banks** around Cross Sq including HSBC and Lloyds, both of which boast cashpoints, and a **chemist** for any blister problems. The **post office** (☎ 01437-720283; shop open Mon-Sat 7.15am-5.30pm, Sun 7.30am-12.30pm) and main **supermarket**, CK's Foodstore (Mon-Sat 7am-10pm, Sun 10am-4pm) meanwhile,

are on New St, just a short walk away. For **Internet access** visit The Bench (see p160) on High Street, which is pricey (£1 for 20 mins, £2.75 per hour) but the connection is fast. The tourist office also offers internet facilities and it's slightly cheaper too at £1 for 30 mins.

Just off Cross Sq, a good place to replace any holey socks or buy any camping equipment is **TYF Outdoor** (☎ 01437-721611, 🖥 www.tyf.com, 1 High St). This is also the place to go for an adrenaline rush since they run sessions on a variety of outdoor activities from surfing (see box p148) and canoeing to climbing and coasteering (see box p83).

Transport

St David's is well served in terms of **buses** as it is on the route for both the Puffin Shuttle Bus, the Strumble Shuttle and the Celtic Coaster. The No 411 (Richards/Acorn) also stops here. There are stops on New St, Goat St and at Grove Car Park and City Hall. For further information see the public transport map and table on pp39-41.

For a **taxi** try Frank (☎ 01437-721731), Tony (☎ 01437-720931), Bob (☎ 01437-720987) or Rob (☎ 01348-837733).

Where to stay

Thanks to the city's fame as a popular tourist and pilgrimage site St David's is full of places to stay. Just off the High St on Anchor Drive is *The Waterings* (☎ 01437-720876, 🖳 www.waterings.co.uk; 3D or T/2F all en suite), which has a mix of twin, double and family rooms, and charges from £40 per person.

For a place with more character the friendly little *Pen Albro* (☎ 01437-721865, 1S/1T/1D), 18 Goat St, offers very comfortable beds for just £20 per person and a hearty breakfast to boot. It's also just a short stagger away from the best pub in town.

On the High St try either *Bryn Awel* (☎ 01437-720082, 🖳 www.brynawel-bb.co.uk; 3D), which has en suite – if slightly cramped – rooms from £30/pp, or the smart *Coach House* (☎ 01437-720632, 🖳 coach_house 15@yahoo.co.uk; 1T/1D/1F), at No 15, which charges the same; they also boast a delightful little cottage round the back which you can stay in for £70 per night. Alternatively *Grove Hotel* (☎ 01437-720341, 🖳 www.thegrovestdavids.co.uk; 1T/4D/2F all en suite), which charges from £40 per person (£50 single occupancy).

More beds can be found along Nun St: *Y-Glennydd Hotel* (☎ 01437-720576, 🖳 www.yglennydd.co.uk) at No 51, 2S/1T/5D/2F) has affordable rooms from £30 per person, or £38 for a single; and *Y-Gorlan* (☎ 01437-720837, 🖳 www.stdavids.co.uk/gorlan, 1S/2D/1T/1F en suite), at No 77, has rooms from £36/pp. Also on Nun St are, at No 7, *Glendower Guesthouse* (☎ 01437-721650, 4D/4T or F) which has B&B from £30 per person; while further down the road, at No 43, is *Alandale Guesthouse* (☎ 01437-720404, 🖳 www.stdavids.co.uk/guesthouse/alandale.htm, 1S/3D/1T) which has en suite rooms from £35 per person.

Sitting all on its own in a quiet location south-west of the city on the lane to Porthclais, the smart *Ramsey House* (☎ 01437-720321, 🖳 www.ramseyhouse.co.uk, Lower Moor, 3D/2T en suite) has beds starting from £35 per person.

If money is no obstacle and you fancy the height of luxury, there's *Warpool Court Hotel* (☎ 01437-720300, 🖳 www.warpoolcourthotel.com; off Goat St) which has 25 rooms. The cheapest single room will set you back around £115, with discounts if you're staying for more than one night.

For a touch of class at a more affordable price go to Cross Sq where the grand *Old Cross Hotel* (☎ 01437-720387, 🖳 www.oldcrosshotel.co.uk, 2S/7T/6D/1F) has en suite rooms from £34 (£38 for a single) per person in low season, rising to £52.50 (£62 single) in high season.

Where to eat

There are all sorts of places to eat in St David's, although many of them can be a bit on the expensive side.

On Cross Sq is one of the cheaper places, *Cartref Restaurant* (☎ 01437-720422, daily 12-2.30pm, 6-9pm; winter times vary), an old yellow and green cottage with a low-slung ceiling. For a full blow-out, try their surf and turf (£11.95), a combination of wholetail scampi and rump steak. They also do some fine curries.

Also on Cross Sq are cheap cakes and sandwiches in the *Square Café* (☎ 01437-720333; daily 10.30am-5pm) at Swn y Don B&B, which doubles as an art gallery.

On the same street, *Jones* (☎ 01437-721001; Mon-Sat 8am-5pm, Sun 9am-5pm) serves up a full Welsh breakfast, while still further up the road is *Cwtch* (☎ 01437-720491; Tue-Sun from 6pm to late) a place that might be short of vowels (the name means 'snug' or 'cosy' in Welsh) but is not short of some delicious meals, including an exquisite fish pie. They charge £20 for two courses, £25 for three.

At the top of the street virtually opposite the tourist office, *Grove Hotel* (see column opposite; daily 12-3pm, 6-9pm) offers fair bar meals and finer fare in their Conservatory restaurant, though the menu was being revamped at the time of writing.

Just as swish, on Nun St, is *Lawton's at No 16* (☎ 01437-720341, 🖳 www.lawtonsatno16.co.uk; opening times vary throughout the year but they usually open Mon-Sat from 6pm), serving some rather unusual dishes including tasty partridge with a rice, walnut, pistachio and raisin

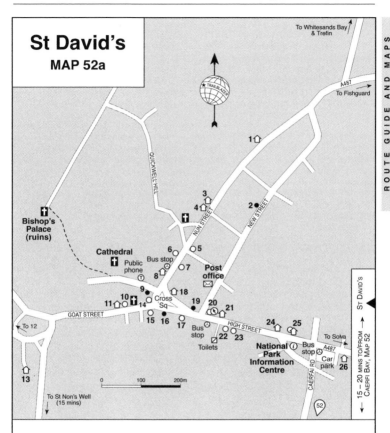

Map 52a — St David's

Where to stay
1 Y-Gorlan
3 Y Glennydd Hotel
4 Alandale Guesthouse
8 Glendower Guesthouse
11 Pen Albro
12 Ramsey House
13 Warpool Court Hotel
18 Old Cross Hotel
21 Coach House
24 Bryn Awel
25 Grove Hotel
26 The Waterings

Where to eat
5 Morgan's Brasserie

6 The Sampler
7 Lawton's at No. 16
10 Farmers Arms
14 Cartref Restaurant
15 Square Café
17 Dyfed Café
20 The Bench
22 Jones' Café
23 Cwtch
25 Conservatory Restaurant

Other
2 CK's Foodstore
9 Thousand Island Expeditions
16 Chemist
19 TYF & Voyages of Discovery

ROUTE GUIDE AND MAPS

stuffing (£18), while nearby the long-estab-lished *Morgan's Brasserie* (☎ 01437-720508, every evening except Tue, 6.30-9pm; open for lunch out of season on Fri, Sat & Sun; 20 Nun St) changes the menu according to the season. Their rack of spring lamb in a redcurrant and balsamic reduction (£19.50) is extremely tasty.

For good pub grub head down Goat St to one of the best pubs in town, the *Farmers Arms* (☎ 01437-720328; noon-2.30pm, 6-9pm), which often serves a fine fish chowder.

A lovely little coffee shop is *The Sampler* (☎ 01437-720757, 17 Nun St, Mar-Oct, Mon-Thur & Sat from 10.30am-5pm) with friendly service and an open fire. Welsh cakes are only 55p or there are fill-ing jacket potatoes from £3.50, toasties

from £3.50. **Fish and chips** to take away can be found at *Dyfed Café* (☎ 01437-720250; Mon, Wed 8am-2pm, Tue, Thur and Fri to 5pm, Sat to 4pm), opposite the TYF outdoor shop.

No summary of the St David's' food scene would be complete, however, with-out mentioning *The Bench* (☎ 01437-721778; Mon-Sat 9am-late Sun 9am-5pm), a wonderfully friendly and busy café-cum-restaurant. Open during the day for snacks including some delicious paninis, hot drinks and their award-winning ice cream, after 6pm they serve some surprisingly sophisticated meals including a delicious Dover sole in mornay sauce (£13.50); while their rhubarb crumble is the perfect way to round off any meal.

CAERFAI BAY TO WHITESANDS BAY   MAPS 52-55

This is a wonderful part of the coast. It is **eight and a half miles (14km, 3-4hrs)**, all of them beautiful, to yet another of Pembrokeshire's fantastic sandy beaches at Whitesands Bay. As the path ventures further west the scenery gets progressively wilder with a real sense of isolation out on the windswept head-lands by Ramsey Sound. From Caerfai Bay the path follows steep vegetated slopes to St Non's Bay, named after St David's mother. Here, just off the coast path, you can see the remains of **St Non's Chapel**, the birthplace of the patron saint and the **Holy Healing Well**. More low cliffs lead to the beautiful little har-bour of **Porthclais** where you can see more fine examples of some lime kilns.

At the wild and lonely **Porthlysgi Bay** a footpath heads north to the camp-site at Pen-cnwc.

PORTHCLAIS & PORTHLYSGI BAY
MAP 53

This lonely stretch of wild coast is dotted with a number of coves and small bays with little in the way of accommodation. However, there are a few farms that offer camping and one or two B&Bs. The Celtic Coaster **bus** stops at Porthclais Harbour; see pp39-41 for details.

At **Porthclais** there is a National Trust **kiosk** and **toilets** as well as a **campsite** at *Porthclais Farm* (☎ 01437 720256; 🖳

www.porthclais-farm-campsite.co.uk) just up the road, heading east from the inlet; prices are £6 per adult. Heading the other way, up the road from the inlet, is *Rhos-y-cribed* (☎ 01437-720336) offering camping for £5/pp.

At **Porthlysgi Bay** you can leave the coast path and by heading north for half a mile on the public footpath reach the *Pen-cnwc Campsite* (☎ 01437-720523, Apr-Oct) with prices at £5 per person.

(Opposite) St David's Cathedral with the ruins of the Bishop's Palace beyond. St David was born at St Non's where the spring and well (**bottom right**) have attracted pilgrims for cen-turies. (Photos © Bryn Thomas). **Bottom left**: Cathedral interior. (Photo © Henry Stedman).

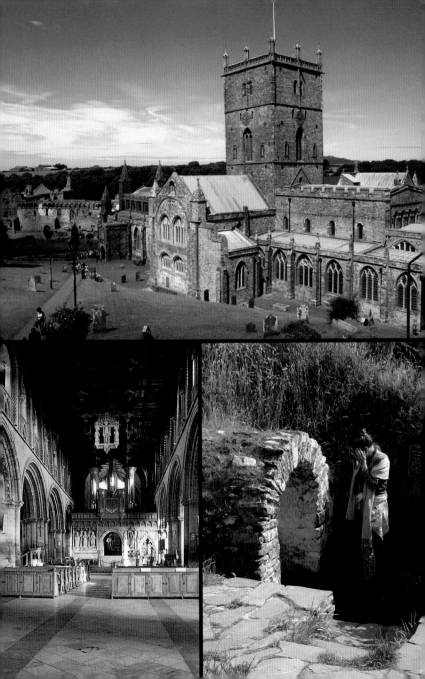

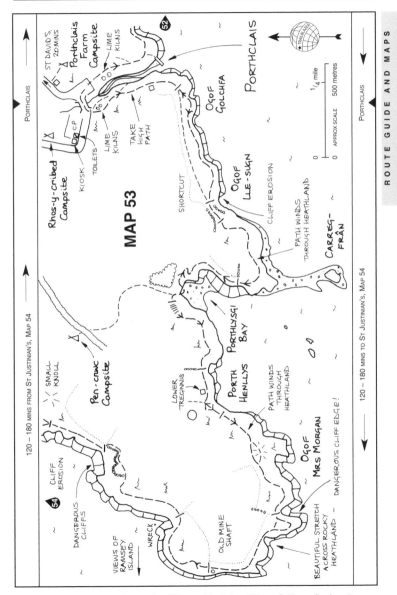

120 – 180 MINS FROM ST JUSTINIAN'S, MAP 54

120 – 180 MINS TO ST JUSTINIAN'S, MAP 54

PORTHCLAIS

PORTHCLAIS

ST DAVID'S 20 MINS

Porthclais Farm Campsite

LIME KILNS

52

PORTHCLAIS

Ogof Golchfa

C.P.

LIME KILNS

TAKE HIGH PATH

Rhos-y-cribed Campsite

KIOSK

TOILETS

MAP 53

Ogof Le-Sugn

CLIFF EROSION

SHORTCUT

PATH WINDS THROUGH HEATHLAND

CARREG-FRÂN

0   ¼ mile
0   500 metres
APPROX SCALE

Pen-cnuc Campsite

SMALL KNOLL

LOWER TREGINNIS

Porthlysgi Bay

PATH WINDS THROUGH HEATHLAND

Porth Henllys

Ogof Mrs Morgan

54

CLIFF EROSION

DANGEROUS CLIFFS

VIEWS OF RAMSEY ISLAND

WRECK

OLD MINE SHAFT

DANGEROUS CLIFF EDGE!

BEAUTIFUL STRETCH ACROSS ROCKY HEATHLAND

(**Opposite**) Fungi flourishing on the cliffs outside Solva. (Photo © Henry Stedman).

ROUTE GUIDE AND MAPS

Staying on the coast path the terrain becomes progressively more barren and wild. Rocky knolls decorate the headland around the tiny cove of **Ogof Mrs Morgan** and low but precipitous cliffs form a twisting savage coastline. Above Ramsey Sound there are fine views over to Ramsey Island. Keep an eye out for seals on the shoreline and schools of dolphins and porpoises further out.

Once past the lifeboat station at **St Justinian's** take extra care along the level cliff top as the narrow path brushes the edge without warning on a number of occasions.

ST JUSTINIAN'S   MAP 54
There is a summer ferry to Ramsey Island (see box p157) and inland there's **camping** along the lane towards St David's at *Rhosson Ganol* (☎ 01437-720361; Apr-Oct), which charges from £5 per person. The **Celtic Coaster** bus stops by the car park; see public transport map and table on pp39-41 for details.

PORTHSELAU   MAP 54
At Porthselau Beach, at the southern end of Whitesands Bay, there is a large caravan and **campsite** at *Pencarnan Farm* (☎ 01437-720324, 🖳 www.pembrokeshire-camping.co.uk, open all year) in a wonderful location overlooking the bay. They charge £11 per person but only take bookings of a week or more during school holidays.

Moving on around the headland the sands of **Whitesands Bay** come into view with the small rocky hills of **Carn Llidi** (see Map 56, p165; where there's a small Neolithic burial chamber) and Carn Perfedd behind.

WHITESANDS BAY (PORTH MAWR)
MAP 55, p164
At the car park by **Whitesands Bay** there is a **phone box**, public **toilets** and a **drinking-water tap** but little else. Those staying at the youth hostel will find a small **shop** at the reception desk. The Celtic Coaster **bus** stops by the beach; see pp39-41 for details.

Despite the name *St David's Youth Hostel* (☎ 0870-770 6042, bookings ☎ 0870-770 8868, 🖳 StDavids@yha.org.uk; Apr-Oct) is not in St David's but here above Whitesands Bay! It's in a great spot below the craggy hill called Carn Llidi in an old farmhouse. Accommodation is in the superbly renovated cowshed – which is a lot more salubrious than it sounds! – with 40

beds at £11 for members. The hostel is self-catering only. To reach it follow the lane up from the car park, turn left by the campsite, bear right then left to Upper Porthmawr and follow the footpath around the hillside.

Whitesands Beach Campsite (☎ 01437-721472; Apr-Oct) is on the left as you walk up from the car park. Prices are from £5 to £7 depending on the size of your tent. *Craig-y-Mor* (☎ 01437-720431, 🖳 www.stdavidsbandb.co.uk; 1T/1S/1D) is a lonely looking house by a golf course with en suite rooms charging £50 per person in high season.

The only place to get **food** is the large *café* in the surf shop at the top of Whitesands Bay car park.

WHITESANDS BAY TO TREFIN   MAPS 55-60

Once again the rugged coastline of the St David's peninsula makes this a wonderful but tough **eleven miles (18km, 5-6hrs)**. From the car park the path climbs up above cliffs and back down to the sandy bay at **Porthmelgan**. For people staying at the youth hostel there is a more direct route from the hostel that avoids having to return to the car park (see Map 55, p164).

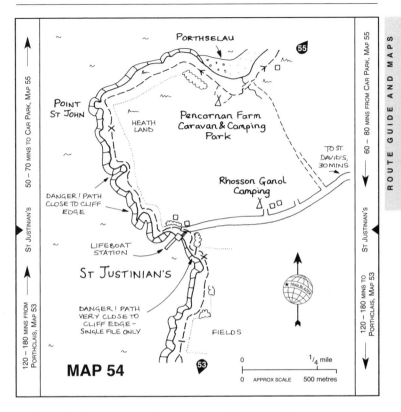

From Porthmelgan the path crosses beautiful slopes of heather to the craggy **St David's Head** jutting into the Atlantic. The path can be rather indistinct in places, crossing rocky heathland to some old fields enclosed by stone walls, though as long as you keep the sea roughly to your left you can't go too far wrong. The route takes a sharp right at **Penllechwen Head** and skirts the pretty coves and bays that make up the coastline until it reaches **Carn Penberry** hill. This small hill is one of several igneous intrusions that crop up on this section of the coastline. Unfortunately, it's also one of the few that you can't walk around; thus for the walker the only way past this obstacle is to climb over its shoulder, rather than around it.

About two miles (3km) from Carn Penberry the path drops down into a small gorge the other side of which there is a sign and footpath leading to Pwll Caerog Campsite & Bunk Barn (see p168; 500 metres from the coast path).

(cont'd on p168)

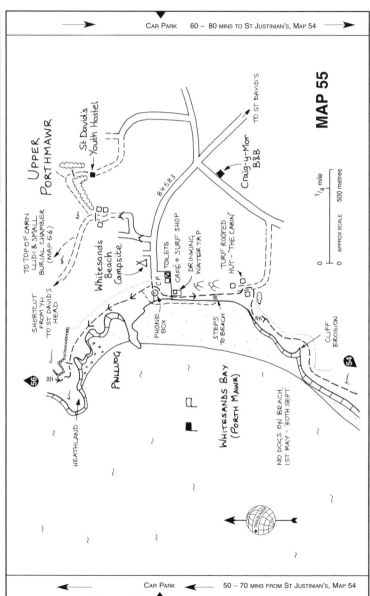

MAP 55

St David's Youth Hostel

UPPER PORTHMAWR

Craig-y-Mor B&B

TO ST DAVID'S

B4583

¼ mile

500 metres

0   APPROX SCALE   0

TO TOP OF CARN LLIDI & SMALL BURIAL CHAMBER (MAP 56)

Whitesands Beach Campsite

TOILETS

CAFÉ + SURF SHOP

DRINKING WATER TAP

TURF ROOFED HUT – 'THE CABIN'

SHORTCUT FROM YH TO ST DAVID'S HEAD

C.P.

PHONE BOX

STEPS TO BEACH

CLIFF EROSION

54

56

PWLLDDOG

HEATHLAND

WHITESANDS BAY (PORTH MAWR)

NO DOGS ON BEACH, 1ST MAY – 30TH SEPT

TRAILBLAZER

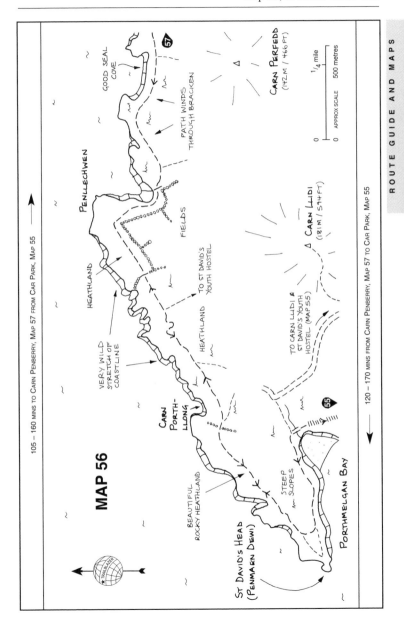

MAP 56

105 – 160 MINS TO CARN PENBERRY, MAP 57 FROM CAR PARK, MAP 55

120 – 170 MINS FROM CARN PENBERRY, MAP 57 TO CAR PARK, MAP 55

GOOD SEAL COVE

57

CARN PERFEDD
(142 M / 466 FT)

PATH WINDS THROUGH BRACKEN

PENLLECHWEN

FIELDS

TO ST DAVID'S YOUTH HOSTEL

HEATHLAND

HEATHLAND

VERY WILD STRETCH OF COASTLINE

CARN LLIDI
(181 M / 594 FT)

TO CARN LLIDI & ST DAVID'S YOUTH HOSTEL (MAP 55)

CARN PORTH- LLONG

55

BEAUTIFUL ROCKY HEATHLAND

STEEP SLOPES

ST DAVID'S HEAD (PENMAEN DEWI)

PORTHMELGAN BAY

0   1/4 mile
APPROX SCALE
0   500 metres

ROUTE GUIDE AND MAPS

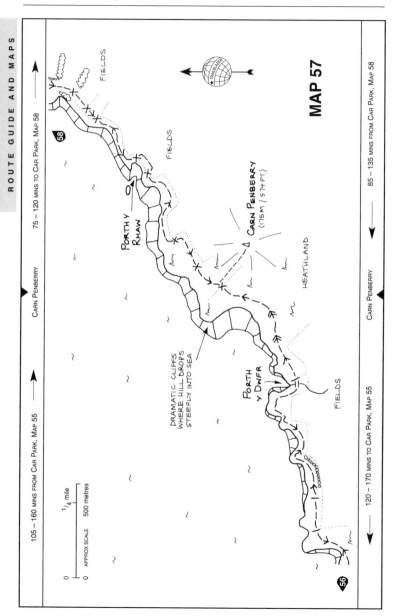

MAP 57

105 – 160 MINS FROM CAR PARK, MAP 55 ⟶

75 – 120 MINS TO CAR PARK, MAP 58

CARN PENBERRY

85 – 135 MINS FROM CAR PARK, MAP 58

120 – 170 MINS TO CAR PARK, MAP 55

CARN PENBERRY

58

CARN PENBERRY
(175M / 574 FT)

FIELDS

FIELDS

HEATHLAND

PORTHY RHAW

PORTH Y DWFR

DRAMATIC CLIFFS
WHERE HILL DROPS
STEEPLY INTO SEA

FIELDS

56

¼ mile

APPROX SCALE   500 metres

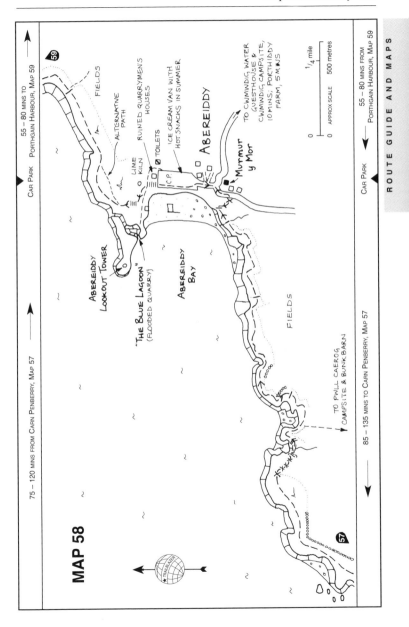

❏ **A lost industry**
A number of ruins can be seen around Abereiddy and Porthgain, evidence of a once-thriving industry. From around 1840 until the 1930s slate, brick and stone were quarried on the cliff tops between the two villages where the old slag-heaps and evidence of the tramway, which carried the slate from the quarry at Abereiddy to the harbour at Porthgain, can still be seen. At Porthgain you can also see the restored brickworks by the tiny harbour.

Look out too for the flooded slate quarry known as 'The Blue Lagoon' as you climb up onto the cliffs above Abereiddy and the ruins of the quarrymen's houses by Abereiddy Bay. The sad remains of these houses which were built in the 1840s are testament to the great storm of January 14, 1938, when the swell of the sea severely damaged five of the homes. The storm damage and an ensuing typhoid epidemic effectively brought the local slate quarry industry to an end.

Yet even to this day the product of the quarry can be seen in Porthgain. One of the boats carrying slate from Porthgain sank in Ramsey Sound. About 100 years later the boat was found on the seabed and the slate was recovered to re-roof the houses of Porthgain.

At the beach of **Abereiddy** you can see the remains of the old quarrymen's houses, destroyed by floods in the 1920s (see box above). As you climb up above the bay you will see **The Blue Lagoon**, a flooded quarry, to the left.

ABEREIDDY   **MAP 58, p167**
Don't expect to find much at this hamlet. In the summer there is usually an ice-cream van in the beach car park selling **drinks and hot snacks**, as well as ice creams. At the far end of the car park is a public **toilet**.

The **Strumble Shuttle** bus (summer only) stops in the car park; see public transport map and table, pp39-41 for details.
Pwll Caerog Campsite and Bunk Barn (☎ 01348-837405, 🖳 www.celtic-camping.co.uk; Apr-Oct), one mile back along the coast path, is a possible place to stay. A sign indicates the point where you have to leave the coast path to reach it. Beds in the barn, where there are showers and kitchen facilities, cost £10 per person plus £2 for bed linen while the campsite pitches are £10 for a two-man tent (£6 for a one-man tent).

Open in the summer only, *Murmur y Mor Guest House* (☎ 01348-831670, 1D/1T) has beds from £25 per person.

A mile up the hill from the bay is the *Cwmwdig Water Guesthouse* (☎ 01348-831434, 🖳 www.cwmwdigwater.co.uk, 1T/2D/1F) which has B&B in converted farmhouse barns from £27 per person or £33 in an en suite room (Half of the rooms are en suite). They also have a good *restaurant* (food served at 7pm daily except Sat May to Sep) which is open to non-residents; booking is essential.

Next door, *Cwmwdig Campsite* (☎ 01348-831376 before 8pm; Mar-Oct) is run by the Camping and Caravanning Club of Great Britain. Each of the 40 pitches costs from £6.60 per person plus a £6.65 pitch fee for non-members.

To get to Cwmwdig from the coast path climb up the lane for 200 yards. Just past Porthiddy Farm take the public footpath on the right. This takes you up to the guesthouse, a big peach-coloured building by the road junction, and the campsite.

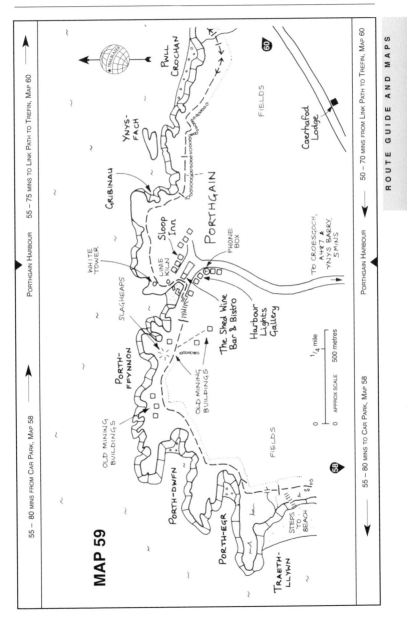

MAP 59

55 – 80 MINS FROM CAR PARK, MAP 58

PORTHGAIN HARBOUR

55 – 75 MINS TO LINK PATH TO TREFIN, MAP 60

55 – 80 MINS TO CAR PARK, MAP 58

PORTHGAIN HARBOUR

50 – 70 MINS FROM LINK PATH TO TREFIN, MAP 60

TRAETH-LLYWN

PORTH-EGR

PORTH-DWFN

PORTH-FFYNNON

OLD MINING BUILDINGS

SLAGHEAPS

WHITE TOWER

LIME KILN

GRIBINAU

YNYS-FACH

PWLL CROCHAN

STEPS TO BEACH

FIELDS

OLD MINING BUILDINGS

The Shed Wine Bar & Bistro

Harbour Lights Gallery

Sloop Inn

PORTHGAIN

PHONE BOX

TO CROESGOCH, A487 & YNYS BARRY, 5 MINS

FIELDS

Caerhafod Lodge

58

60

0   ¼ mile
APPROX SCALE
0   500 metres

The path follows a nice level cliff top around the beautiful beach of **Traeth-Llywn** and past a few coves to arrive at some old quarry buildings, slate slag heaps and evidence of the old mine tramway on the cliffs above the village of **Porthgain**.

PORTHGAIN MAP 59, p169

This is an unusual little place with a great pub, a modern café and an explosion of art galleries. Up on the hill is an old, disused stone quarry that hints at the stone industry of the 19th century. The tiny harbour was used to export stone for building projects elsewhere. Nowadays the village is home to tourists and artists, whose work can often be seen in the **Harbour Lights Gallery**. The **Strumble Shuttle** bus stops by the Sloop Inn; see pp39-41 for details.

The *Sloop Inn* (☎ 01348-831449, 🖳 www.sloop.co.uk) is one of the best pubs on the whole trail. Easily spotted on the far side as you drop down into the village, it usually has a trail of smoke coming from the chimney. It is a lovely rustic old inn dating from 1743. In the past it was, no doubt, a popular haunt for the quarrymen but is now a regular stop-off for coast-path walkers.

The inn does good food daily (breakfast 9.30-11am, lunch 12-2.30pm, dinner 6-9.30pm) and the bar is open daily 9.30am-11pm. All in all, an essential stop on the coast path.

Decent competition for the Sloop is provided by *The Shed Wine Bar & Bistro* (☎ 01348-831518, 🖳 www.theshedporthgain.co.uk; summer daily 10.30am-5pm, Tue-Sun 6pm-late, winter open Fri, Sat & Sun eves subject to number of bookings; booking essential), which was awarded the title of AA Wales Seafood Restaurant of the Year in 2006 – and deservedly so, as this family-run establishment not only cook the fish, they catch it too from their own boat!

Accommodation in Porthgain is thin on the ground. *Ynys Barry* (☎ 01348-831180, 🖳 www.ynysbarry.com; 4D/2T) is a series of holiday cottages and twin or double-room en suite lodges that can be rented for one night for £50 (no reduction for single travellers). Breakfast is not offered, other than fruit and cereal, but as you can have breakfast at the Sloop Inn that's not a problem.

From Porthgain the path follows gentle cliffs to the little bay of **Aber Draw**. This is the first of the access routes to Trefin, climbing up the steep road ahead, but if you're not staying at Caerhafod Lodge (see opposite), a better idea is to continue along the coast path until you see the signpost for the youth hostel – unless since researching this guide it has been removed because the hostel itself has closed. This is the path that takes you into **Trefin**.

TREFIN MAP 60

Trefin (pronounced 'Tre-feen', like 'ravine') is a quiet little village sitting on top of a windswept hill. It feels as if you have stepped back in time when you first set foot in the place and is worth visiting either for a quick pint or an overnight stop.

The best way to get to the village from the coast path is by the footpath from the cliffs at Trwyn Llwyd. Alternatively you can come straight up the steep road from the bay at Aber Draw.

Services

The **post office**, which has rather irregular opening times, is not very obvious. It's the small pebble-dashed bungalow on the left as you enter the village by the steep road from the coast. Be warned that there is no shop in the village.

Buses leave outside Oriel y Felin Gallery Tearooms. Both the Strumble Shuttle and Richards Brothers No 411 service (Mon-Sat only) call in here en route between St David's and Fishguard; for fur-

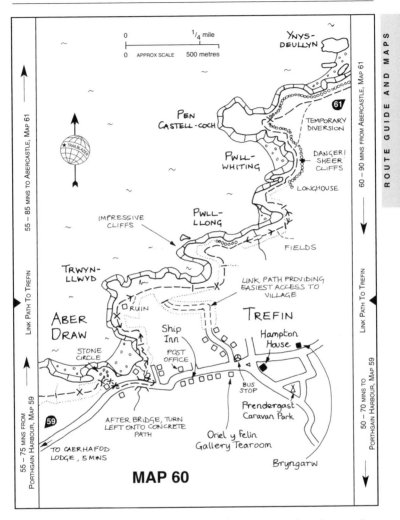

MAP 60

ther details see the public transport map and table, see pp39-41.

Where to stay

Just down the lane from where the former YHA hostel used to be is the *Prendergast Caravan Park* (☎ 01348-831368, 🖥 www

.prendergastcaravanpark.co.uk; open Apr-Sep) which has a **campsite**. Prices start at £9 per night for two adults.

There is a **bunkhouse** near the village of **Llanrhian**; *Caerhafod Lodge* (☎ 01348-837859, 🖥 www.caerhafod.co.uk, open all year) is a wonderful, friendly place with

ROUTE GUIDE AND MAPS

five en suite dormitories and a self-catering kitchen. It has a capacity for 23 people; £13.50 per person. From the point where the coast path joins the road before Trefin, follow the road uphill in the St David's direction; the bunkhouse is about half a mile up the road on the left.

In the centre of the village there is B&B at *Hampton House* (☎ 01348-837701, 📧 viv.kay@virgin.net; 1S/1T/1D) with rooms from £28 per person. *Bryngarw Guest House* (☎ 01348-831211, 🖥 www .bryngarwguesthouse.co.uk, Abercastle Rd, 4D/2T en suite) is a little way out of the village. It has rooms starting at £35 per person, with a £10 surcharge for people on their own.

Where to eat
The *Ship Inn* (☎ 01348-831445, food daily noon-3pm, 6-9pm) is the last place for a pint before Goodwick 19 miles (30km) away. The food's only average, but it's filling.

Despite the loss of the popular Glan-y-mor Gallery Tearooms to Fishguard, the village has not lost out, for in its place has come *Oriel y Felin Gallery and Tearoom* (☎ 01348-837500; 🖥 www.oriel-y-felin .com; Easter-Oct Tue-Sun 11am-5pm), run by friends of the owners of Glan-y-mor. The same winning ingredients are all there: tasty and reasonably priced snacks in a warm and cosy tearoom with lots of local art – paintings, pottery, ceramics and jewellery – decorating the walls and the display cases. A really worthwhile stop.

TREFIN TO PWLL DERI   MAPS 60-63

These **nine and a half miles (15km, 3¹/₂-4¹/₂hrs)** begin by following a beautiful line of snaking cliffs to the hamlet of **Abercastle** sitting at the end of yet another pretty cove. There are no facilities for the walker apart from a public lavatory, though the **Strumble Shuttle** bus does stop here; see pp39-41 for details.

Just before Abercastle you should keep an eye out for the stones of **Carreg Sampson** marking the site of a neolithic burial chamber, or *cromlech*, dating back 5000 years. It is only a short detour from the coast path and is the most impressive cromlech on the path. Look out for the signpost just before the coast path drops down the steps to the cove.

From Abercastle the path climbs up through cliff-top fields and past the bay at **Pwllstrodur**. If you want to stop for a dip in the sea the beaches at Abermawr and Aber-Bach are nice enough but it's much better to wait until you get to **Pwllcrochan**. This is a fantastic location for a swim; well sheltered with a backdrop of sheer cliffs. It's all the more interesting because the only way to get to it is by climbing down a rope hanging over a short section of cliff. It's not quite as dangerous as it sounds but you should be careful as you climb down. (Note, this is not an official part of the route, nor is it recommended by the park authorities. As such, the author and publisher accept no responsibility for potential accidents.) Since climbing over cliffs isn't everybody's cup of tea the beach is usually pretty quiet. Look out for the path leading to the rope at the southern end of the bay.

After a swim it's back to the hard grind. The path climbs relentlessly uphill to gain the long ridge leading to Pwll Deri. This rugged ridge of heather and rocky bluffs provides great views of the Pembrokeshire countryside to the east but even more outstanding are the 100-metre (300ft) cliffs, covered in bracken and scrub, which plunge down into the sea. It all culminates in the wonderful circle of cliffs around **Pwll Deri**. If the weather's good, it's worth sitting down on top of the ridge to take in the view.   *(cont'd on p176)*

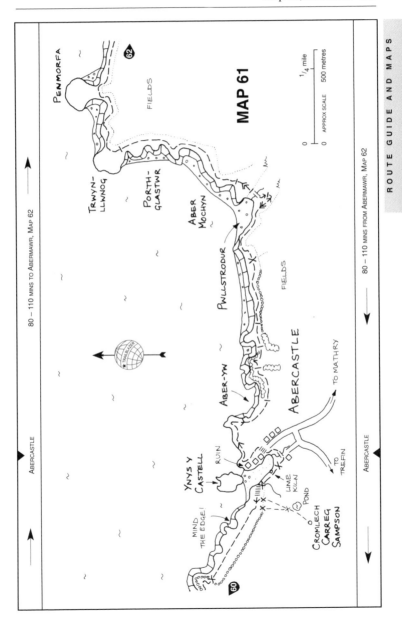

80 – 110 MINS TO ABERMAWR, MAP 62

ABERCASTLE

ABERCASTLE

62

PENMORFA

TRWYN-LLWNOG

PORTH-GLASTWR

ABER MOCHYN

PWLLSTRODUR

FIELDS

FIELDS

ABER-YW

ABERCASTLE

TO MATHRY

TO TREFIN

RUIN

LIME KILN

POND

CROMLECH CARREG SAMPSON

YNYS Y CASTELL

MIND THE EDGE!

60

MAP 61

¼ mile

0   APPROX SCALE
0   500 metres

80 – 110 MINS FROM ABERMAWR, MAP 62

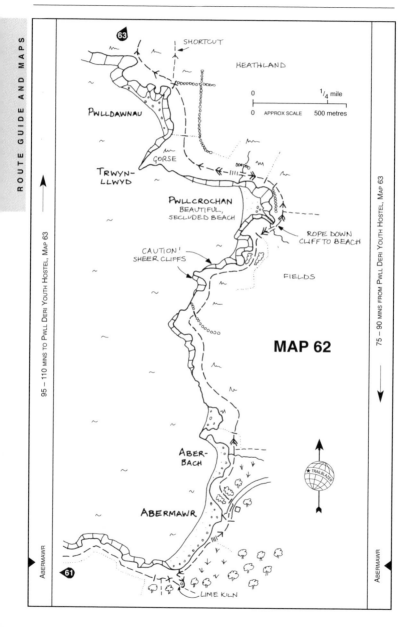

ROUTE GUIDE AND MAPS

63

SHORTCUT

HEATHLAND

0   1/4 mile

0   APPROX SCALE   500 metres

PWLLDAWNAU

GORSE

TRWYN-
LLWYD

PWLLCROCHAN
BEAUTIFUL,
SECLUDED BEACH

ROPE DOWN
CLIFF TO BEACH

CAUTION!
SHEER CLIFFS

FIELDS

MAP 62

ABER-
BACH

★ TRAILBLAZER

ABERMAWR

61

LIME KILN

95 – 110 MINS TO PWLL DERI YOUTH HOSTEL, MAP 63

75 – 90 MINS FROM PWLL DERI YOUTH HOSTEL, MAP 63

ABERMAWR

ABERMAWR

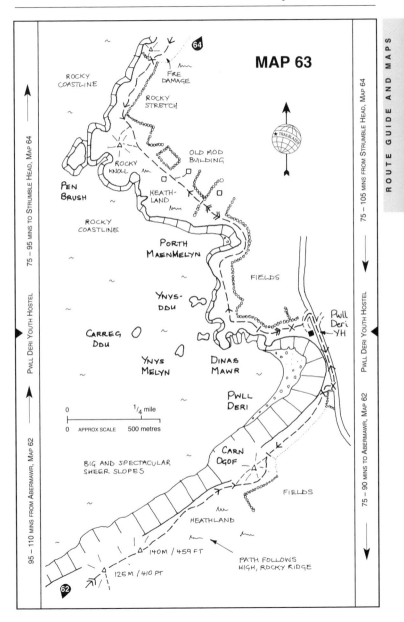

MAP 63

ROCKY
COASTLINE

FIRE
DAMAGE

ROCKY
STRETCH

OLD MOD
BUILDING

ROCKY
KNOLL

PEN
BRUSH

HEATH-
LAND

ROCKY
COASTLINE

PORTH
MAENMELYN

FIELDS

YNYS-
DDU

Pwll
Deri
YH

CARREG
DDU

YNYS
MELYN

DINAS
MAWR

PWLL
DERI

0   ¼ mile

0   APPROX SCALE   500 metres

CARN
OGOF

BIG AND SPECTACULAR
SHEER SLOPES

FIELDS

HEATHLAND

△ 140M / 459 FT

△ 125 M / 410 PT

PATH FOLLOWS
HIGH, ROCKY RIDGE

62

64

★ TRAILBLAZER

75 – 105 MINS FROM STRUMBLE HEAD, MAP 64

75 – 90 MINS TO ABERMAWR, MAP 62

PWLL DERI YOUTH HOSTEL

75 – 95 MINS TO STRUMBLE HEAD, MAP 64

95 – 110 MINS FROM ABERMAWR, MAP 62

PWLL DERI YOUTH HOSTEL

PWLL DERI   MAP 63, p175

Pwll Deri Youth Hostel (☎ 0870-770 6004 for information, ☎ 0870-770 8868 for bookings, Apr-Oct, 31 beds). It is surely one of the most impressive locations for a youth hostel, sitting precariously 125 metres (410ft) above the sea. It can be found just off the lane that skirts the cliff tops. After a hard day's walk, sitting in the conservatory with your dinner admiring the sun setting over the sea is a great way to chill out. On a clear day you can see southern Ireland. The hostel is self-catering only and charges £11 each for members.

PWLL DERI TO FISHGUARD   MAPS 63-68

The coast along these **ten and a half miles (17km, 4-5hrs)** is wild and in places rough going. The cliffs are less sheer and sometimes relatively low but they are rugged and hide countless rocky coves and bays.

The path begins by crossing through wild country of rocky hillocks, grass and heather, passing a barren headland with fine views all around. Parts of the trail here can be boggy when the weather is bad. Just past a narrow cleft in the cliffs the path comes to the car park at **Strumble Head** where the white lighthouse can be seen on the island just off the headland. The path continues through heathland and bracken to **Porthsychan Bay** where a footpath heads inland for the **campsite** at *Fferm Tresinwen* (see below).

STRUMBLE HEAD   MAP 64

The **Strumble Shuttle** bus stops here; see pp39-41 for details.

Three miles (5km) further north along the coast path there is **camping** for a pittance (£4 per night for two people and a tent) on the road inland at *Fferm Tresinwen* (☎ 01348-891238). It can be found by either following the road inland from Strumble Head for about a mile or following the coast path east from Strumble Head as far as Porthsychan Bay where a footpath leads from the coast path to the campsite.

At **Carreg Wastad Point** make sure you take the quick detour to the top of the heathery hill to see the stone commemorating the last invasion of Britain, when a French fleet landed at this point on 22 February 1797.

Around the bay of **Aber-Felin** the path passes through some pretty woodland before winding its way up and over rough hillocks with the cliffs becoming less severe, eventually tapering to gentle heathery slopes at **Penanglas**. Here the path swings southwards through a number of old fields before joining the residential road, New Hill.

As the road starts to descend more steeply, a zig-zagging path drops down onto Quay Road which leads into the centre of **Goodwick**.

GOODWICK (WDIG)   MAP 67, p181

Goodwick is often considered to be an extension of Fishguard but it's really a separate town. Its main claim to fame is its role as a ferry port, shipping holidaymakers to and from Ireland. It may be somewhat overshadowed by its bigger twin but it does have plenty of eating places and accommodation, most notably the very grand Fishguard Bay Hotel, originally built for passengers when the ferry route to Ireland opened in 1906.

Since then it has been used to house the film crew of *Moby Dick* (cont'd on p180)

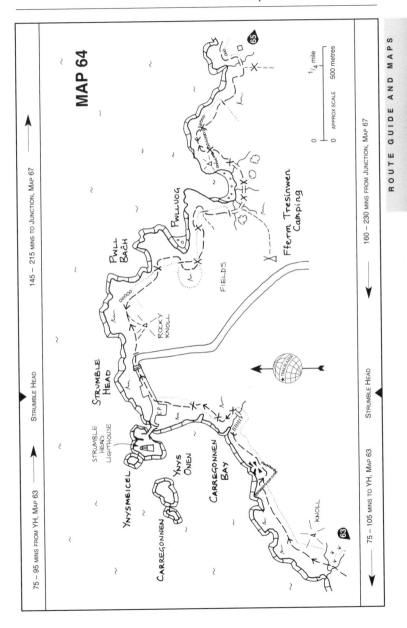

MAP 64

75 – 95 MINS FROM YH, MAP 63 ——— STRUMBLE HEAD

145 – 215 MINS TO JUNCTION, MAP 67

STRUMBLE HEAD LIGHTHOUSE

YNYSMEICEL

YNYS ONEN

CARREGONNEN

CARREGONNEN BAY

STRUMBLE HEAD

ROCKY KNOLL

PWLL BACH

PWLLOG

FIELDS

Fferm Tresinwen Camping

KNOLL

65

63

160 – 230 MINS FROM JUNCTION, MAP 67

STRUMBLE HEAD

75 – 105 MINS TO YH, MAP 63

0 ——— 1/4 mile
APPROX SCALE
0 ——— 500 metres

ROUTE GUIDE AND MAPS

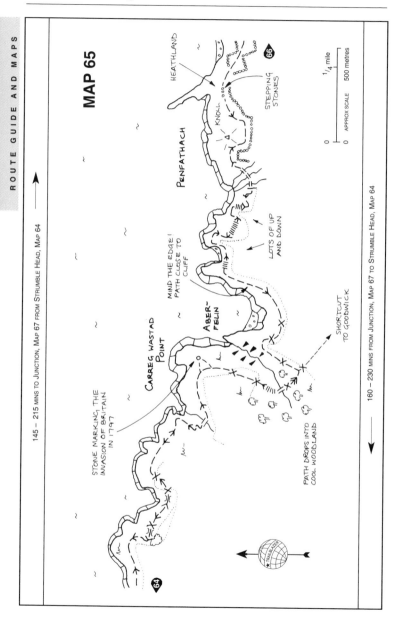

MAP 65

145 – 215 MINS TO JUNCTION, MAP 67 FROM STRUMBLE HEAD, MAP 64

160 – 230 MINS FROM JUNCTION, MAP 67 TO STRUMBLE HEAD, MAP 64

HEATHLAND

PENFATHACH

KNOLL

STEPPING STONES

66

1/4 mile

0

0   APPROX SCALE   500 metres

LOTS OF UP AND DOWN

MIND THE EDGE! PATH CLOSE TO CLIFF

ABER-FELIN

CARREG WASTAD POINT

STONE MARKING THE INVASION OF BRITAIN IN 1797

SHORTCUT TO GOODWICK

PATH DROPS INTO COOL WOODLAND

TRAILBLAZER

64

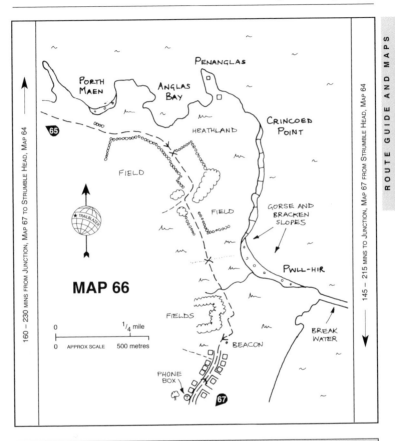

❑ The last invasion of Britain

On 22 February 1797 four French sailing vessels, led by the American Colonel Tate, anchored off Carreg Wastad Head, west of Fishguard. This was the beginning of the last invasion of Britain, a somewhat half-hearted and short-lived affair. The 1400 or so Frenchmen occupied the stretch of coast around Strumble Head for a grand total of two days. The story goes that they got so drunk on stolen beer that the locals soon overpowered them, finally surrendering on the sands of Goodwick on 24 February 1797.

The hero of the whole affair was one Jemima Nicholas who, to this day, is something of a local folk hero. Armed with her pitchfork she single-handedly rounded up 12 Frenchmen and is now honoured by having a local ale named after her. A memorial stone to the last invasion stands at Carreg Wastad Point (see Map 65).

(cont'd from p176) which was filmed in Lower Fishguard, and, later, the men who constructed one of the Milford Haven oil refineries.

Services
The **tourist information centre** (☎ 01348-872037, 🖳 fishguardharbour.tic@pembrokeshire.gov.uk; Apr-Oct daily 9.30am-5pm, to 6pm in the school summer holidays, Nov-Mar 10am-4pm) is in the **Ocean Lab Centre** (daily 10am-5pm) on Fishguard Rd. There is also an **internet café** here (£2 per 30 minutes), though it's free in the library in Fishguard.

As you come into the town centre you will see a **chemist** standing next to a small **shop** and **newsagent**. A little further on is the **post office** (☎ 01348-872842; Mon, Tue, Thur, Fri 9am-5.30pm, Wed & Sat to 1pm; shop open Mon-Sat 9am-5.30pm, Sun 10am-1pm).

Transport
The **Strumble Shuttle** bus stops in the Square; the No 410 town service also runs from the Square to Fishguard. Fishguard **train station** is actually here in Goodwick, by the ferry terminal. However, at the time of writing there was only one service a day to Cardiff, timed to link in with the ferry. See the public transport map and table, pp39-41.

Goodwick is where the **ferry** leaves for Ireland. Adventurous sorts could take a day-trip over to sample the Guinness. The catamaran takes less than two hours to Rosslare while the ferry takes under four hours. Passenger-only fares start from £17 on the ferry. Contact Stenaline Ferries (see box p41) for further details.

Where to stay
In the centre of town *Glendower Hotel* (☎ 01348-872873, 🖳 glendowerhotel@hotmail.com; 3S/1D/6T/1F all en suite) charges £39 for a single, doubles/twins are £34.50/pp for two sharing. Also by The Square is the *Hope & Anchor* (☎ 01348-872314; 🖳 www.hopeandanchorinn.co.uk; 4D/1F) with very smart en suite rooms with flat-screen TVs from £35 per person.

On top of the hill, about half a mile

from town, is the very welcoming *Brynawel Country House* (☎ 01348-874155, 🖳 brynawel@amserve.net, 2T or D/1F). They provide free transport for coast-path walkers between St Dogmael's and St David's if staying two nights or more, meaning you can base yourself here for several days while tackling the entire northern section of the coast path – useful if you're catching the train home from Goodwick. Phone to confirm a booking and to arrange a lift from Goodwick when you arrive. What's more, if you are coming by car they will happily keep your car in a safe place for the duration of your stay. The rate is from £29.50 per person for bed and breakfast.

For complete pampered luxury (though at a price), *Fishguard Bay Hotel* (☎ 01348-873571, 🖳 www.fishguardbayhotel.co.uk, 59 en suite rooms) is a grandiose building set in woodland at the end of Quay Rd. Built a century ago when a room would set you back five shillings, these days a room starts at £60 for a single (£70 for single occcupancy of a double) or £80-95 (the exact tariff depending on whether you've got a sea view) in a double. Make sure you wipe your hiking boots before you enter.

Where to eat
On the corner of The Square is the *Hope and Anchor* (see column opposite; daily 11.30am-3.30pm, 6-11pm) with similarly basic but good value and tasty fare.

Next door is the *Farmhouse Kitchen* (☎ 01348-873907; Tue-Sat 7-10pm) where the menu is constantly changing. They do a good three-course menu for £13.95 (£18.50 on Fri and Sat evening). Continuing past these, near the post office is the *No 10 Café*, offering sandwiches and simple snacks. The owners of *Masala* (☎ 01348-873616; daily 5-11pm), an Indian restaurant and takeaway, also own *Gary's Takeaway* (daily 5-11pm), next door, serving fish and chips, kebabs and burgers.

At the other end of the spectrum is the restaurant (daily 7-9pm) at *Fishguard Bay Hotel* (see above), which is open to non-residents. The bar menu is served Mon-Sat 12-1.45pm.

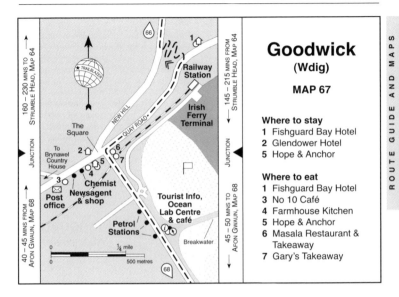

ROUTE GUIDE AND MAPS

Goodwick
(Wdig)

MAP 67

Where to stay
1 Fishguard Bay Hotel
2 Glendower Hotel
5 Hope & Anchor

Where to eat
1 Fishguard Bay Hotel
3 No 10 Café
4 Farmhouse Kitchen
5 Hope & Anchor
6 Masala Restaurant & Takeaway
7 Gary's Takeaway

Once past the information centre the coast path follows the tarmac path known as **Marine Walk**. This effectively bypasses much of the residential part of **Fishguard**. Arriving at the Slade, a small lane lined with pretty cottages, you have a choice: left and down to continue along the route to Lower Fishguard; or up and right to bring you into the centre of the main part of town.

FISHGUARD (ABERGWAUN)
Map p182
Fishguard is a surprisingly amenable place. It is big enough to provide everything you need and small enough to maintain a quiet charm. This is the capital of 'Last Invasion Country' (see box p179); the peace treaty was signed at the Royal Oak Inn on Market Sq.

The main town of Fishguard sits on high ground above Fishguard Harbour but down the hill to the north of the town, where the Afon Gwaun drains the Cwm Gwaun valley and the Preseli Hills, is **Lower Fishguard**.

This pretty quayside village comes as a pleasant surprise. It was the setting for Dylan Thomas's *Under Milk Wood* and was also used in the 1956 film *Moby Dick*.

Services
Market Sq is the hub of the town. Continuing up the High St you'll find the library, the new home of the **tourist information centre** (☎ 01348-873484, ✉ fish guard.tic@pembrokeshire.gov.uk; Mon-Sat 9.30am-5.30pm, Thur to 6pm, Sun 10am-4pm). The **post office** (Mon-Fri 9am-5.30pm, Sat to 12.30pm) is on West St and there is a **supermarket** on High St.

If you're searching for supplies on a Saturday the fortnightly **farmers' market** (9am-2pm) is well-worth visiting; it's held in the supermarket car park on Main St.

Transport
Buses leave from Market Sq. Richards' No 410 town service goes to Goodwick as does the No 411, the No 412 stops at Dinas and

ROUTE GUIDE AND MAPS

Newport en route to Cardigan. Fishguard is on the route for both the Strumble Shuttle and the Poppit Rocket services. Fishguard **train station** is not actually in Fishguard but in Goodwick (see p180). See the public transport map and table, pp39-41, for full details.

Where to stay
Campers should head out of Fishguard to *Fishguard Bay Caravan & Camping Park* (see Map 69; ☎ 01348-811415, ☐ www .fishguardbay.com, Mar-Nov) where a pitch for one person costs £8.50 (£13 for two). It is situated two miles (3km) east of Fishguard; the coast path goes straight through it.

In town, budget travellers will appreciate *Hamilton Backpackers Lodge* (☎ 01348-874797, ☐ www.fishguard-back packers.com; 21/23 Hamilton St; 21 beds). It's a rough and ready place run by a friendly Australian guy who keeps it ticking over in a very informal way; it's open all year. It's a useful stop if you arrive late in the day since there is no curfew. Rates: £14 for a bunk, £18 per person in a double, £16 in a triple and £15 in a quad, with a simple make-it-yourself breakfast of tea and toast available.

On Main St is the smart Georgian *Manor Town House Hotel* (☎ 01348-873260, ☐ www.manortownhouse.com; 1S/1T/3D/1F) which has B&B accommodation from £35 and some cracking views over the harbour below.

Cartref Hotel (☎ 01348-872430, ☐ www.cartrefhotel.co.uk, 15-19 High St, 4S/2T/2D/2F en suite) has rooms for £41 (single) to £65 (double). On Market Sq *Abergwaun Hotel* (☎ 01348-872077, 2S/4T/4D/2F all en suite) charges from £20 per head plus £3.95 for breakfast.

On Vergam Terrace, the continuation of West St, *Inglewood* (☎ 01348-873475, 13 Vergam Terrace, 2D/1T) offers B&B from £25-30 per person. Further along is *Tara Hotel* (☎ 01348-872777, ☐ www.tara-hotel.co.uk; 1S/2T/2D/2F all en suite) with rooms from £27.50 per person in a double, £35 for the single.

Where to eat
Probably the most popular place – and justifiably so – is the *Royal Oak Inn* (☎ 01348-872514; daily noon-2pm, 6-9pm; open winters lunchtime and Fri & Sat eves only, 6.30-9pm), a rustic pub on Market Sq with an extensive menu of hearty home-cooked food. Occasionally, your dining will be accompanied by the sound of folk music during one of their popular evenings.

For something cheap but filling try the *Ship and Anchor* (☎ 01348-872362, Mon-Sat 11am-3pm, 5.30-8.30pm, Sun noon-3pm only, closed in eves). It's the big pink building on High St and does bacon and onion

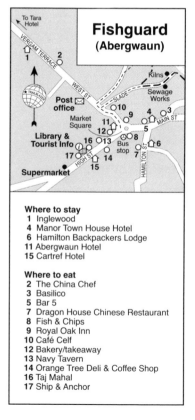

Fishguard
(Abergwaun)

To Tara Hotel

VERGAM TERRACE

WEST ST

Kilns
Sewage Works

Post office

Market Square

Library & Tourist Info

SLADE

Bus stop

HIGH ST

MAIN ST

HAMILTON ST

Supermarket

Where to stay
1 Inglewood
4 Manor Town House Hotel
6 Hamilton Backpackers Lodge
11 Abergwaun Hotel
15 Cartref Hotel

Where to eat
2 The China Chef
3 Basilico
5 Bar 5
7 Dragon House Chinese Restaurant
8 Fish & Chips
9 Royal Oak Inn
10 Café Celf
12 Bakery/takeaway
13 Navy Tavern
14 Orange Tree Deli & Coffee Shop
16 Taj Mahal
17 Ship & Anchor

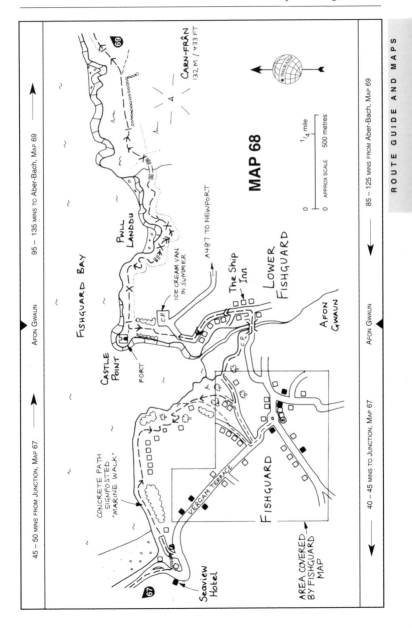

baguettes for £1.95 as well as more substantial meals. Close by is *Taj Mahal* (☎ 01348-874593, 22 High St, daily 6-11.30pm) for typical Indian dishes. You can get a takeaway until midnight.

Nearby is the *Navy Tavern* (☎ 01348-875120; food served daily 12noon-3pm, Sun-Tue & Thur/Fri 7-9pm) which does a decent afternoon tea that you can eat in their peaceful back garden, while opposite is the *Orange Tree Deli and Coffee Shop* (☎ 01348-875500; Mon-Sat 9am-4pm).

A new Italian, *Basilico* (☎ 01348-871845; Tue-Sat 6.30-9pm), has opened at 3 Main St; the large menu includes such treats as *agnello marinato*, an Italian twist on lamb, flavoured with lemon and rosemary (£12.50). *Bar 5* (☎ 01348-875050; Tue-Sat 10.30am-3pm, 7-11pm, Sun 12noon-4pm), another new place on Main St, is thriving in an old Georgian townhouse. A large establishment with restaurants on three floors, a bar and an outside terrace overlooking the old town below, Bar 5's décor is contemporary and chic, though the food, much of

which is locally produced, reared or caught, remains reasonably priced.

The first place you come to on the way into town is *Celf* (☎ 01348-873867, 🖳 www.westwalesartscentre.com; Mon, Wed-Sat 10am-4.30pm), a smart café-cum-gallery at 16 West St that has a small but regularly changing menu of fine lunches starting at around £8.95; they also open for dinner on Fri and Sat (6.30-10pm).

Opposite Hamilton Backpackers is *Dragon House Chinese Restaurant* (☎ 01348-872004; Wed-Mon 5-11pm) for takeaway Chinese food, and another Chinese, *The China Chef* (☎ 01348-873221; daily 5.30-11pm), on Vergam Terrace. There is a **fish and chip** place on Main St and a cheap and cheerful **bakery-cum-takeaway** on the main square next to the Abergwaun.

On the way out of Fishguard heading east you pass the *Ship Inn* (☎ 01348-874033; food served daily 12noon-11pm) in Lower Fishguard, a good place for a pint though they don't do food.

FISHGUARD TO NEWPORT   MAPS 68-72

It's **eleven miles (18km, 4½-5Hrs)** if you follow the entire coast path via the peninsula known as Dinas Island. Cheats, or those in a hurry, can take the shortcut marked on Map 70, bringing the distance down to nine miles (14km, 3½-4hrs).

The pretty fishing village of **Lower Fishguard** with its colourful houses lining the quay below the hillside and boats bobbing in the harbour contrasts greatly with the bustling main town on top of the hill.

From the top of the steep climb up the main road the path passes through gorse bushes to the remains of the 220-year-old **Fishguard Fort**.

Another mile and a half (2km) and the path brings you directly into Fishguard Bay Caravan Park (see p182) where it is possible to camp. The path continues along the edge of steep, high cliffs all the way to the tiny sheltered beach of **Aber-Bach** and, around 30 minutes later, the minuscule settlement of Pwllgwaelod.

PWLLGWAELOD & DINAS CROSS
MAP 70

At **Pwllgwaelod** there is a **drinking-water tap** next to the public **toilets** in the car park. In the summer (2-3/day) the **Poppit Rocket** stops in the car park before heading to

Dinas Cross; see pp39-41 for details. There's nowhere to stay here but there is *The Old Sailors Restaurant* (☎ 01348-811491, Thur-Tue 11am-6pm, booking essential Fri and Sat) with tasty lobster and crab lunches.

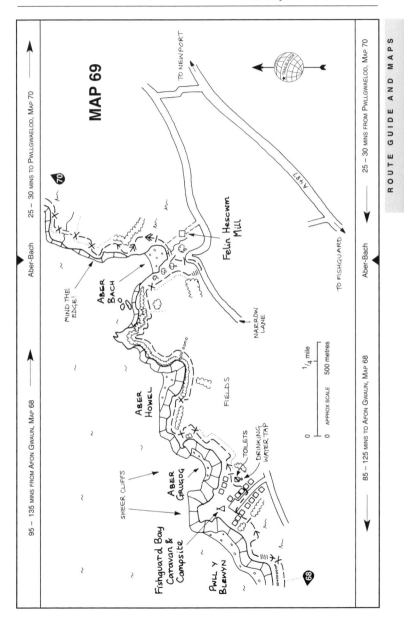

The village of **Dinas Cross** is a short detour from the coast path. It can be reached by walking up the lane from Pwllgwaelod through Brynhenllan to the main road and turning right (20 mins from the coast path). Here there is a service station with a mini **supermarket**, **post office** and an **off-licence**.

There is also a **fish and chip shop** (☎ 01348-811660, open Tue-Sat 12-2pm, 5-9pm); you can phone ahead to place your order. Next door is the ***Freemasons Arms*** (☎ 01348-811243; open daily 12noon-11pm) where you can treat yourself to a pint.

Along the lane between Brynhenllan and Dinas you will find B&B at *Dolwern* (☎ 01348-811266, 1S/1T/2D), with rooms from £22 per person, and the *Ship Aground Inn* (☎ 01348-811261, daily noon-2pm, 6.45-9pm) serving good pub grub.

At Pwllgwaelod you must decide if you want to include the peninsula of **Dinas Island** in your walk. If the answer is no follow the well-made straight path through the valley to Cwm-yr-eglwys.

If the answer is yes take the easy to follow path which climbs steadily through heather and bracken all the way to the 142-metre (466ft) Pen y Fan, the summit of **Dinas Head**. The path continues around the peninsula above high slopes of bracken before passing through bushes and trees to emerge at **Cwm-yr-eglwys** (Church Valley) named after the church which lies in ruins by the beach. With everything squeezed into such a narrow valley the effect is claustrophobic so it is a relief to escape by walking up the steep lane out of the village.

After ten minutes or so of lung-busting ascent the path can be found sneaking between high hedges on the left next to a house. The path is well hidden by hedges and trees until you reach cliffs above the cove at **Fforest**. The cliffs along the next section are sheer and in places overhanging. The path can be very close to the edge so watch your step.

The next cove is a real beauty. The turn-off to Tycanol campsite (see p190) is just before the boathouse here. The unspoilt nature of the area makes it quite a rarity. Unlike most of these coves there is no road and no houses, just woodland, a marsh and a stony beach. From here the path continues along the edge of precipitous cliffs to **Parrog**, where it's worth stopping at Morawelon Coffee Shop (see p191), and the edge of Newport town where it briefly crosses the shingle, mud and sand on the seafront.

Where the path passes the salt marsh and some woodland there are two lanes, both of which provide access to the centre of **Newport**. The first leads up to the national park information centre, while the second takes you to the youth hostel.

NEWPORT (TREFDRAETH) MAP 72

Rising behind Newport are the Preseli Hills. This is bluestone country from where the stones for the inner circle of Stonehenge were transported.

The hill directly behind the town is Carn Ingli rising to 319 metres (1046ft). From the top you can see the mountains of Snowdonia on a clear day.

The town itself is small and friendly. The **Norman castle** and church at the top were built along with the original town in the 12th century when the Norman invader Robert Martin chose the spot beside the Newport estuary to set up home. Unfortunately the castle is privately owned so visitors must content themselves with a view from the outside. *(cont'd on p190)*

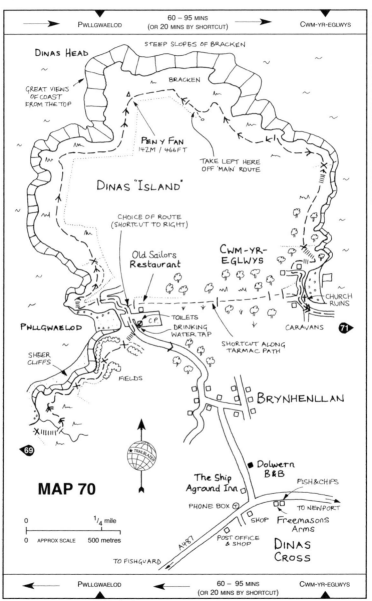

PWLLGWAELOD → 60 – 95 MINS (OR 20 MINS BY SHORTCUT) → CWM-YR-EGLWYS

STEEP SLOPES OF BRACKEN

DINAS HEAD

BRACKEN

GREAT VIEWS OF COAST FROM THE TOP

PEN Y FAN 142M / 466FT

TAKE LEFT HERE OFF 'MAIN' ROUTE

DINAS "ISLAND"

CHOICE OF ROUTE (SHORTCUT TO RIGHT)

Old Sailors Restaurant

CWM-YR-EGLWYS

CHURCH RUINS

PWLLGWAELOD

C.P.

TOILETS

DRINKING WATER TAP

CARAVANS

71

SHORTCUT ALONG TARMAC PATH

SHEER CLIFFS

FIELDS

BRYNHENLLAN

69

★ TRAILBLAZER

MAP 70

Dolwern B&B

The Ship Aground Inn

FISH & CHIPS

PHONE BOX

TO NEWPORT

SHOP

Freemasons Arms

0   1/4 mile

0   APPROX SCALE   500 metres

A487

POST OFFICE & SHOP

DINAS CROSS

TO FISHGUARD

← PWLLGWAELOD ← 60 – 95 MINS (OR 20 MINS BY SHORTCUT) CWM-YR-EGLWYS

ROUTE GUIDE AND MAPS

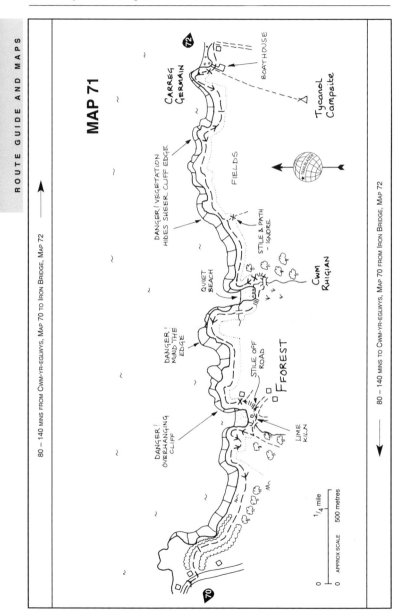

MAP 71

80 – 140 MINS FROM CWM-YR-EGLWYS, MAP 70 TO IRON BRIDGE, MAP 72

80 – 140 MINS TO CWM-YR-EGLWYS, MAP 70 FROM IRON BRIDGE, MAP 72

72

CARREG GERMAIN

BOAT HOUSE

Tycanol Campsite

FIELDS

DANGER! VEGETATION HIDES SHEER CLIFF EDGE

STILE & PATH - IGNORE

CWM RHIGIAN

QUIET BEACH

DANGER! MIND THE EDGE

STILE OFF ROAD

FFOREST

LIME KILN

DANGER! OVERHANGING CLIFF

¼ mile

500 metres

APPROX SCALE

0

0

70

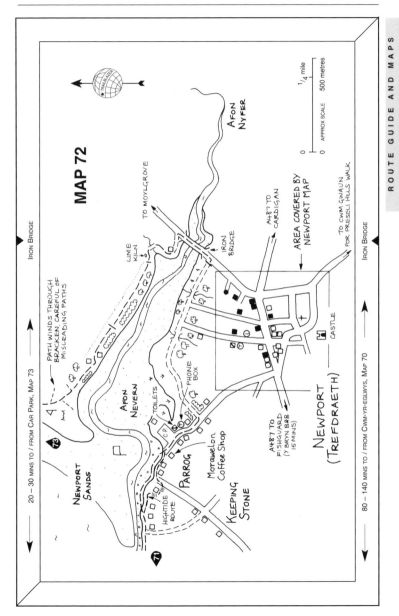

On Lower St Mary St is another Carreg, or burial chamber, one of many that can be found in this part of Wales. **Carreg Coetan** is typical, consisting of several standing stones surmounted by a capstone, and is perhaps of greater interest for its location, in an unassuming residential corner of Newport surrounded by bungalows.

Before you leave town check the **West Wales Eco Centre** (☎ 01239-820235, 🖳 www.ecocentre.org.uk; Apr-Oct, Mon-Fri 9.15am-4.45pm, admission free) next to the youth hostel on Lower St Mary's St. It has displays and demonstrations on renewable energy and conservation. Entrance is free.

In terms of facilities, Newport is a surprisingly well-equipped little town. Almost everything you could possibly need can be found in the compact centre. It's the perfect place to stay before the tough final leg of the journey to St Dogmaels.

Services

The **tourist information centre** (☎ 01239-820912, NewportTIC@pembrokeshire coast.org.uk; Easter-Oct Mon-Sat 10am-5.30pm lunch 1-1.45pm, also in summer Sun 9.45am-1.15pm) is also the **National Park Information Centre**. They plan to install **internet** soon but until then you'll have to rely on the library's service (Mon 2-5pm, Wed 10am-1pm, Fri 10am-noon and 2-5pm). If you're in Newport on one of the days when the library's shut you could try the Eco Centre as they have Internet access though it's only meant to be for those researching ecological issues. However, if they're quiet they will usually let you use their terminal for £2.50 per hour.

The **post office** (☎ 01239-820200; Mon-Fri 9am-5.30pm, Sat 9am-1pm) is on the corner of Long St and the main road, Bridge St. The **bank** on Bridge St has a cashpoint. The best place for provisions is the Spar **supermarket** (daily 8am-10pm) on Market St. Alternatively Newport Garage's **mini-market** is on Bridge St.

Dirty socks can be washed at the **laundrette** (9am-9pm, open daily; dryers 50p for 10 mins), and there's a **chemist** (☎ 01239-820239) on Market St.

Transport

The Poppit Rocket **bus** stops at Parrog Car Park and by the Castle Hotel; Richards Brothers' No 412 service also stops in Newport; for details see the public transport map and table, pp39-41.

Where to stay

Tycanol Campsite (Map 71; ☎ 01239-820264, 🖳 www.caravancampingsites.co .uk/pembrokeshire/tycanolfarm.htm; Apr-Oct) is 200 yards from the coast path. Turn inland just before the boat house by Carreg Germain. It costs £6 per person but there is also a great **bunkhouse** – more like a rudimentary, rustic apartment and completely charming – in the loft of their barn, for which they charge just £12 per person.

Newport Youth Hostel (☎ 0870-770 6072; 🖳 newport@yha.org.uk, Lower St Mary St), a converted schoolhouse with 28 beds costing £12.50 for members. The hostel is self-catering only but this is not a problem since there are plenty of places serving food in Newport.

There are some good places to stay along East St. Recommended is the *Golden Lion* (☎ 01239-820321, 🖳 www.golden lionpembs.co.uk; 7D/3T/2F) which has en suite rooms from £39.50 in the pub itself, with three more double rooms over the road in the cottage (not en suite). Rates are £32.25 per person for two sharing, or it's £39.50 for single occupancy. Dogs are also welcome for a £5 charge, and the ambitious owners also offer a baggage-transfer service; see their website for further details.

Further along the road *LlysMeddyg Guest House* (☎ 01239-820008, 🖳 www .doctorscourt.com; 2T/2D/2F) has en suite rooms starting at around £45-65 per person. On the same road *Cnapan Country House* (☎ 01239-820575, 🖳 www.cnapan.co.uk; 2D/3T en suite) charges £40 per person, with a £7 single occupancy supplement.

On Bridge St is another good pub-cum-hotel with very comfortable en suite rooms from £27.50 single, £25 per person in a double: *Gwesty'r Castell* (Castle Hotel; ☎ 01239-820742; 2S/2D/1F) is a pleasant place where the owners are very welcoming and helpful.

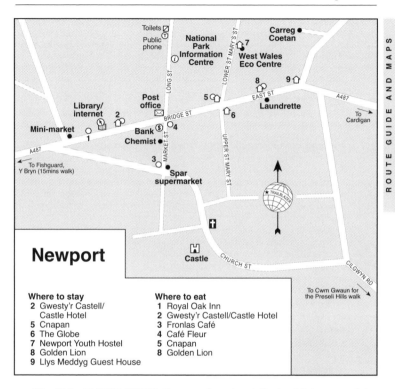

Toilets
Public phone
National Park Information Centre
Carreg Coetan
West Wales Eco Centre
LONG ST
LOWER ST MARY'S ST
Post office
EAST ST
Laundrette
5
8
9
Library/internet
BRIDGE ST
2
Bank
Chemist
MARKET ST
4
Mini-market
1
A487
To Fishguard, Y Bryn (15mins walk)
3
Spar supermarket
UPPER ST MARY ST
A487
To Cardigan
TRAILBLAZER

Newport

Castle
CHURCH ST
CILGWYN RD
To Cwm Gwaun for the Preseli Hills walk

Where to stay
2 Gwesty'r Castell/ Castle Hotel
5 Cnapan
6 The Globe
7 Newport Youth Hostel
8 Golden Lion
9 Llys Meddyg Guest House

Where to eat
1 Royal Oak Inn
2 Gwesty'r Castell/Castle Hotel
3 Fronlas Café
4 Café Fleur
5 Cnapan
8 Golden Lion

ROUTE GUIDE AND MAPS

The Globe (☎ 01239-820296, Upper St Mary St; 1D/1T) has comfortable rooms at £50 for two sharing (£35 for single occupancy); discounts for a stay of more than one night are available, which may come in useful as the landlady also offers a pick-up or drop-off service covering the last, lengthy stretch to Cardigan.

To the west of Newport on the road to Dinas Cross is the smart, 4-star *Y Bryn* (☎ 01239-820288; 🖥 www.brynbedandbreakfast.co.uk; 2D/1F), with two en suite doubles overlooking the sea, and one huge room with private bathroom and views towards the Preseli Hills. Rates are £30 per head, or £35 single occupancy.

Where to eat

Newport is completely spoilt with great

places to eat. For breakfast or a snack try one of the coffee shops; the first one you come to as you walk towards the town on the coast path is actually in Parrog: the *Morawelon Coffee Shop* (☎ 01239-820565; daily 8.30am-5pm) does a variety of snacks and light lunches, has a sun-trap of a garden out the back and good views over Newport Beach from the front. You can't miss it; it's on the seafront near the yacht club. Call in, even if you're not stopping in the village.

In the centre of the town is *The Canteen* (☎ 01239-820131, Market St; Mon 10am-5pm, Tue-Sat to 9.30pm, Sun 12noon-4pm) where you could have polenta and mozarella with aubergine for £12.

Further up Market St opposite Spar supermarket *Fronlas Café* (☎ 01239-820351; daily 9am-9pm) does breakfasts and afternoon snacks; it also serves evening meals (from 7pm, Wed-Sat, booking essential). Back down on East St, look out for the *Golden Lion* (see p190; daily 6.30-9pm), which does very good, hearty food and has friendly bar staff.

Another good choice is the *Royal Oak Inn* (☎ 01239-820632, food served daily 11am-9.30pm), on Bridge St, where they know how to knock up a good curry and

have a winning way with fish too. The traditional pub is an unlikely-looking curry house but their extensive Indian menu should be enough to convince you.

Alternatively there is *Castle Hotel* (see p190, daily 12-2pm, 6.30-9.30pm, Bridge St) with local food, real ales and a roaring log fire. For a straightforward restaurant *Cnapan* (see p190; Wed-Mon) does high-quality, if slightly expensive, evening meals.

Walking in the Preseli Hills (Mynydd Preseli) and Cwm Gwaun

The Preseli Hills rise behind Newport, dissected by the deep Cwm Gwaun glacial valley. This little-known area is well worth exploring if you have time to spare as it provides some wonderful secluded walking away from the more popular coast. This is bluestone country. The rock here was transported all the way to Salisbury Plain for the construction of Stonehenge by some miracle of Druidian engineering. There are Iron-Age hill-forts and standing stones dotted all along the crest of the hills with fantastic views over the coastline and the sweep of Cardigan Bay. The Preseli Hills are divided into three distinct parts. On the northern side is the lowest line of hills reaching 337m (1105ft) on Carningli Common above Newport. The higher Myndd Preseli to the south reaches a height of 536m (1758ft) at Foel Cwmcerwyn, while the heavily wooded Cwm Gwaun valley separates the two. The circular walk outlined below starts in Newport and takes in the Cwm Gwaun valley before returning over the ridge of the lower hills via the distinctive peak of Carningli.

Safety Do not underestimate these hills. They may be relatively low but they are exposed and the weather can change suddenly as with the rest of Britain's western hills. The ridge is a broad one with few distinctive landmarks and little in the way of signposts and other waymarks, making it very inhospitable in bad weather. Take the OS Outdoor Leisure Map 35 of North Pembrokeshire (yellow cover) and a compass in case the cloud comes down. Warm waterproof clothing and plenty of food and water for the day are also essential.

A circular walk (see map opposite) This walk is about **11 miles** (17.5km) and takes about **4-6 hours** (please note, the times below are cumulative). From Newport follow the road up Church St with the castle to your right and the church to the left. Continue up Cilgwyn Rd. Stay on the lane following the signs for Cwm Gwaun. The lane now heads downhill to a sharp right-hand corner. Continue up the hill, ignoring the left turn. The lane eventually meets another lane at a T-junction where you should turn right. After passing the tiny disused quarry on your left the road drops down with a fine view of the valley ahead. At the sharp right-hand bend it's time to leave the road and head along the woodland track through the gate to your left (1-1½hrs). This beautiful stretch of path passes through some impressive beech forest where red squirrels and buzzards can frequently be spotted. The path passes a number of ruined houses hinting at a time when the Cwm Gwaun was more heavily populated.

(Opposite) Top: The path winds its way through bracken and gorse beneath Carn Penberry (see p166). **Bottom**: Seal basking on the shore, Penllechwen. (Photos © Henry Stedman).

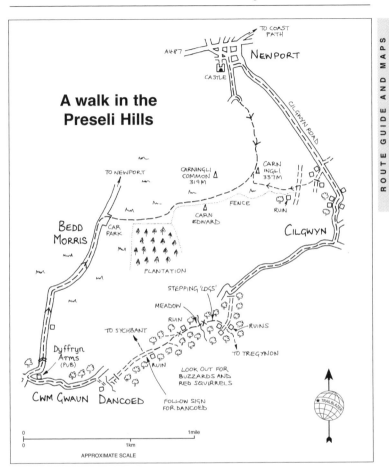

A walk in the Preseli Hills

TO COAST PATH

A487

NEWPORT

CASTLE

CILGWYN ROAD

TO NEWPORT

CARNINGLI COMMON △ 319M

CARN INGLI 337M

FENCE

RUIN

△ CARN EDWARD

CILGWYN

BEDD MORRIS

CAR PARK

PLANTATION

STEPPING 'LOGS'

MEADOW

RUIN

RUINS

TO SYCHBANT

TO TREGYNON

Dyffryn Arms (PUB)

RUIN

LOOK OUT FOR BUZZARDS AND RED SQUIRRELS

CWM GWAUN DANCOED

FOLLOW SIGN FOR DANCOED

TRAILBLAZER

0   1mile
0   1km
APPROXIMATE SCALE

Keep to the path on the edge of the forest, passing fields on your right, eventually reaching the farm at Dan Coed (2-2¾hrs) where you have to rejoin the lane. It is a short walk along the road to the eccentric **Dyffryn Arms** (☎ 01348-881305; open daily 11am-11pm; 2½-3¼hrs) where you can get beer poured from a jug and passed through a hatch in what is effectively Bessie, the landlady's, living room. It's a good spot to eat your lunch, although the pub itself doesn't do food. After a break it's time for the steep climb up to the hilltop. Turn right after the pub and climb the hairpin lane, reaching the bleak

---

(Opposite) Top: The ruined church at Cwm-yr-eglwys (see p186). **Bottom**: The impressive rock striations at Cemaes Head (see p199). (Photos © Henry Stedman).

windswept moor at Bedd Morris where there is a car park and fine views of Dinas Head on the coast (3-4hrs). At the car park follow the track through the heather. In bad visibility a compass will be needed. Head directly east until you come to a fence. Follow the fence line, passing the rocks of Carn Edward on the right. From the end of the fence head up onto the 337m (1105ft) rocky top of Carn Ingli (3¹/₂-5hrs), an interesting little hill with views over Newport on an otherwise featureless upland moor. Look out for the hut circles on the ridge leading to the top. To get back to Newport follow the obvious path north down the slopes and join the track which takes you back onto Church Rd (4-6hrs).

NEWPORT TO ST DOGMAELS   MAPS 72-79

There's nothing like leaving the best till last but there's always a catch. This is the toughest section of the entire walk. If you have come all the way from Amroth you will either be feeling fitter than ever or you will be feeling 30 years older and will find these last **sixteen miles (26km, 5¹/₂-7¹/₂hrs)** pretty strenuous.

The cliffs are bigger here, the distances longer, there is nowhere to get any food, nowhere to get any water and only one place to stay until you get to Poppit Sands. These are all ingredients for a tough day, so count on taking at least two to three litres of water with you and more if it's a hot day. That one place to stay is in the village of Moylgrove (see p197) near Ceibwr Bay. If you intend to stay there you are well advised to book in advance. Alternatively, you can, of course, walk up to Moylgrove and catch the Poppit Rocket (see p41) to Cardigan or Newport, then return to Moylgrove the next day in order to complete the walk. This alternative, of course, involves a bit of pre-planning and knowledge of local bus times – but it does neatly divide the walk in two.

After crossing the iron bridge over the **Afon Nyfer** the path follows the northern edge of the estuary, through bushes and bracken and across a golf course to a car park next to **Newport Sands**. Here there is a small **café**, **toilets** and a **drinking-water tap**; the **Poppit Rocket** also stops here (see pp39-41).

This is where the hard stuff begins. The path climbs up onto high cliffs, passing through a beautiful heathland nature reserve. In the summer this area is alive with butterflies. The path continues above very high, steep slopes of bracken and around some spectacular bays sheltered by terrifying barren cliffs, climbing steadily higher and higher to reach 150 metres (492ft) where the hill of **Foel-Gôch** plunges into the sea.

Once past a couple of huge old landslips, which are no doubt still vulnerable to collapse, the path drops down to lower cliffs, eventually arriving at the spectacular formations around the **Witch's Cauldron**. A great wedge of rock lies just offshore trapping a finger of the sea below the cliffs. The path, rather worryingly, passes very close to the nasty drop down into this pool. Watch your step. Further on is the Witch's Cauldron itself, a sea cave where the roof has collapsed. The result is a beautiful cove with a natural bridge making it appear separate from the main body of the sea.

A little further on is **Ceibwr Bay** with its shingle beach; a good halfway point for lunch. The village of **Moylgrove** is along the valley road; the only accommodation for miles lies just beyond the village.

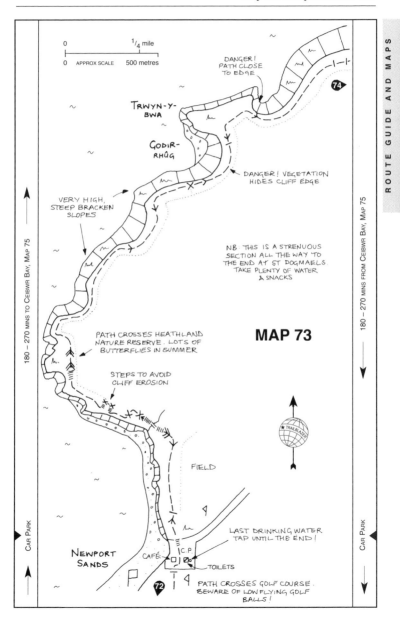

0   ¼ mile

0   APPROX SCALE   500 metres

DANGER! PATH CLOSE TO EDGE

74

TRWYN-Y-BWA

GODIR-RHÛG

DANGER! VEGETATION HIDES CLIFF EDGE

VERY HIGH, STEEP BRACKEN SLOPES

NB: THIS IS A STRENUOUS SECTION ALL THE WAY TO THE END AT ST DOGMAELS. TAKE PLENTY OF WATER & SNACKS

MAP 73

PATH CROSSES HEATHLAND NATURE RESERVE. LOTS OF BUTTERFLIES IN SUMMER

STEPS TO AVOID CLIFF EROSION

★ TRAILBLAZER

FIELD

180 – 270 MINS TO CEIBWR BAY, MAP 75

180 – 270 MINS FROM CEIBWR BAY, MAP 75

CAR PARK

CAR PARK

LAST DRINKING WATER TAP UNTIL THE END!

C.P.

NEWPORT SANDS

CAFÉ

TOILETS

72

PATH CROSSES GOLF COURSE. BEWARE OF LOW FLYING GOLF BALLS!

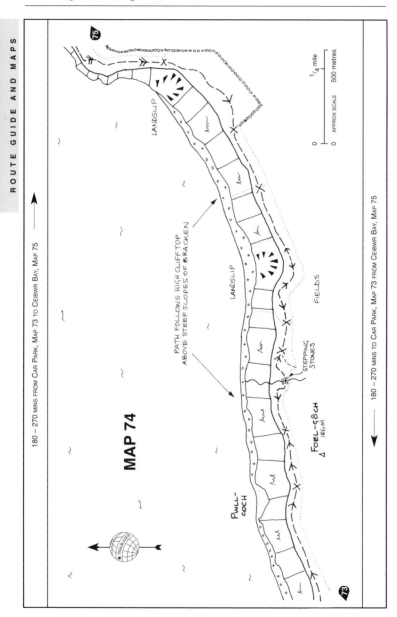

180 – 270 MINS FROM CAR PARK, MAP 73 TO CEIBWR BAY, MAP 75 →

MAP 74

PATH FOLLOWS HIGH CLIFFTOP
ABOVE STEEP SLOPES OF BRACKEN

LANDSLIP

LANDSLIP

FIELDS

STEPPING
STONES

FOEL-GÔCH
△ 186 M

PWLL-
COCH

TRAILBLAZER

¼ mile
0
0   APPROX SCALE   500 metres

← 180 – 270 MINS TO CAR PARK, MAP 73 FROM CEIBWR BAY, MAP 75

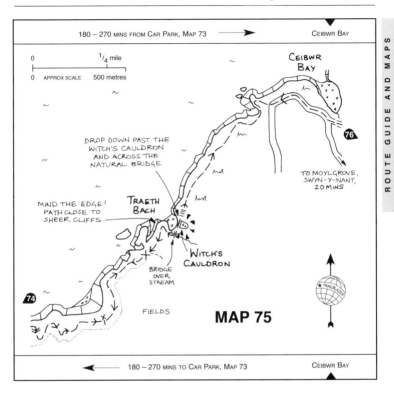

MOYLGROVE (TREWYDDEL)
OFF MAP 75

This pretty hamlet lies about half a mile up the lane through the valley from **Ceibwr Bay**. There's a public lavatory and also a natural spring where you can fill water bottles.

The very welcoming *Swyn-y-Nant* (☎ 01239-881244; 🖳 www.moylegrove.co.uk; 2D/1T), is uphill from the car park in the centre of the village in the direction of Newport. All the rooms are either en suite or have private bathroom and the charge is £29 per person per night.

In the summer there is a tearoom at *Penrallt Garden Centre and Nursery* (☎ 01239-881359; Mon-Sat 10am-5pm, Sun to 4.30pm) where you can find light snacks, tea and coffee. You can reach it by following the track inland from the beach and climbing the path up the steep wooded nose of the hill in front. It sits at 100 metres above sea level so you might want to hide your rucksack in some bushes at the bottom to avoid carrying it.

The Poppit Rocket **bus** (see pp39-41) stops at the entrance to the car park in Moylgrove Village.

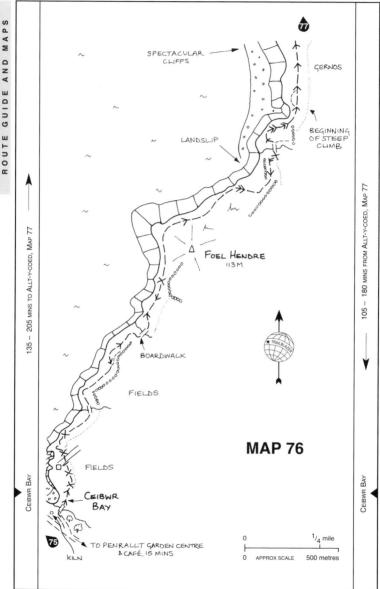

ROUTE GUIDE AND MAPS

SPECTACULAR CLIFFS

GERNOS

LANDSLIP

BEGINNING OF STEEP CLIMB

FOEL HENDRE
113 M

TRAILBLAZER

BOARDWALK

FIELDS

MAP 76

FIELDS

CEIBWR BAY

135 – 205 MINS TO ALLT-Y-COED, MAP 77

105 – 180 MINS FROM ALLT-Y-COED, MAP 77

CEIBWR BAY

CEIBWR BAY

TO PENRALLT GARDEN CENTRE & CAFÉ, 15 MINS

KILN

0		1/4 mile
0	APPROX SCALE	500 metres

77

75

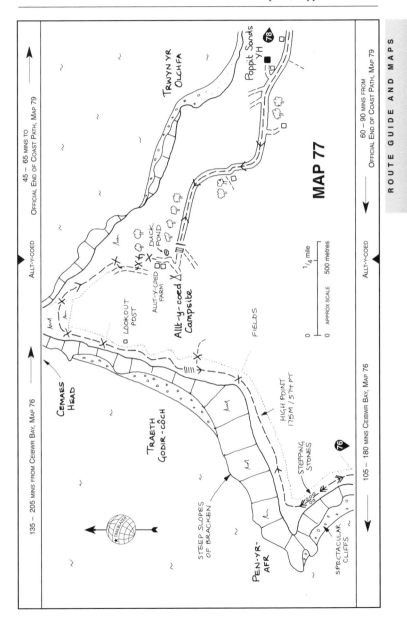

Ahead are wonderful twisted folds of rock dropping into the sea. After skirting around the flanks of **Foel Hendre** spectacular cliffs come into view. The impressive folding of the rock in these cliffs will have geologists drooling at the mouth. The path here begins to spasm in a series of excruciating descents and ascents. In places it climbs quite improbably steep slopes.

Once above the aforementioned cliffs the path swings to the east reaching the highest point of the entire coast path at 175 metres (574ft). The steep slopes of bracken that sweep down to the sea certainly make you feel a long way up.

Soon the path passes an old **lookout building** and drops down to the broad **Cemaes Head** before heading south to Allt-y-coed Farm and Campsite (see below) where the track joins a country lane. The lane leads steadily downhill to the lifeboat station and car park at **Poppit Sands**, where there's a plaque commemorating the opening of the path in 1970 by local war correspondent, journalist and broadcaster Wynford Vaughan Thomas.

POPPIT SANDS (DRAETH POPPIT)
MAPS 77 & 78

Poppit Sands refers to the scattering of houses that stretch from Allt-y-coed Farm all the way down the lane to the car park and the RNLI lifeboat station next to Poppit Sands itself, an enormous beach that fills the mouth of the Afon Teifi estuary. There's a **phone** by the car park and a **café**. The Poppit Rocket **bus** stops at the entrance to the car park and Richards' No 407 service calls here 5-6/day (Mon-Sat); see pp39-41 for details.

The official end of the path is still a mile and a half (2km) from Poppit Sands but there are plenty of places to stay along this stretch leaving very little to do the next morning. The first place you come to after rounding Cemaes Head is *Allt-y-coed Farm* (Map 77; ☎ 01239-612673). The coast path runs right through the farmyard. Just up the slope past the duck pond is their **campsite** offering pitches all year for £5 per person. From the farm the path joins the narrow Poppit Sands Lane.

Half a mile further on is *Poppit Sands Youth Hostel* (☎ 0870-770 5996, 🖳 poppit@yha.org.uk, open all year) overlooks the Sands less than an hour short of the end of the trail. It is self-catering only, has 34 beds at £14 for members and gets very popular in the summer.

If you hadn't already noticed you are now in the Welsh-speaking part of Pembrokeshire, but you certainly will if you go to *Webley Hotel* (☎ 01239-612085; 🖳 www.webleyhotel.com; 8D/1F), about half a mile down the road from Poppit Sands. B&B is £37.50 per person; single occupancy is £55.

They also have a field where you can **camp**; there are toilets and running water but the shower block won't be ready till 2008. Currently, it's £5 per night. In the bar (open daily 11am-3pm, 6-11pm, food served daily 12-2.30pm, 6-8.30pm) there's reasonable food, much of it home-cooked and including daily specials; prices start from £4.95.

And so the path continues on to **St Dogmaels**, where the coast path officially ends. Though purists may want to keep on walking to Cardigan to cross the **Afon Teifi** – the river that marks the border between Pembrokeshire and its neighbour, Ceredigion – the official end of the coast path is the unassuming slipway at the northern end of St Dogmaels.

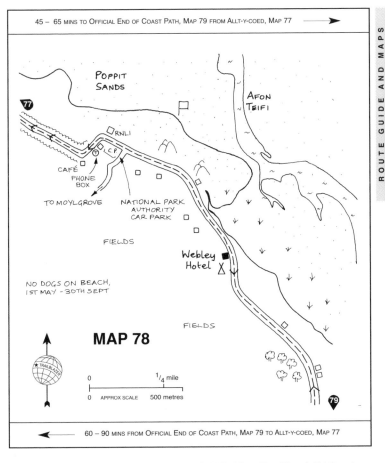

45 – 65 MINS TO OFFICIAL END OF COAST PATH, MAP 79 FROM ALLT-Y-COED, MAP 77

POPPIT SANDS

AFON TEIFI

77

RNLI

C.P.

CAFÉ

PHONE BOX

TO MOYLGROVE

NATIONAL PARK AUTHORITY CAR PARK

FIELDS

Webley Hotel

NO DOGS ON BEACH, 1ST MAY – 30TH SEPT

FIELDS

MAP 78

★ TRAILBLAZER

0   1/4 mile

0   APPROX SCALE   500 metres

79

60 – 90 MINS FROM OFFICIAL END OF COAST PATH, MAP 79 TO ALLT-Y-COED, MAP 77

ST DOGMAELS (LLANDUDOCH)
MAP 79

St Dogmaels is stretched along a dogleg in the river estuary. The coast path ends at the slipway at the northern limit of the village but the main centre is further south.

Before rushing through on your way to Cardigan it's worth taking a look at the old **abbey ruins** which can be found in the main part of the village. Head down the hill and look behind the **post office** (☎ 01239-

612563; Mon, Tue, Thur & Fri 9am-1pm, 2-5.30pm, Wed & Sat 9am-noon).

There is a small convenience **shop** (Mon-Sat 7am-10pm, Sun 8am-8pm) here but Cardigan, on the other side of the river, has far more to offer.

Both the Poppit Rocket and Richards' No 407 **bus** services stop here en route to Cardigan; see pp39-41 for details. Alternatively you can phone for a **taxi**: Cardi Cabs (☎ 01239-621399).

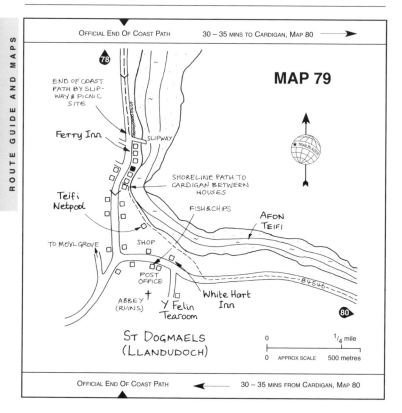

78

END OF COAST
PATH BY SLIP-
WAY & PICNIC
SITE

MAP 79

Ferry Inn   SLIPWAY

★ TRAILBLAZER

SHORELINE PATH TO
CARDIGAN BETWEEN
HOUSES

Teifi
Netpool

FISH & CHIPS

AFON
TEIFI

TO MOYL GROVE

SHOP

POST
OFFICE

ABBEY †
(RUINS)   Y Felin
Tearoom

White Hart
Inn

B4546

80

ST DOGMAELS
(LLANDUDOCH)

0   ¹/₄ mile
├─────────────────────┤
0   APPROX SCALE   500 metres

Right by the end of the path, *The Ferry Inn* (☎ 01239-615172; food served Mon-Fri 12-2pm, 6-9pm, Sat/Sun 12-9pm, daily 12-9pm in high season) is the perfect spot for a celebratory pint. *Teifi Netpool Inn* (☎ 01239-612680, Fri-Sun 12noon-2pm, daily 6-8.30pm) is another good place to kick the boots off and congratulate yourself with a pint or two. It has typical pub food and does a good plate of fish and chips.

There is a *fish and chip shop* (Tue-Thur noon-2pm, 5-8.30pm, Fri & Sat to 9.30pm) next to the post office and a little further down the hill is another good pub, the *White Hart Inn* (☎ 01239-612099, daily 12.30-9pm except Tue to 2.30pm) with decent pub grub. Down the road opposite is *Y Felin* (☎ 01239-613999, Mon-Fri 10.30am-5pm), a tea room with the unusual selling point of having one of the last working water mills left in Wales, which you can tour around and which produces traditional stoneground flour that they use in their scones and cakes.

For more accommodation, shops and transport options, Cardigan, just a little over a mile away, is a better bet than St Dogmaels. To reach it, catch one of the buses (see p41) that run between the Two or, if you prefer to walk, turn left at the central junction in St Dogmaels to follow the B4546 road down to the bridge across the **Afon Teifi**.

CARDIGAN (ABERTEIFI)   MAP 80

Cardigan is a mile (2km) beyond the end of the coast path. If you are using public transport to get home Cardigan is the place to go. There are also a number of places to spend the night and recover before heading home the next day.

Services

The **tourist information centre** (TIC; ☎ 01239-613230, ✉ cardigantic@ceredigion .gov.uk, Bath House Rd; Mon-Sat 10am-1pm, 2-5pm) is in the Theatr Mwldan building. There are plenty of **banks** and all the **shops** you need along High St as well as the **post office** (Mon-Fri 9am-5.30pm, Sat 9am-12.30pm). Down Quay St, off High St at the river end, is a Somerfield **supermarket**. The **library**, on the fourth floor of the mini-mall next to the tatty indoor market, has free **Internet access**, though you may have to wait a while for a terminal.

Transport

The all-essential **bus stop** is on Finch Sq. The Poppit Rocket goes from here to St Dogmaels, and ultimately Fishguard, whilst Richards'/Acorn's Bus No 412 goes to Haverfordwest via Newport and Fishguard, and the No 407 goes to St Dogmaels and Poppit Sands. If you have left your car at the start of the path take Midway Motors' service No 430 to Narberth, then Silcox's No 381 to Tenby and finally their No 350 or 351 to Kilgetty or Amroth. See the public transport map and table, pp39-41, for details.

Where to stay

A very friendly place to stay is *The Highbury* (☎ 01239-613403, Pendre, 2S/1OD). They have comfortable rooms and serve big breakfasts in a sunny conservatory. Prices start from £20 in the single rooms; in the doubles, all of which are en suite, it's £50.

There are more affordable B&Bs along Gwbert Rd: *Brynhyfryd Guest House* (☎ 01239-612861, 2S/2T/3D) costs from £22

per person in a standard room, or £23.50 for an en suite; and *Garth* (☎ 01239-613085, ✉ joyevans.garth@tiscali.co.uk; 1S/2T/2D/1F), which charges from £24/pp. Both are about five minutes on foot from the town centre.

The *Black Lion* (☎ 01239-612532, ✉ www.theblacklioncardigan.com; 3S/5D/2T/2F), on High St, charges £40 for a single, and £30 for two sharing a double. On St Mary St, *Angel Hotel* (☎ 01239-612561; 2S/5T/1D/1F) charges £20/pp for room only, some of which are en suite. The hotel is currently undergoing a lot of renovations, so prices and facilities may well have changed by the time you read this.

Where to eat

Abdul's Tandoori Spice (☎ 01239-621416, daily 5-11.45pm) is hidden down Quay St by the river, opposite Somerfield supermarket. This is an award-winning restaurant with very friendly waiters and a menu that takes a good half-hour to read. Book your table in advance because it is very small and the locals like it a lot. They do takeaway as well.

The *Black Lion* (see above; food served daily 12-2pm, 6-9pm) has an extensive menu while the *Angel Hotel* (see above; food served Mon-Sat 8am-8pm) also does food for non-residents. For something quick and easy there are a number of takeaway places and coffee shops along High St and Pendre; try *The Castle Café* (☎ 01239-621882; Mon-Wed 8.30am-4pm, Thur-Sat to 9pm), on the corner with Quay St, or *Cardi Café* (☎ 01239-614199; Mon-Sat 7am-5pm), which is well-worth hunting down for its excellent all-day breakfasts for £3.75. The *Cardigan Arms* (☎ 01239-614969) is, despite its name, just a café though the menu's cheap and the portions large. At the old theatre, which also houses the TIC (see column opposite), you will find the *Theatr Mwldan Café* (Mon-Sat 10am-5pm). *Quick Chip* (☎ 01239-621671; Mon-Sat 11.30am-9pm, Sun 4.30-7.30pm), in front of the castle, is a cheap and cheerful option. Also on Pendre is ***Happy City Chinese*** (☎ 01239-612273; Sun-Thur 5-10.30pm, Fri/Sat 5-11pm).

To let your hair down after the long walk the best place for a drink is the very Welsh ***Red Lion*** (☎ 01239-612482, daily 11am-12midnight), tucked behind Finch Sq. The friendly bar staff are only too happy to welcome strangers despite this being very much a locals' hangout. Be prepared for some strong Welsh singing once the beer starts flowing.

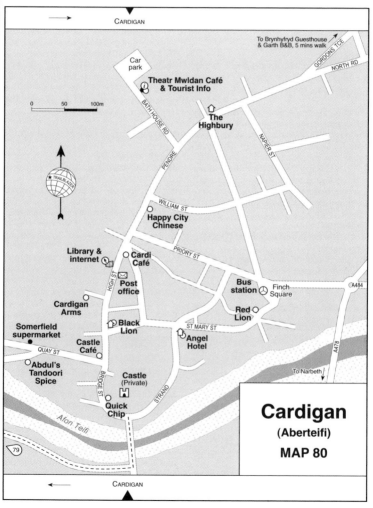

Cardigan
(Aberteifi)
MAP 80

INDEX

[bold type = map reference]
Aber Bach *see* Little Haven
Aber Draw 170, **171**
Aber-Felin 176, **178**
Aber Llydan *see* Broad Haven
Aberdaugleddau *see* Milford
  Haven
Abereiddy **167**, 168
Abergwaun *see* Fishguard
Aberteifi *see* Cardigan
access rights 45-8
accommodation 10-13, 65-6
  see also place name
Afon Nyfer **189**, 194
Afon Teifi 200, **201**
Amroth **69**, 70, **70**
Angle 99-100, **102**
Angle Bay **102**, **103**, 106
annual events 23
ATMs 16, 24

Backpackers' Club 34, 35
baggage carriers 18
banks 16, 17
Barafundle Bay 88, **89**
bed and breakfasts (B&Bs) 12,
  13, 14, 21, 25, 28
Bedd Morris **193**, 194
Benton Castle 112, **113**
birds 36, 58-62, 134
blisters 50
Blue Lagoon **167**, 168
boots 31
Borough Head 138, **141**
Bosherston 90, **91**, 94
Bosherston Lily Ponds 57, 90, **91**
Brandy Bay 138, **141**
Broad Haven 142-4, **143**
Broad Haven (nr Bosherston)
  88, **89**
budgeting 20-21
bunkhouses 12, 20, 25, 27
buses 39, **39**, 40-1
business hours 16

Caerfai Bay 155, **155**
Caldey Island 74
camping/campsites 10, 20, 25, 26
camping gear & supplies 14, 33
Cardigan 203-4, **204**
Carn Llidi 162, **165**
Carn Penberry 163, **166**
Carreg Sampson, cromlech
  172, **173**

Carreg Wastad Point 176, **178**
cash machines, *see* ATMs
Castlemartin 94, 96, **97**
Ceibwr Bay 194, 197, **197**, **198**
Cemaes Head **199**, 200
Cilgetti, *see* Kilgetty
Cleddau Bridge 116, **117**
cliff tops 49 (safety), 63 (flowers)
clothing 31-2
coaches 37, 38
coasteering 83
compasses 33
conservation organizations 54, 55
costs 20-1
Country Code 47
Countryside Council for Wales
  (CCW) 44, 53-4
Cresswell Quay 112, **113**
currency 16
Cwm Gwaun 57, 192, **193**
Cwm-yr-eglwys 186, **187**

Dale 126, **131**, 132
Daugleddau Estuary 111-2, **113**
David, Saint 156
day walks 29
daylight hours 22
Dinas Cross 186, **187**
Dinas-Fawr **151**, 152
Dinas Island 186, **187**
Dinbych y Pysgod, *see* Tenby
direction of walk 27
disabled access 20
distances 24
dogs, walking with 19
Draeth Poppit *see* Poppit Sands
drinking water 14-15
Druidstone Haven 144, **146**

eating places 25
economic impact, 42-3
EHIC 16
East Blockhouse 96, **101**
Elegug Stacks 90
emergency services 17, 51
emergency signal 48
environmental impact 43-5
equipment 30-4

ferries 37, 41
field guides 36
firing ranges, *see* MoD ranges
first-aid kit 32
Fishguard 181-2, **182**, **183**, 184

flora and fauna 56-64, 134
flowers 63-4
Foel-Gôch 194, **196**
Foel Hendre **198**, 200
food 14-15, 48
food stores 25
footwear 31
Fort Popton **103**, 106
Freshwater East 86, **87**
Freshwater West 96, **98**, **99**
Friends of Pembrokeshire
  National Park 35, 55

Gann estuary 126, 129, **130**, 132
Garron Pill 112, **113**
Gelliswick Bay 123, **124**
Giltar Point 79, **81**
Goodwick 176, 179, 180, **181**
Grassholm Island 54, 58, 134
Green Bridge of Wales 90, **95**
Greenala Point 86, **88**
group/guided tours 18
guesthouses 13, 21
Guttle Hole 96, **101**

Haroldston Chins 144, **145**
Hazelbeach 118, **119**
Herbrandston 124-6, **125**
Heritage Coast 53
history of path 9
holiday cottages 13
hostels 11-12, 14, 20, 25, 27
hotels 13, 14, 21
Hundleton 106, **107**
hyperthermia 51
hypothermia 50

inns 13, 21
itineraries 23-9

Kilgetty 66-7, **67**

lambing 46
Landshipping 111
Landsker Borderlands 111-12
Last Invasion of Britain 179
Lawrenny 111-2, **113**
length of path 9
Lindsway Bay **127**, 128
liquid natural gas (LNG)
  terminals 123
litter 43
Little Haven 142, **143**
Llandudoch *see* St Dogmael's

Llanismel *see* St Ishmael's
local transport 38-41, **39**
Long Distance Walkers'
  Association 35
Lower Fishguard 181, **183**, 184
Lydstep 82, **82**
Lydstep Haven 82, **82**

maintenance of path 44
Manorbier 84, **84**
Manorbier Bay 83, **85**
Manorbier Castle **84**, 84, **85**
map keys 6
maps 33
Marloes 134, 138, **139**
Marloes Sands 133, **136**
Martin's Haven 133, **137**
Merrion 94, **95**
Milford Haven 118-20, **121**, 122
Mill Bay 133, **135**
minimum impact walking 42-8
money 16-17, 33
MoD firing ranges 81, 89, **91**,
  93, 101
Monk Haven 128-9, **129**
Moylgrove 197
Musselwick 129, **130**
Musselwick Sands 133, **139**
Mynydd Preseli *see* Preseli Hills

national holidays 16
National Trails 46
national transport 36-8
nature conservation 52-5
Newgale 148, **149**
Newgale Sands 145, **147**
Newport 186, **189**, 190-2, **191**
Newport Sands **189**, 194
Neyland 116, **117**
Nolton Haven 144, **146**

Ogof Mrs Morgan **161**, 162

Parrog 186, **189**
Pembroke (Penfro) 108-11, **109**
Pembroke Castle 108, **109**
Pembroke Dock 114-6, **115**
Pembrokeshire Coast National
  Park Authority 35, 44, 53
Penanglas 176, **179**
Penally 80, **80, 81**
Poppit Sands 200, **201**
Porth Mawr *see* Whitesands Bay
Porthclais 160, **161**
Porthgain **169**, 170

Porthlysgi Bay 160, **161**
Porthmelgan 162, **165**
Porthselau 162, **163**
Porthsychan Bay 172
post offices 16, 17, 24
Preseli Hills 56, 57, 192-4, **193**
public transport, *see local
  transport*
pubs 13, 14, 15, 16
Pwll Deri **175**, 176
Pwllcrochan (nr Fort Popton)
  104, 106
Pwllcrochan 172, **174**
Pwllgwaelod 184, **187**
Pwllstrodur 172, **173**

Raggle Rocks 133, **136**
rail services 36, 37, 41
rainfall 22
Ramblers' Association 34, 35
Ramsey Island 54, 57, 153
Ramsey Sound 56
rates of exchange 16
real ales 15
Rickeston Bridge 127, **128**
right to roam 46
Roundhouse, The, 144, **146**
route finding 10
route maps, using the 65-6
rucksacks 30

safety, outdoor 48-51
Sainffraid *see* St Brides Haven
Sampson Cross **92**, 94
Sandy Haven **125**, 126, **127**
Sandy Haven Pill 126, **127, 128**
Saundersfoot 72-4, **72**
school holidays 16
seasons 21-2
self-guided holidays 18
services 18
side trips 28
Skokholm Island 54, 58, 134
Skomer Island 53, 54, 56, 58,
  60, 134
Skrinkle Haven **82**, 83
sleeping bags 33
smoking 17
Solva (Solfach) **151**, 152-3, **153**
St Ann's lighthouse 133, **135**
St Brides Haven 138, **140**
St David's 156-60, **159**
  Cathedral 156
St David's Head 163, **165**
St Dogmael's 201, 202, **202**

St Govan's Chapel 90, **91**
St Ishmael's 128, **129**
St Justinian's 162, **163**
St Non's Chapel/Well **155**, 160
Stack Rocks 90, **95**
Stackpole Quay 88, **88**
Stepaside 68, **68**
Strumble Head 176, **177**, 179
Summerhill 68, **69**
surfing 148
Swanlake Bay **85**, 86

telephones 17
temperature 22
Tenby 74-9, **77**
Thorne Island 99, **101**
Ticklas Point 138, **141**
tide tables 50
time needed 10, 26-8
tour groups 18-19
tourist information centres 24,
  35; *see also place name*
town facilities 24-5
Traeth Llywn **169**, 170
travel insurance 16
travellers' cheques 17
trees 62-3
Trefdraeth *see* Newport
Trefin 170-2, **171**
Trewent Point 86, **87**

village facilities 24-5

Wales Tourist Board 35
walking companies 18-19
walking times 65
Warren 94, **95**, 96
Watch House Point 128, **129**
water, drinking 14-15, 48
Watwick Bay 133, **135**
waymarking 10
Wdig *see* Goodwick
weather forecasts 50
weekend walks 29
weights and measures 17
Welsh vocabulary 34
West Angle Bay 96, **101**
Westdale Bay **131**, 133
Whitesands Bay 162, **164**
wild camping 10, 45
Wildlife Trust West Wales 54, 55
Wiseman's Bridge 71-2, **71**
Witch's Cauldron 194, **197**

Youth Hostels Association 11

TRAILBLAZER GUIDES – TITLE LIST

Adventure Cycle-Touring Handbook	1st edn out now
Adventure Motorcycling Handbook	5th edn out now
Australia by Rail	5th edn out now
Azerbaijan	3rd edn out now
The Blues Highway – New Orleans to Chicago	2nd edn out now
China Rail Handbook	1st edn early 2008
Coast to Coast (British Walking Guide)	2nd edn out now
Cornwall Coast Path (British Walking Guide)	2nd edn out now
Corsica Trekking – GR20	1st edn early 2008
Dolomites Trekking – AV1 & AV2	2nd edn out now
Inca Trail, Cusco & Machu Picchu	3rd edn out now
Indian Rail Handbook	1st edn late 2007
Hadrian's Wall Walk (British Walking Guide)	1st edn out now
Himalaya by Bike – a route and planning guide	1st edn early 2008
Japan by Rail	2nd edn out now
Kilimanjaro – the trekking guide (includes Mt Meru)	2nd edn out now
Matterhorn and the Haute Route	1st edn early 2008
Mediterranean Handbook	1st edn out now
Nepal Mountaineering Guide	1st edn late 2007
New Zealand – The Great Walks	1st edn out now
North Downs Way (British Walking Guide)	1st edn out now
Norway's Arctic Highway	1st edn out now
Offa's Dyke Path (British Walking Guide)	2nd edn out now
Pembrokeshire Coast Path (British Walking Guide)	2nd edn out now
Pennine Way (British Walking Guide)	1st edn out now
The Ridgeway (British Walking Guide)	1st edn out now
Siberian BAM Guide – rail, rivers & road	2nd edn out now
The Silk Roads – a route and planning guide	2nd edn out now
Sahara Overland – a route and planning guide	2nd edn out now
Sahara Abenteuerhandbuch (German edition)	1st edn out now
Scottish Highlands – The Hillwalking Guide	1st edn out now
South Downs Way (British Walking Guide)	2nd edn out now
South-East Asia – The Graphic Guide	1st edn out now
Tibet Overland – mountain biking & jeep touring	1st edn out now
Tour de Mont Blanc	1st edn early 2008
Trans-Canada Rail Guide	4th edn out now
Trans-Siberian Handbook	7th edn out now
Trekking in the Annapurna Region	4th edn out now
Trekking in the Everest Region	4th edn out now
Trekking in Corsica	1st edn out now
Trekking in Ladakh	3rd edn out now
Trekking in the Pyrenees	3rd edn out now
West Highland Way (British Walking Guide)	2nd edn out now

www.trailblazer-guides.com

TRAILBLAZER'S LONG-DISTANCE PATH (LDP) WALKING GUIDES

We've applied to destinations which are closer to home Trailblazer's proven formula for publishing definitive route guides for adventurous travellers. Britain's network of long-distance trails enables the walker to explore some of the finest landscapes in the country's best walking areas and they are an obvious starting point for this series. These are guides that are user-friendly, practical, informative and environmentally sensitive.

● Unique mapping features

In many walking guidebooks the reader has to read a route description then try to relate it to the map. Our guides are much easier to use because walking directions, tricky junctions, places to stay and eat, points of interest and walking times are all written onto the maps themselves in the places to which they apply. With their uncluttered clarity, these are not general-purpose maps but fully edited maps **drawn by walkers for walkers**.

● Largest-scale walking maps

At a scale of just under 1:20,000 (8cm or $3^1/_8$ inches to one mile) the maps in these guides are bigger than even the most detailed British walking maps currently available in the shops.

● Not just a trail guide – includes where to stay, where to eat and public transport

Our guidebooks are a complete guide, not just a trail guide. They include: what to see, where to stay (pubs, hotels, B&Bs, campsites, bunkhouses, hostels), where to eat. There is detailed public transport information for all access points to each trail so there are itineraries for all walkers, both for hiking the route in its entirety and for day walks.

West Highland Way *Charlie Loram* ISBN 978-1-873756-90-4, £9.99
2nd edition, 192pp, 53 maps, 10 town plans, 40 colour photos

Pennine Way *Ed de la Billière & Keith Carter* ISBN 978-1-873756-57-7, £9.99
1st edition, 256pp, 135 maps & town plans, 40 colour photos

Coast to Coast *Henry Stedman* ISBN 978-1-873756-92-8, £9.99
2nd edition, 224pp, 108 maps & town plans, 40 colour photos

Pembrokeshire Coast Path *Jim Manthorpe* ISBN 978-1-905864-03-4, £9.99
2nd edition, 208pp, 96 maps & town plans, 40 colour photos

Offa's Dyke Path *Keith Carter* ISBN 978-1-905864-06-5, £9.99
2nd edition, 208pp, 88 maps & town plans, 40 colour photos

South Downs Way *Jim Manthorpe* ISBN 978-1-873756-95-9, £9.99
2nd edition, 192pp, 60 maps & town plans, 40 colour photos

Hadrian's Wall Path *Henry Stedman* ISBN 978-1-873756-85-0, £9.99
1st edition, 192pp, 60 maps & town plans, 40 colour photos

North Downs Way *John Curtin* ISBN 978-1-873756-96-6, £9.99
1st edition, 192pp, 60 maps & town plans, 40 colour photos

The Ridgeway *Nick Hill* ISBN 978-1-873756-88-1, £9.99
1st edition, 192pp, 53 maps & town plans, 40 colour photos

Cornwall Coast Path *Edith Schofield* ISBN 978-1-873756-93-5, £9.99
2nd edition, 224pp, 112 maps & town plans, 40 colour photos

'*The same attention to detail that distinguishes its other guides has been brought to bear here*'. **The Sunday Times**

TRAILBLAZER
British Walking Guides

Pembrokeshire Coast Path – AMROTH TO CARDIGAN

MAP KEY

Map 1 – p67	Map 18 – p100	Map 41 – p139	Map 53 – p161	Map 67 – p181
Map 1a – p68	Map 19 – p101	Map 42 – p140	Map 54 – p163	Map 68 – p183
Map 1b – p69	Map 20 – p102	Map 43 – p141	Map 55 – p164	Map 69 – p185
Map 2 – p71	Map 21 – p102	Map 44 – p141	Map 56 – p165	Map 70 – p187
Map 2a – p73	Map 22 – p103	Map 45 – p143	Map 57 – p166	Map 71 – p188
Map 3 – p75	Map 23 – p104	Map 46 – p145	Map 58 – p167	Map 72 – p189
Map 3a – p77	Map 24 – p105	Map 47 – p147	Map 59 – p169	Map 73 – p195
Map 4 – p79	Map 25 – p107	Map 48 – p148	Map 60 – p171	Map 74 – p196
Map 5 – p81	Map 26 – p109	Map 49 – p149	Map 61 – p173	Map 75 – p197
Map 6 – p82	Map 27 – p115	Map 49a – p150	Map 62 – p174	Map 76 – p198
Map 7 – p83	Map 28 – p117	Map 50 – p151	Map 63 – p175	Map 77 – p199
Map 8a – p84	Map 29 – p119	Map 51 – p154	Map 64 – p177	Map 78 – p201
Map 8 – p85	Map 30 – p120	Map 52 – p155	Map 65 – p178	Map 79 – p202
Map 9 – p87	Map 31 – p121	Map 52a – p159	Map 66 – p179	Map 80 – p204
Map 10 – p88	Map 32 – p124			
Map 11 – p89	Map 33 – p125			
Map 12 – p91	Map 34 – p127			
Map 12a – p92	Map 34a – p128			
Map 13 – p93	Map 35 – p129			
Map 14 – p95	Map 36 – p130			
Map 15 – p97	Map 37 – p131			
Map 16 – p98	Map 38 – p135			
Map 17 – p99	Map 39 – p136			
	Map 40 – p137			

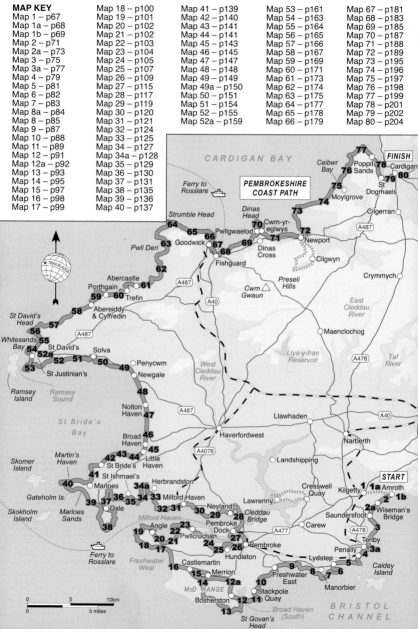